Youth Organizing for
Reproductive Justice

REPRODUCTIVE JUSTICE: A NEW VISION FOR
THE TWENTY-FIRST CENTURY

*Edited by Rickie Solinger (senior editor),
Khiara M. Bridges, Laura Briggs, Krystale
E. Littlejohn, Ruby Tapia,
and Carly Thomsen*

Youth Organizing for Reproductive Justice

A Guide for Liberation

Chris A. Barcelos

UNIVERSITY OF CALIFORNIA PRESS

University of California Press
Oakland, California

Library of Congress Cataloging-in-Publication Data
Names: Barcelos, Chris A., author.
Title: Youth organizing for reproductive justice : a guide
    for liberation / Chris Barcelos.
Other titles: Reproductive justice ; 11.
Description: Oakland, California : University of
    California Press, [2024] | Series: Reproductive justice:
    a new vision for the 21st century ; 11 | Includes
    bibliographical references and index.
Identifiers: LCCN 2024021693 (print) | LCCN 2024021694
    (ebook) | ISBN 9780520390072 (cloth) | ISBN
    9780520390089 (paperback) | ISBN 9780520390096
    (ebook)
Subjects: LCSH: Reproductive rights—United States—21st
    century. | Youth protest movements—United
    States—21st century.
Classification: LCC HQ766.5.U6 B48 2024 (print) |
    LCC HQ766.5.U6 (ebook) | DDC 323.0835097309/05—
    dc23/eng/20240820
LC record available at https://lccn.loc.gov/2024021693
LC ebook record available at https://lccn.loc
    .gov/2024021694

Manufactured in the United States of America
33 32 31 30 29 28 27 26 25
10 9 8 7 6 5 4 3 2 1

For Stevie

CONTENTS

ACKNOWLEDGMENTS

To all the young people who are working toward our collective liberation: thank you for your leadership and solidarity.

Writing a book does not happen without the labor—paid or unpaid, visible or invisible—of many people beyond the author. Thank you to Cathy Hannabach, Rachel Fudge, and the team at Ideas on Fire for their skillful editing and indexing services. I cannot overstate how much I recommend their services to other scholars. Thank you to all the coffeeshop employees, Boston Public Library staff, and University of Massachusetts Boston professional and classified staff whose labor made the writing of this book possible. A shout-out to James McMaster for reviewing my memories of that sweaty day. Thank you as well to Shoshana Ehrlich for fact checking the legal history of youth access to abortion. Finally, I am grateful to Shaun Trujillo for his assistance with the archives of the Civil Liberties and Public Policy Program / Collective Power for Reproductive Justice at Hampshire College.

An enormous thank-you to Tamara Marzouk for her support in contacting the young activists interviewed for this book. To Alyssa, Diana, Hanan, Jaden, Samar, and Viviana: thank you for your time, your stories, and your work.

I feel fortunate every day to work at the UMass Boston, where I have the very best students and colleagues one could hope for. Their insights and support made this book possible. If I thanked all of my students here, the list would be far too long and I would inevitably forget someone. So, to all of my students: thank you for the opportunity to learn from you. The biggest thanks to my colleagues Chris Bobel, Elora Chowdhury, Shoshana Ehrlich, Amani El Jack, Aaron Lecklider, Marisol Negrón, Denise Patmon, Heike Schotten, Cedric Woods, and many others for their unfaltering support. Thank you also to the College of Liberal Arts Office of the Dean for a generous start-up funding package that provided the financial resources necessary to bring this project to fruition.

Thank you, Rickie Solinger for inviting me to write this book, and to Naomi Schneider, Aline Dolinh, and all staff at the University of California Press for their work in taking it from idea to print.

I am so honored to have the art of Cristy C. Road on the front cover of this book: thank you so much for this beautiful image.

I am deeply grateful to the following members of my family for countless interruptions during the writing of this book: my beloved life companion Stevie, Wondernicks, Patti, and Bernadette.

Finally, to my partner Davey: I am so deeply lucky to spend my life herding cats with you. Thank you for sticking with me through everything.

Introduction

Framing Youth and Reproductive Justice

On a scorching hot day in early June 2020, I parked my tiny black car in the middle of a busy highway overpass in Madison, Wisconsin. It was one of about two hundred parked cars on a road where motorists usually sped by at seventy miles per hour. Paint on the side of our vehicles and signs in our windows read things like "DEFUND THE POLICE" and "SAY HER NAME." George Floyd had recently been murdered by the Minneapolis police, and the growing COVID-19 pandemic was causing devasting loss of life, especially among people of color, economically marginalized people, and incarcerated people. The occupation of the highway was organized by a local nonprofit organization called Freedom Inc., an organization led by and serving Black and Southeast Asian people that works with low- to no-income communities of color. Their mission is to "achieve social justice through coupling direct services with leadership development and community organizing that will bring about social, political, cultural, and economic change resulting in the end of violence against women, gender-nonconforming and transgender folks, and children within communities of color."[1] The action that brought us all together on that unbearably hot pavement was part of Freedom Inc.'s broader efforts to support youth-led organizing. It was also part of the national Movement for Black Lives (M4BL) Week of Action.[2] Communities all over the United States were engaged in similar protests that week and all summer long. These uprisings were set in motion by the police murder of George Floyd, but they built on years of Black- and youth-led resistance against policy brutality and state violence. For instance, Freedom Inc.'s Youth Squad had long been working on a campaign to remove police officers from the Madison public schools. During this action on the highway overpass, we disrupted traffic at rush hour and then caravanned throughout the city to the home of one person with the power to meet our demands: the president of the school board.

Two friends, also college professors, rode with me, all of us sweating under our face masks. Our commitment to showing up as adult *accomplices* to youth working to get cops out of their schools tempered our concerns about COVID transmission.[3] Nevertheless, following several months of stay-at-home orders in the winter and spring of 2020, it felt strange to be in a car with people who didn't live in your household. We quickly pulled masks aside to wipe our sweat in between replying to call-and-response chants: *If we don't get it / Shut it down! Money for schools / Not police!* As the parade of cars snaked through the streets, we shouted out the windows and honked the horn on beat. The organizers hadn't let us know where we were going—for our safety and to avoid tipping off our target. Shortly before sunset we parked our cars and spilled into a suburban neighborhood, carrying small American flags with "#FUCK12" written on them in marker (a euphemism for "fuck the police"). We gathered at the end of a quiet cul-de-sac outside the home of school board president and former Madison police officer Gloria Reyes. Despite the Freedom Youth Squad's repeated actions over the past year—including disrupting school board meetings and testifying about the harm that cops in school caused to Black youth, other youth of color, LGBTQ youth, and disabled youth—Reyes ignored their demands and stayed committed to keeping police officers in the city's schools. People crowded the street, fanning themselves with their protest signs. Organizers handed out water bottles and snacks. There were youth, adults, college students—many of them members of the LGBTQ community, and many more people of color than you would normally see together in heavily segregated Madison.

Mahnker Dahnweih, Freedom Inc.'s community power–building coordinator, stood closest to Gloria's home and held a bullhorn to lead us in chants of *Do you want your job, Gloria?! Because our children are dying! Our children are being pushed out of school!* and *Our children are being harassed!* It took what seemed an eternity for the school board president to emerge from her house. Eventually she came outside wearing light summer pajamas, but stayed at the end of her driveway, away from the crowd. Dahnweih communicated our demands clearly: end the school's contract with the police department. M Adams, Freedom Inc's co–executive director, cleaned the mouthpiece of a bullhorn with a disinfectant wipe and handed it to Reyes. She refused to answer whether she would remove the cops from the city's schools and accused the organizers of disrupting her peace at home.

"You come to my house and yell at me—"
"People are dying!"
"You're gonna come to my house and not let me speak?!"
"Shame! Shame!"

Adams asked if any Black girls in the crowd wanted to come up and speak as Reyes continued to state that she would "reconsider" the issue of police in schools but would not give an answer right there and then. Some people in the crowd called her out on her lack of solidarity as a person of color. Others noted that she had been ignoring their demands for years. Eventually the tired, sweaty crowd dispersed, but not before we planted dozens of #FUCK12 American flags in Reyes's front yard. Later that night, Freedom Inc. posted this message on their Facebook page, along with the contact info for the members of the Madison school board:

> Today, we practiced #CommunityControl by caravanning to MMSD [Madison Metropolitan School District] school board President Gloria Reyes house and demanding #PoliceFreeSchools. Gloria has the power to fire the police from our schools—just as the Minneapolis school board did earlier this week. Tell her to put this item on the agenda during the school board meeting THIS MONDAY. Tell all of the school board members to vote to END THE CONTRACT WITH POLICE!

It was at the end of an emotionally heavy day when I emailed each member of the school board. I had recently watched the police take my own child out of a city school in handcuffs for what in my view was a bad judgment call but the school considered a felony crime. As a parent, I knew that cops didn't belong in schools. Firing off emails, I dared to allow myself to imagine how my family's situation might have been different had the school called a peer crisis counselor instead of the police.

At first glance, the protest over cops in schools may not seem directly related to the topic of this book: youth and reproductive justice. Abortion or contraceptive access might be the first issues that come to mind when we hear "youth" and "reproduction."

Maybe we think about teen pregnancy and parenting or school-based sexuality education. However, as a vision, framework, and social movement, reproductive justice helps us shift toward a broader understanding of reproductive politics. SisterSong Women of Color Reproductive Justice Collective defines reproductive justice as "the human right to maintain personal bodily autonomy, have children, not have children, and parent the children we have in safe and sustainable communities."[4] Reproductive justice helps us to shift to a broad political vision that moves beyond a singular, rights-based focus on white, cisgender women's access to abortion. Youth—especially youth of color, LGBTQ youth, and disabled youth—cannot maintain personal bodily autonomy when the police patrol the halls of their schools. Adults cannot parent their children in safe and sustainable communities when a quick trip to the corner store can result in being shot down by police. As Monica Simpson, Sister-Song's executive director, puts it, "If our environments are being plagued by police violence, state-sanctioned violence, [or] vigilantes who feel like they need to take the law into their own hands, that is not creating a safe environment for our children."[5] Getting cops out of schools is reproductive justice.

Historian Laura Briggs argues that *all* politics are reproductive politics. She chronicles how the major political issues in the United States over the past forty years—from welfare reform to "crack babies" to gay marriage—are at their core a form of reproductive politics. Linking all of these issues together is neoliberalism, a cultural and economic system that emphasizes individual responsibility and a scaling back of social supports. In *Youth Organizing for Reproductive Justice*, I apply Briggs's assertion that there "is no outside to reproductive politics" to youth organizing in the new millennium.[6] *All* youth organizing is reproductive justice organizing, whether it is campaigning for accurate and affirming school-based sex ed, supporting transgender youth's access to gender-affirming care, resisting the criminalization of Black youth, or exposing the violence of the foster care system. The central, unifying feature that links together this organizing, especially organizing by youth of color and queer and trans youth, is a focus on a shared marginal relationship to power. The youth organizing described in this book demonstrates a coalitional approach to politics and a vision of collective liberation that links bodily autonomy, self-determination, freedom from violence, support for alternative family formations, and the disruption of gender and sexual normativity— ideas at the core of the reproductive justice vision.

Theorizing all youth political organizing as reproductive justice organizing helps us to connect issues that seem distinct but are fundamentally linked. Medical scholar Melissa Gilliam notes that the deficit framing of youth—especially the narrative of Black and brown youth as "at risk"—combined with the (white) feminist discourse on reproductive "choice" and "rights"—limits the possibility of youth sexual and reproductive freedom. She argues that approaching youth through the reproductive justice (RJ) lens helps to answer the question: "Which inequitable practices and which social and political systems must change in order to create the necessary conditions such that all people have reproductive freedom?"[7] The chapters that follow use the frameworks *women of color feminisms* and *queer of color critique* to help us understand how youth in the new millennium resist the interlocking social and political systems that limit bodily autonomy and self-determination. Wherever possible, I make connections to related political frameworks that can help us to better understand youth organizing and reproductive justice, such as abolition feminism and disability justice. Taken together, these frameworks demonstrate the interconnections between issues generally understood to be related to reproductive justice—such as youth access to abortion, contraception, and sexuality education—as well as issues we don't generally think of as related, such as the livability of transgender youth or the so-called juvenile justice system. There are many other issues linked to youth and reproductive justice that are beyond the scope of this book, such as intersex justice, sex work, gun violence, the occupation of Palestine, and the climate crisis.

Theorizing all youth organizing as reproductive justice organizing provides a number of valuable lessons. This broad approach centers theory from the margins and centers youth of color and queer and trans youth in particular. When I teach or give talks, I am often asked how we should think about the enormity and connectedness of the struggles we're fighting and the injustices we are working against. My answer is always the same: look to the young people, especially the Black, Indigenous, brown, queer, and/or trans young people. Their abolitionist, anti-racist, and gender-inclusive understandings of interlocking systems of oppression have a lot to teach grown folks, as do their strategies of resistance. The youth organizing described in this book is a powerful tool for understanding how our struggles are connected and advances a view of collective liberation in which *none* of us are free until *all* of us get free.

Youth Organizing for Reproductive Justice also intervenes in the academic literature on both youth organizing and reproductive justice. Despite nearly three decades of scholarship on the reproductive justice movement and many more decades of research on youth social movements, the scholarship on youth movements has had little to say about reproductive justice organizing, and the scholarship on reproductive justice has mainly focused on adults. For instance, research on youth social movements has focused on the role of college campuses in student organizing, political identity formation, the supposed decline in political mobilization among people, and the role of the internet and social media in youth organizing. Although this research has covered youth organizing around immigration, the environment, gun violence, and so on, comparatively few studies have considered issues of reproductive freedom in youth movements.[8] Similarly, although several books and hundreds of articles now document and analyze the reproductive justice movement more generally, these works have primarily centered on RJ issues pertaining to adults and political organizing among adults.[9]

I conducted the research for this book through archival research and digital ethnography of youth organizing in the United States from approximately 2002 to 2024. I had already been following and documenting youth and reproductive justice movements as part of my professional and political work, so I simply began formally collecting and analyzing news articles, reports, and issue briefs in addition to closely following youth and RJ organizations and projects on social media. The analyses in this book are based on my knowledge as a scholar and organizer in various social movements and, like all knowledge production, reflect my own positionalities and political commitments and are therefore partial and incomplete. My analytic and pedagogical strategy is to bring the movement into more people's lives, and to bring more people into the movement.

KEY CONCEPTS AND THEORETICAL FRAMEWORKS

Before we explore how youth organizing in the new millennium is a form of reproductive justice organizing, it is useful to establish a working vocabulary of the concepts and theoretical frameworks used in this book. First, I provide a brief overview of the concepts of reproductive justice for readers new to the framework. Next, I review what this book means by "youth" and the contested issue of who society considers a youth. I then examine how scholars and activists have critiqued assumptions about youth, politics, and resistance. Finally, I discuss the related theoretical frameworks that animate this book: women of color feminisms and queer of color critique.

Reproductive Justice

Activists, scholars, and the media have increasingly shifted from the term *reproductive rights* to the term *reproductive justice*, and use of the latter has grown exponentially. For example, in 2005 "reproductive justice" was mentioned in English-language newspapers and magazines just 12 times; by 2010 that number had grown to 46 and by 2019 it had grown to 222. Attention to reproductive justice has grown in academic journals, with only 11 mentions in 2005 and 218 by 2020.[10] News outlets that focus on reproductive health politics have also changed their names; for instance, in 2016 the reproductive politics news sites RH Reality Check changed its name to Rewire News in order signal that its coverage was about more than just reproductive health. Similarly, in 2020 the National Latina Institute for Reproductive Health changed its name to the National Latina Institute for Reproductive Justice.

The term *reproductive justice* was first coined by a group of Black feminist activists in 1994. Frustrated that the reproductive rights movement had centered the needs of white women; had divorced reproductive rights from social, economic, and racial justice; and didn't promote the leadership of women of color, they formed a new vision for reproductive politics.[11] They articulated this new vison by applying the concept of human rights to US-based issues (for the most part, activists had used the human rights framework to talk about issues outside the United States).[12] In 1997, sixteen women of color organizations formed SisterSong Women of Color Reproductive Justice Collective to serve as an umbrella organization connecting multiple groups working on issues related to reproduction and social justice. Today, SisterSong continues to be a leader in advancing the reproductive justice vision and movement.[13] Feminist activists and scholars have written many detailed books and articles about the origins and history of reproductive justice.[14] Here, I briefly sketch out the concept of reproductive justice for readers new to the idea.

In a pivotal 2005 article, Asian Communities for Reproductive Justice (now called Forward Together), a founding member of the SisterSong Collective, laid out the differences between reproductive health, rights, and justice.[15] These distinctions were crucial in naming the limitations in the reproductive health and rights approaches and articulating RJ as a strategy that includes and extends them both. The document defined *reproductive health* as a service delivery approach focused on addressing unmet reproductive health care needs. Its goal is to eliminate reproductive health inequities by improving access to safe, affordable, accessible, and quality health care. Because it focuses on individuals and their reproductive health needs, it doesn't necessarily get at the root causes of *why* people don't have access to health care in the first place. *Reproductive rights* is a legal and advocacy approach focused on maintaining the individual legal right to abortion, contraception, and so on. The approach uses legislative strategies (e.g., promoting federal or state laws that enhance reproductive choice or preventing laws that erode it) and legal strategies (e.g., suing the government for allowing unjust laws to be implemented). Like the reproductive health approach, reproductive rights works at the level of the individual person, as demonstrated by the popular slogan "My body, my choice."

In contrast, the *reproductive justice* approach is a vision, framework, and social movement with a goal of collective power. Activists and scholars describe it as a *vision* that helps articulate a long-term idea of the world we want to create—a world in which people can decide if, when, and how they make their families. They also conceptualize RJ as a *framework* that provides a lens and agenda for understanding reproductive politics. Through the reproductive justice framework, we can make sense of how racism, classism, sexism, homophobia, transphobia, ableism, ageism, xenophobia, and so on affect reproductive health and rights. Finally, scholars and activists understand RJ as a *social movement* that brings together individuals and organizations working to advance reproductive freedom through policy advocacy, culture shift, grassroots organizing, and leadership development.[16] This isn't to say that all reproductive justice organizers and scholars easily agree on the definition and objectives of reproductive justice. As sociologist Zakiya Luna notes in her book tracing the history of SisterSong, there's even some disagreement about when and how the term emerged. She also details that during the early years of SisterSong—and the

RJ movement more generally—there were growing pains and tensions around a number of issues, such as how the movement understood and adopted concepts like human rights and social justice.[17] Scholars and organizers in the movement have also debated issues such as how much to center or decenter abortion, the role of nonprofit organizations and funding agencies in the movement, the relationship to the mainstream reproductive rights movement, and racism, homophobia, transphobia, ableism, and other forms of oppression within the movement.

Youth

Although it might seem relatively straightforward, who we consider a "youth" is actually quite complicated. I often use the category of youth to illustrate for my students the concept of social construction, or how the meaning of something is shaped through social processes and institutions. I ask them, "At what age are you no longer a youth?" Some students easily shout out "eighteen," and others look puzzled and say, "I thought they changed it to twenty-four?" Another will offer that a person is no longer a youth once they have children of their own, get married, or are financially independent from the adults who raised them. Others will note how the conditions of racism, class exploitation, homophobia, and transphobia often force young people to take on adult responsibilities at a young age, a process known as *adultification*. That my students' answers differ so much demonstrates how the category *youth* is slippery. It means different things to different people, and it changes throughout time and place. Institutions like the law, schools, and the health care system play a role in constructing who is and who is not a youth. For instance, in the United States, 18 years of age is considered the "age of majority" allowing young people to legally vote, own property, and live on their own. In many US states, people under 18 years old cannot legally consent to having sex.[18] The United Nations defines youth as individuals between 15 and 24 years of age.[19] The World Health Organization defines youth as ages 15–24 and "young people" as 10–24. The American Academy of Pediatrics has historically classified anyone under 21 years of age as a youth.[20] Conversely, the Centers for Disease Control and Prevention's biennial survey of youth health, the Youth Risk Behavior Surveillance System, considers youth to include people in grades 9–12 of high school.[21]

The idea of youth as a particular developmental or chronological part of the life course is a relatively recent social construction. Although we now generally consider youth to be a time of significant physical, psychological, and social change, prior to the 1900s there was no concept of youth as we currently understand it. In the United States, the concept began to take shape through psychological literature and changing social conditions during the early twentieth century. Rapid industrialization, the spread of compulsory schooling, and other social changes altered the way adults thought about young people and created new ways of managing them, from organized recreation such as the Boy Scouts to punitive "treatment" such as the juvenile justice system.[22] This new understanding of youth as a time of naturally occurring cognitive, psychosocial, and pubertal growth was also tied to ideas about modernity; that is, the category of youth reflected ideas about social progress and people as self-determining, independent, rational individuals. As youth studies scholar Nancy Lesko argues, in this era "adolescence became a social space in which to talk about the characteristics of people in modernity, to worry about the possibilities of social changes, and to establish policies and programs that would help create the modern order and citizenry."[23] In other words, the idea of "youth"—and young people themselves—became a container to hold social anxieties about a changing world.

Lesko demonstrates that ideas about who a "youth" was or what "normal" youth behavior involved were tied to ideas about race and social progress. Scientists began to frame youth in an evolutionary framework that mirrored the scientific racism also prevalent at the time: (white) youth were in need of the sorts of protection and cultivation that would enable them to progress from innocent children to productive adults. As a result, we began to think about youth as living in the future, rather than the present, because they exist in the discourse of "growing up": they are not children but not yet adults.[24] Young people of color and economically marginalized youth, however, were generally not granted the same innocence as white, property owning–class youth. For example, reproductive justice scholar Natalie Lira uncovers how working-class Mexican-origin youth in California were disproportionately confined in state institutions during the mid-1900s. Young women of color were institutionalized for "feeblemindedness," which was often code for having broken social norms such as having sex outside marriage. Young men of color were institutionalized for their real or perceived criminal activity. Both young Mexican-origin men and women were more likely than white youth to be sterilized without their consent.[25] As *Youth Organizing for Reproductive Justice* shows throughout, the social construction of some youth as bad or deviant has serious consequences for their reproductive autonomy.

Education scholars Eve Tuck and K. Wayne Yang contend that youth is a social location, rather than a chronological or developmental phase. Like Tuck and Yang's work, this book understands youth as a structural, historical, and political location in that "youth is a legally, materially, and always raced/gendered/ classed/sexualized category around which social institutions are built, disciplinary sciences created, and legal apparatuses mounted."[26] "Youth" is always already political. It is deeply wrapped up in social processes and institutions that co-create the meanings of race, class, gender, sexuality, and other axes of difference. Who we consider to be a youth, how we understand youth as an organizing feature of social life, how we interact with and best support youth—these are all deeply political issues. Depending on where they live and their access to resources, youth may or may not be able to consent to sexual activity, access an abortion, or become legally emancipated from their guardians when they have children of their own. In some US states, youth can be charged as an adult in criminal proceedings and sentenced to long prison terms in adult correctional facilities. In some states, legislators have made it a crime for a health care professional to provide gender-affirming care for transgender youth. In addition, in most states, minors cannot access an abortion without parental notification or a judicial bypass, a process in which a young person must attend court proceedings to ask a judge for permission to have the procedure.

For the most part in the United States, social institutions such as the family, the law, the educational system, and the health care system construct youth as passive, inferior, and deficient.[27] In this view, youth cannot be trusted to make decisions about their bodies, their education, or their futures. It assumes that youth are "broken" or "bad" and in need of adult intervention. These examples illustrate what education scholars Keri DeJong and Barbara Love call *youth oppression*. Also referred to as *adultism*, youth oppression is "the systematic subordination of younger people as a targeted group, who have relatively little opportunity to exercise social power through restricted access to the goods, services, and privileges of society, and denial of access to participation in the economic and political life of society."[28] Youth activism scholar Hava Rachel Gordon analyzes how adultism shows up in youth organizing. She argues that when young people engage in collective power, adults may implicitly and explicitly thwart their work and view their political organizing as "precocious, transgressive, and out-of-bounds of proper adolescent behavior."[29] This is a deficit model approach to youth, one that focuses on what's "wrong" with them. In contrast, an asset- or strengths-based model emphasizes young people's skills, knowledge, and resources, even in the face of adultism. Gordon argues that the idea of youth as "citizens in the making" is key to maintaining age as a system of oppression and youth as a subordinated group. In this model, adults may acknowledge young people's political participation but only in the future tense, when they eventually become adults.[30] Viewing reproductive injustices through the lens of youth oppression or adultism helps us to understand how ageism is a form of social power that affects the reproductive autonomy and health of young people.

In this book, "youth" refers to anyone who considers themselves to be a young person but for the most part refers to people under twenty-five years of age. I'm less concerned with the ages of the young people discussed in this book, though, than I am with youth as a social category that tells us something about a shared marginal relationship to power. This relationship is always structured by interlocking systems of oppression such as white supremacy, cissexism, ableism, adultism, and so on. When we say oppressions are "interlocking," we are referring to how they are mutually reinforcing, rely on one another, and are difficult to disentangle. For example, when society shames a young woman of color for having a baby as a teenager, this is racism, sexism, and adultism all playing out simultaneously. I focus on organizing by and for youth, especially multiply marginalized youth, but I'm also cautious not to romanticize youth organizing (more on this below). This book is about youth of all genders organizing for reproductive justice. It centers youth of color and LGBTQ youth because these young people are often the most impacted by interlocking systems of oppression. They have also engaged in some of the fiercest and most effective youth organizing.

Again, "youth" is always a raced, classed, and gendered category. For example, in recent years, service providers have shifted from the phrase "pregnant and parenting young women" to "expectant and parenting youth." This shift is intended to engage young cisgender men in service provision for young families and also makes the term more inclusive of trans and nonbinary parents who are not women. These are important goals, but the neutral language can sometimes hide the fact that most often the category refers to young women of color who are pathologized for early childbearing. Likewise, while many activists, scholars, and organizations have begun to use more gender-inclusive language when talking about reproduction (e.g., "pregnant people"), others have resisted this change on the false accusation that it erases women.[31] Language is always about power.

Organizing and Resistance

Youth *organizing* and *resistance* are also contested concepts. *Organizing* generally refers to some kind of coordinated effort in response to power imbalances or social inequality. Youth might organize to get cops out of their schools or change state policies on health care access for minors. This organizing could take such forms as engaging in political education, sit-ins, or protest or lobbying elected officials or forming affinity groups. Whereas organizing is something we can concretely name and do, *resistance* is harder to pin down. In the words of Michelle Fine, a renowned scholar of youth and social action, "Resistance is an epistemology, a line of vision, theorizing and analysis; it does not require intent and it does not guarantee victory, it simply presumes the human yearning for dignity and action."[32] By *epistemology*, Fine means that resistance is a theory of knowledge or a way of understanding how society works. As a strategy of theory and analysis, resistance helps us to imagine the world we want to live in. According to Fine, resistance theory recognizes "that oppression births structural violence but also critical resistance, despair, anger and also desire."[33] Resistance comes in many forms and may not always be recognizable as such. For example, education scholar Jessica Ruglis uses participatory action research in schools to argue that dropping out of school can be an active or subconscious form of resistance effort "to preserve one's humanity, elevate one's self to a higher level of life and go further away from death (physical, mental, spiritual, and psychic, etc.)."[34]

In terms of the relationship between resistance and organization, education scholar Pedro Noguera thinks of organizing as the highest form of resistance. For him, when we decide that "'we're going to focus on a particular issue, and we're going to plot a strategy to address that issue,' then we are engaged in genuine praxis."[35] We might think of resistance as way of thinking and feeling that inspires us to engage in organizing. However, *Youth Organizing for Reproductive Justice* doesn't neatly separate organizing and resistance. They are often entwined processes, and the following chapters weave together theories about how youth push back against power and the concrete actions they take to do so.

It can be easy to romanticize youth activism because adultism encourages us to imagine youth as apolitical or passive subjects in the face of social transformation. As Pedro Noguera and Chiara Cannella note, researchers "have characterized young people as passive participants in larger events, as spectators, ground troops, and victims, but rarely as actors with the ability to influence the course of events."[36] Individual young people such as Swedish climate activist Greta Thunberg or Pakistani girls' education activist Malala Yousafzai make for media-worthy inspirational stories of young people saving the world. However, this cultural obsession with a few high-profile young people obscures the significant work of young people in communities that do not have the ear of the international media and the resources it brings. It also draws on the legacy of a singular, charismatic leader in social movements, rather than collective action. In addition, it neglects the ways that youth resistance and organizing can be used as tools to consolidate, rather than challenge, power. Tuck and Yang caution us that organizations and researchers tend to "obscure understandings of youth resistance which may not align so neatly with established assumptions about civic participation and social movements."[37] Put another way, we must be aware of how particular adult-approved or -supported forms of resistance and organizing are privileged over others—especially those that are messy or unruly or that are not led by socially acceptable young people.

It's important to think critically about youth organizing and challenge taken-for-granted assumptions. First, youth organizing is often a strategy for addressing social problems that youth themselves did not create. In this sense, the burden is on youth to "fix" adult-made problems like poor-quality schooling, lack of access to health care, or the punitive criminal legal system.[38] A great deal of youth organizing takes place through nonprofit organizations; for example, when a community-based youth development organization gets a grant to train youth leaders to organize a peer health outreach program. Scholars and activists have critiqued how the *nonprofit industrial complex* takes the radical politics out of social movement work.[39] Essentially, because nonprofits are beholden to the individual donors and government grants that give them the money to run their programs, the work becomes all about the priorities of those in power and loses its radical edge. Youth activism scholar Soo Ah Kwon describes how nonprofit organizations often view youth organizing as a strategy for solving social problems like crime, school dropout, or unintended pregnancy. By marking youth, especially youth of color, as "at risk," such programs are a strategy to manage perceived youth deficits and regulate their lives. In seeking to empower youth, nonprofit programs often promote individual-level solutions (leadership development, signing petitions) to structural-level problems (racism, homophobia). Kwon calls this process "affirmative governmentality," referring to the ways that nonprofits "are called upon to regulate as well as empower 'at-risk' young people to exercise responsibility and self-government."[40] Nonprofit organizations can thus depoliticize political action and instead regulate the lives of young people affected by interlocking social oppressions.

We must also be attentive to the ways that adults commodify or fetishize youth organizing and young activists. In cautioning against this fetishization, writer and activist Yasmin Nair argues that nonprofit organizations often view LGBTQ youth as a way to garner funding because foundations and the government frequently invest money in youth-focused projects, though not usually with the goal of redistributing power. However, youth involved with these organizations are often "commodified and fetishized as potential revenue sources, but little is actually done to address the systemic issues that cause real harm to them." "Very often," she writes, "I hear fellow activists talk about 'youth' as if 'youth organizers' are some other-worldly creatures who will deliver us all from the evils facing the world. Say the word 'youth' in certain organizing circles, and everyone immediately steps back and refuses to engage in any critique of their practices."[41] In these situations, nonprofit organizations exploit youth organizing while activists position youth resistance as something that we cannot and should not critique.

Sociologist Jessica K. Taft, who studies girls' social movements in the United States and Latin America, acknowledges that critiquing youth organizing can pose risks. Adults all too often dismiss the idea that youth can produce knowledge or bring about social change. However, she also cautions us against the fetishizing of youth movements through "wowing," or over-eagerly celebrating the fact that young people are organizing at all without meaningfully engaging in the content of their political ideas and actions.[42] Taft encourages adults to think about youth organizing outside the binary of romanticizing-fetishizing and dismissing-undermining. Instead, she says, "we need stories that allow us to think deeply together about how to create intergenerational democratic communities that work collaboratively in the pursuit of social justice."[43]

With all these important critiques in mind, the chapters that follow tell stories about youth organizing for reproductive justice that involve success, contradiction, and sometimes fail-ure. I use examples both from youth organizing that takes place through nonprofit organizations and outside them. These are stories about individual youth activists and collective groups of youth organizers. Profiles spotlight fierce youth activists work-ing on the various issues described in the book. Many of these youth are on the older side, mainly for the reason that adultism makes it harder to find and speak to youth under age eighteen (who must receive parent or guardian consent). Although the focus is on youth, I provide many examples of youth working in solidarity with adult accomplices, including scholars and repro-ductive justice organizations.

Women of Color Feminisms and Queer of Color Critique

One of the effects of the uprisings in the summer of 2020 was that ideas and concepts around social justice have become avail-able to more and more people. The increase in attention to and visibility of issues related to social power and oppression is a good thing. At the same time, as concepts like *anti-racism, inter-sectionality, abolition,* or *reproductive justice* grow in popularity, we must take care to ground these concepts in their political and intellectual histories. To begin with, reproductive justice is based in the activist and intellectual tradition of *women of color feminisms,* an approach that builds knowledge from the particular vantage points of women of color. Terms such as *people of color* (POC) and *women of color* (WOC) are contested categories about which there is not always consensus. Loretta Ross, one of the founders of SisterSong, argues that "women of color" is a "solidarity definition [and a] commitment to work in collabo-ration with other oppressed women of color who have been minoritized."[44] Similarly, Zakiya Luna explains, "'Women of color' refers to both an identity and a political stance that, together, advance the idea that women and marginalized racial/ethnic groups experience oppression due to *both* their race and their gender, among other identities."[45]

Some activists and scholars argue that "people of color" homogenizes the experiences of those who are not white and reinforces the default nature of whiteness and white privilege. Similarly, as micha cárdenas points out, women of color feminism has historically meant *cisgender* women of color, thereby excluding the voices, analyses, and movements of transgender women of color.[46] Critiques of the term *people of color* prompted terms such as BIPOC, which usually stands for "Black, Indigenous, (and other) people of color." The term is intended to highlight the histories and experiences of Black and Indigenous people in the United States and the particular forms of oppression related to enslavement and settler colonialism. However, as Andrea Plaid and Chris Macdonald-Denis point out, there is confusion about which groups the term BIPOC actually includes, and when "you insist on naming Black people separately from other people of color, as BIPOC does, you are in effect claiming that Black people aren't people of color, though Black people coined the term."[47] This book recognizes that these terms will always be in contention. In the following chapters I use the words *women, youth*, and *people of color* as political terms of solidarity (in Ross's understanding) despite their imperfections and impossibilities.

The intellectual and activist work of women of color feminisms began to take shape in the 1960s and 1970s in response to the mainstream feminist movement.[48] Composed mostly of white, cisgender women who saw equality with men as their main goal, the mainstream movement excluded the needs and perspectives of women of color. Through both scholarship and activism, women of color feminisms advanced a vision of collective power grounded in the lived experiences of minoritized women. For example, Cherríe Moraga and Gloria Anzaldúa's notion of "theory in the flesh" built a political analysis from the concrete realities experienced by women of color. Their world-changing edited volume, *This Bridge Called My Back: Writings by Radical Women of Color,* first published in 1981, remains one of women of color feminism's key texts. Among other crucial pieces, the book includes Audre Lorde's groundbreaking essay and speech "The Master's Tools Will Never Dismantle the Master's House." Lorde argued that we cannot break down systems of oppression like racism and patriarchy without building our own tools of analysis, "for the master's tools will never dismantle the master's house. They may allow us temporarily to beat him at his own game, but they will never enable us to bring about genuine change."[49]

Audre Lorde also declared that "there is no such thing as a single-issue struggle because we do not live single-issue lives."[50] Here she called attention to the concept that we would later call *intersectionality,* a framework for analyzing how social identities and systems of oppression intersect with each other. For example, a young Latina trans woman experiences both transphobia, racism, and adultism simultaneously—and she can't separate "Latina" from "trans" in her understanding of her identities. Legal scholar Kimberlé Crenshaw coined the term in her 1991 article, "Mapping the Margins: Intersectionality, Identity Politics, and Violence against Women of Color," but the origins of the concept can be traced further back in time. For example, in 1977 the Combahee River Collective Statement, written by the

Boston-based Black lesbian feminist socialist group of the same name, called for an "integrated analysis and practice based upon the fact that the major systems of oppression are interlocking."[51] More recently, political theorist Jennifer Nash has cautioned against the idea that we can trace intersectionality to one specific group or piece of writing. She also criticizes how intersectionality has been called on to do to the work of "fixing" or "saving" white-dominated feminist thought and action.[52]

Similar to the way women of color feminisms constitute a distinct intellectual and activist project (not just a retooling of white feminism), the tradition of *queer of color critique* is not just a variation of white-dominated queer theory and activism. Scholars Grace Kyungwon Hong and Roderick Ferguson describe queer of color critique as "emerging from women of color feminism rather than deriving from a white Euro-American gay, lesbian, and queer theory tradition."[53] They also note the shared roots of queer of color critique and women of color feminisms in texts like *This Bridge Called My Back* and the Combahee River Collective Statement. Queer of color critique is an intellectual and political project grounded in the struggles and world making of LGBTQ people of color. Like women of color feminisms, it focuses on the knowledges and experiences of people multiply marginalized at the intersections of race, ethnicity, nation, gender, sexuality, and so on. As anthropologist Martin Manalansan explains, queer of color critique provides a "view from below" whose task is to "understand the traffic and travel of sexual matters, how certain bodies matter and certain bodies are located on the wayside."[54] Centering activism, scholarship, and cultural production by and for queer and trans people of color, this framework helps us analyze how racialization is a key part of the social regulation of sexuality and reproduction.

Queer of color critique and women of color feminisms offer us tools with which to think about how power, oppression, and resistance operate. In particular, these frameworks help us to theorize collective liberation and coalitional politics. In her influential 1997 article, "Punks, Bulldaggers, and Welfare Queens: The Radical Potential of Queer Politics?" political scientist Cathy Cohen argued for a coalitional form of politics through which shared marginal relationship to power—not just individually held identities—organizes our analyses. She suggests that "the process of movement building be rooted not in our shared history of identity, but in our shared marginal relationship to dominant power which normalizes, legitimizes, and privileges."[55] This analysis and vision helps us to understand how our own liberation is bound up in one another's. As the Combahee River Collective wrote in 1977, "If Black women were free, it would mean that everyone else would have to be free since our freedom would necessitate the destruction of all the systems of oppression." Centering those at the middle of interlocking systems of power illustrates how not only our struggles but also our freedoms are linked.

Women of color feminisms and queer of color critique are the main approaches that animate this book, but many other related, complementary frameworks share their political commitments. As one example, disability justice has many of the same epistemological and strategic foci as reproductive justice, including a commitment to bodily autonomy and a critique of choice- and rights-based discourses. Both frameworks were born of women and queer of color organizing. Both challenge an individualistic focus on rights and choice and instead direct attention to the interlocking systems of power that constrain self-determination and bodily autonomy.[56] Disability scholar Alison Kafer points out that the movements for disability justice and reproductive justice focus on cross-movement organizing because of their deep connection to the politics of race, class, sexuality, health care, and social services.[57] Historically, tensions have arisen between disability rights and reproductive rights over genetic testing and selective abortion—for instance, the right to terminate a pregnancy due to a fetal diagnosis that may result in a disability versus the right of disabled people to live with dignity and support. Yet, as scholars Dorothy Roberts and Sujatha Jesudason argue in their call for cross-movement solidarity between reproductive and disability justice, an intersectional analysis of the issues each movement faces can "reveal and create commonalities among people who are affected by the same matrix of domination."[58]

As overarching theoretical frameworks that link together the thematic chapters, women of color feminisms and queer of color critique demonstrate how all youth justice in the new millennium is reproductive justice. Analyzing youth RJ as a coalitional form of politics grounded in the struggles and world making of people of color and queer and trans youth allows us to see how seemingly disparate issues such as the school-to-prison pipeline and transgender youth's access to gender-affirming care are reproductive justice issues alongside abortion access and support for pregnant and parenting teens. As the 2020 report "A Young People's Reproductive Justice Policy Agenda" demonstrates, youth organizers and their co-conspirators frame reproductive justice in this broad sense. Rather than understanding reproductive or racial justice issues as separate, young people view their connections as inextricable. The report explains that there is a "focus on race in each of the issue areas, instead of creating a narrow and separate category of racial justice issues. The same is true of gender, sexuality, economic status, immigration status, and other identities."[59] In other words, youth organizing for reproductive justice centers on a shared marginal relationship to power, rather than viewing reproductive injustice in narrow issue- or identity-based terms, and thus demonstrates the power of a coalitional approach to political organizing.

WHO AM I TO WRITE THIS BOOK?

My words in this book are not the only way of thinking about youth organizing and reproductive justice. They are written from my perspective as someone who has both participated in and conducted research on RJ movements. I don't believe in "experts," and we must always consider who gets to be considered a producer of knowledge. In referring to RJ "activists and scholars" throughout this book, I am not suggesting that activists and scholars are mutually exclusive groups; many people are both. Instead, I use this phrase to acknowledge the all too often ignored political thought and work of people from outside formal academic institutions.

Women of color feminisms and queer of color critique ask us to pay attention to how power moves around the social world. In line with these traditions, it's important to name who I am as the author of this book about youth organizing for reproductive justice. It has become common in social justice circles to begin a social media post, lecture, workshop, or piece of writing with a list of the author's privileged and marginalized identities. This is a well-intentioned but nonetheless flawed attempt to wrestle with power and privilege. Scholars call this sort of reflection on how our social positionalities affect our research "reflexivity." Although it is important and necessary to identify how your experiences of marginalization and privilege impact your world-view, doing so poses the danger of flattening difference and making something complex appear very neat and tidy. The messiness of experience, identity, and power makes it tricky to simply list your identities and claim stable truths about the social world and your place in it.

With these limitations in mind: I'm writing this book because I am scholar who studies youth, reproductive justice, and political organizing. I teach college courses on reproductive justice, sexuality education, queer of color critique, and feminist public health. I conduct social research on topics including youth pregnancy and parenting, queer sexualities, transgender health, social movements, and political education. Because I make my living as a university professor, part of my job includes writing books. Reproductive justice activists and scholars who work in nonprofit organizations or in grassroots organizing rarely get to write books as an official part of their job. My job of teaching college courses and conducting research doesn't alone qualify me as the "best" person to write about youth and reproductive justice—it just means I have the resources and time to do so. In addition, the fact that I no longer have care responsibilities for dependent children or elders means that I have had the "luxury" of working on it as part of a predictable writing routine, instead of during scattered moments when another person's bodymind didn't need my attention.

My very unusual experience of being a high school dropout turned teen parent turned university professor greatly affects my analyses. I am no longer a young person, but becoming a young parent was and has always been a big part of how I understand the world. It was this experience that politicized me and opened my consciousness to question power and oppression. I come from a family with one brown parent and one white parent; I generally, though not always, move through the world experiencing the benefits of white privilege. I hold a complicated social class background, having been raised middle-class but later becoming, in my own words, a welfare queen, and then later becoming a university professor. My queer gender and sexuality motivate my politics as does my complicated racial-ethnic and class background. These positionalities have resulted in my familiarity with the experience of marginalization *and* the people and institutions that produce it. The workings of power that structure my experiences of oppression and privilege are far too complicated to do justice to in these paragraphs, but they undoubtedly affect what I write about and how I do so.

WHO THIS BOOK IS FOR AND HOW TO READ IT

This book is for anyone who wants an introduction to issues surrounding youth, reproductive justice, and political organizing. To read this primer, you do not need to have prior knowledge about the topics to engage with the book. However, even those familiar with reproductive justice will benefit from the case studies, activist spotlights, and focus on praxis (putting thought into action). This material will be especially useful for students, who can take the material they learn in the classroom and apply it to their organizing efforts. Beyond the classroom, the book has a lot to offer activists and reproductive justice organization staff. For instance, you could use the book as part of employee training or onboarding or in youth leadership development programs. Both youth and adult accomplices can benefit from the material and analyses in this book. The material generally focuses on youth, reproductive justice, and political organizing in the United States in contemporary times. However, it also understands sexuality, reproduction, and politics in a transnational frame. As queer sociologists Ghassan Moussawi and Salvador Vidal-Ortiz describe this frame, "To treat the United States as a transnational site of study means to recognize its settler colonial history and its geopolitical role."[60] In *Youth Organizing for Reproductive Justice*, this means that although I'm writing about the United States, I'm also thinking about how, for instance, early sex education efforts were part of US military intervention overseas or how today's abortion activists adapt tactics employed in social movements in Latin America.

At its core, *Youth Organizing for Reproductive Justice* is a pedagogical book. *Pedagogy* refers to the art and philosophy of teaching and learning. By calling this book pedagogical, I intend that it help build readers' knowledge and perspectives on youth and reproductive justice. *Youth Organizing for Reproductive Justice* can also help readers develop skills for working in solidarity for reproductive justice by strengthening our vision, framework, and movement. I believe that learning should bring joy and pleasure, but it is not always fun and easy. This book may challenge you and bring you to your "learning edge" by pushing you out of your comfort zone. That's a good thing!

Each chapter focuses on a different issue related to youth and reproductive justice. The book begins with issues that might seem obviously connected to reproductive justice, such as abortion and teen parenting, and then moves toward ones that readers may not have considered before, like gender-affirming care and the school-to-prison pipeline. I begin the following text by laying out a broad overview of youth reproductive justice issues that focus on historical, legal, and political contexts. Next, I review what we know from research on the issues; for example, why youth seek an abortion without parental consent and how gender-affirming care improves mental health. Chapters also showcase youth organizing around the issue. It's not possible in this primer to provide an exhaustive overview of the many, many forms that youth organizing for reproductive justice takes. I focus on exemplars from the past fifteen years that help illustrate both the possibilities and limitations of youth organizing.

Chapters also contain "spotlight boxes" where I profile youth activists, organizations, and campaigns. The spotlights are brief case studies that further illustrate the themes of each chapter. People, projects, and organizations have been spotlighted rather than included in the main text if I had less archival material about them or if they were related to the chapter theme but not part of the core focus. The youth organizer spotlights are the product of a collaboration with Advocates for Youth, a US-based nonprofit organization that "partners with young people and their adult allies to champion youth rights to bodily autonomy and build power to transform policies, programs and systems to secure sexual health and equity for all youth."[61] I provided them with the chapter themes and asked them to invite exceptional youth working on those issues to an interview for the project. Each chapter also includes a spotlight box with how-to information on different aspects of organizing, such as issue selection or choosing a tactic. You can read the chapters in any order or read some and not the others. In the spirit of sitting with the discomfort of potentially generative learning experiences, I invite you to avoid skipping over the chapters you think you already know everything about, as well as to read chapters that may lie outside your main areas of interest. My hope is that you learn as much from reading this book as I did from writing it.

CHAPTER ONE

Abortion Access and Beyond

The first time I ever got carded for something as a legal adult was the day after my eighteenth birthday. I got carded for an abortion. The receptionist behind the counter at the clinic asked for an ID, and I enthusiastically handed her my license. "This is the first time since I turned eighteen that I've had to show my ID for something!" I exclaimed. The receptionist did not seem to appreciate my dark humor as she photocopied my ID and told me to take a seat.

It wasn't a coincidence that I was getting an abortion the day after my eighteenth birthday; in fact, it was quite intentional. When I missed my period earlier that summer, I didn't think much of it. Periods were sometimes irregular, and I was on the pill. When I missed a second period and got a positive pregnancy test, I didn't hesitate to schedule an abortion. This was the 1990s and the internet wasn't really a thing yet, so it meant calling all the numbers on the handout the teen clinic had given me. I quickly realized that scheduling the appointment wouldn't be easy. I called clinics all around southern New Hampshire, where I lived at the time, and none would schedule the procedure without first charging for an ultrasound to confirm the length of gestation. They were concerned the pregnancy was past twelve weeks' gestation and would require a slightly different abortion procedure. The ultrasound would cost several hundred dollars, which I couldn't afford, in addition to the price of the procedure itself. I was able to find a clinic in nearby Massachusetts that would schedule an appointment without an ultrasound, but at the time, a law in that state required unmarried minors under eighteen to obtain the notarized or in-person consent of both parents. If that wasn't possible, the only way to get an abortion was to go to court and get permission from a judge, a process called a "judicial bypass."[1]

I was only a couple of weeks away from turning eighteen, so I decided to schedule the appointment in Massachusetts for the day after my birthday. This decision also meant that the procedure was costlier and riskier (but only *very* slightly so—abortion is an incredibly safe medical procedure, less risky than giving birth or having your wisdom teeth removed).[2] The whole process of getting the appointment was stressful, frustrating, and scary. It was also the first time I began to think about the politics of reproductive health care access. I was fortunate that I was able to navigate the situation relatively easily, and that "fortune" was due to the privilege I held as someone who spoke English and had US citizenship, a car, and enough money saved up to pay for the procedure. Only four years later New Hampshire would enact a parental notification law of its own. Over the next decade, states across the United States enacted countless restrictions on abortion access for minors *and* adults, including mandatory waiting periods, mandatory unnecessary ultrasounds, requirements that providers share false information about abortion risks, bans on certain types of abortion procedures, and provider-targeted laws that resulted in the mass closure of clinics. During this time, although abortion was still *technically* legal in all US states, these laws limited access so severely that abortion care was *effectively* banned in many areas of the country.

After many years of escalating restrictions on and attempts to outright ban abortion, in June 2022 the US Supreme Court, now stacked with ultraconservative justices, issued its decision in *Dobbs v. Jackson Women's Health*. This decision overturned the 1973 decision in *Roe v. Wade* and the 1993 decision in *Planned Parenthood v. Casey*, officially ended the constitutional right to abortion in the United States, and allowed states to ban the procedure altogether. It's important to note, however, that the attacks on abortion access that youth activists are fighting in the new millennium are rooted in a long history of reproductive oppression. They did not start, nor will they end, with the escalating abortion bans that preceded the end of *Roe*.[3] As the disability justice organization Sins Invalid explains in its solidarity statement "Reproductive Justice Is Disability Justice," abortion bans can be traced back to the "violent control [that] began with exploration, conquest and colonization of Indigenous lands and practices, and through chattel slavery and dehumanization through torture of Black people."[4] Rather than locating abortion bans' origin in the 2010s or 2020s, Sins Invalid reminds us of their roots in much older histories of reproductive control, including the theft of Indigenous families' land and enslaved people's forced reproduction.

Abortion has often taken center stage in the fight for reproductive freedom—and for good reason. People cannot decide if, when, and how to create a family without access to abortion. Some of those new to learning about reproductive politics may assume that abortion access is the primary—or only—objective of movements for reproductive freedom. This misconception is due to the historical conflation of "reproductive rights" with "abortion rights" and the ways that a pro-choice movement dominated by white, owning-class, cisgender women framed "choice" as the right to choose abortion and contraception. The reproductive justice vision, framework, and movement that women of color organizers birthed in the mid-1990s was an act of resistance to this narrow framing of choice. Women of color activists and scholars pushed back against the idea that fighting for the individual right to *not have* children was the only goal of reproductive freedom. As scholar Jael Silliman wrote in 2002, the emphasis on individual choice "obscures the social context in which the state regulates populations, disciplines individual bodies, and exercises control over sexuality, gender, and reproduction."[5] Women of color have long been fighting against coercive contraceptive and sterilization practices, the state-sanctioned removal of Black and Indigenous children from their homes, the stigmatization of women who receive public assistance benefits, and so on. Thus, the expansive vision of reproductive justice includes abortion access, but it also focuses on the right to *have* children and raise them in safe and supportive communities.

Although abortion is not the singular focus of reproductive justice organizing, historically it has been—and continues to be—an important part of our interconnected struggles. Because it is an issue some readers may have more familiarity with, I discuss it before moving on to other topics that may seem less central to reproductive justice, such as youth criminalization. Youth access to abortion has a lot to teach us about interconnected struggles for bodily autonomy. Attempts to control youth access to abortion are part of larger systems of social control explored throughout this book: white supremacist, adultist, transphobic attempts to regulate the bodies of marginalized young people. For instance, the attempts to criminalize abortion patients and providers that escalated in the years before *Roe* was overturned are intimately connected to the criminalization of trans youth in health care and youth of color in schools. By shifting our focus to youth organizing and resistance surrounding abortion, we can more fully appreciate how struggles for abortion access are also struggles for racial justice, queer justice, and youth justice more broadly. This chapter first reviews the history of youth access to abortion in the United States by exploring how laws regulating abortion have disproportionately harmed young people. Next, it describes what we know from research on youth experiences of accessing abortion and how restricting abortion access reproduces inequality. Before, during, and since the overturn of *Roe v. Wade*, young people have sparked vibrant campaigns not only to expand access to abortion but also to reimagine abortion care and access. This section profiles the full-spectrum doula movement, mutual aid, and digital activism as exemplars of how young people have organized to build creative strategies surrounding abortion access and care.

A BRIEF HISTORY OF RESTRICTING MINORS' ACCESS TO ABORTION

In the weeks following the leak of the *Dobbs* decision draft in May 2022, news outlets around the country focused on stories about what it was like to get an abortion before it was legal in all US states. Articles under headlines such as "They Had Secret Abortions Pre-*Roe*; Now They Feel Compelled to Speak Out" and "Women Share Their Experience of Getting an Abortion before *Roe* Made It Legal" remembered days when women visited clandestine providers, traveled out of the country, or attempted to self-manage an abortion without effective methods.[6] Loretta Ross told the *New York Times* about her abortion that took place three years before the *Roe* decision—when the procedure was legal in the District of Columbia but parent permission was required. She was sixteen years old, the mother of a young child, and a college student at Howard University. Her mother wanted her to drop out of college and continue the pregnancy. As Ross explained, "By the time I had gone through all the fighting with my mom, and all the delays, I was in my third trimester. I had to have a saline abortion, where they inject this huge—it felt like a mile long—needle into your stomach, and induce labor."[7]

Before *Roe v. Wade* (and since 2022), a patchwork of different state-level laws could mean that crossing a line on a map presented a very different set of barriers to getting an abortion. *Roe* established a constitutional right to abortion but specified that states had cognizable interests in protecting the health of the pregnant person or the fetus, interests that grew in significance as a pregnancy progressed. To manage this tension between an individual person's constitutional right to abortion and the interests of the state, the Court established the "trimester framework." In the first trimester of pregnancy (approximately 12–14 weeks' gestation), the state did not have a sufficiently compelling interest in restricting abortion. In the second trimester (approximately 13 to 27 weeks' gestation), the state's interest in protecting the health of the pregnant person became sufficiently compelling as to warrant restrictions aimed at protecting the health of the pregnant person; and at fetal viability in the third trimester (approximately 27 to 40 weeks' gestation), the state's interest in protecting potential life was deemed sufficiently compelling to justify banning abortion, except if necessary to protect the patient's life and health.

Roe v. Wade made no distinctions about the age of the person seeking the abortion. However, courts and state legislatures began to impose restrictions on abortion access almost immediately after the decision, and laws aimed at youth were among them. In 1976, the US Supreme Court struck down a Missouri law that required a person seeking an abortion to obtain spousal consent if married and parental consent if a minor. The Court ruled that the parental consent requirement was unconstitutional, but it also signaled that it might accept a less intrusive law. Three years later in the case of *Bellotti v. Baird,* the Court stressed that while minors do have a constitutional right to an abortion, "the peculiar vulnerability of children; their inability to make critical decisions in an informed, mature manner; and the importance of the parental role in child rearing" meant that minors' decision-making autonomy could be limited by requiring the involvement of a parent or a judge.[8] In a series of similar cases in the early 1980s, courts tried to sort out the legality of requiring the consent of one or both parents or simply requiring their notification.

Historian Rickie Solinger points out that the late 1970s were a time of great anxiety about youth sexuality and reproduction, among parents and politicians alike. This time period was also when researchers, policy makers, and the general public began to understand teenage pregnancy as a social problem in need of fixing. The anxiety around teen pregnancy emerged as white teenagers began having babies at increasing rates: white and middle-class families began to see teen pregnancy as something affecting *their* children. Solinger argues that "as teenage girls became threatening emblems of sexual and reproductive insubordination, politicians and others devoted national and community resources to reestablishing parental authority."[9] (I would add that this adultist urge to establish authority was also about maintaining white supremacy through positioning certain families as deviant and others as deserving of support.) Parental involvement laws offered one way to reestablish this authority. In 1992, the US Supreme Court issued its ruling in the pivotal abortion case *Planned Parenthood v. Casey,* which drastically changed the legal standard set out in *Roe v. Wade.* Instead of *Roe*'s trimester framework, *Casey* ruled that states could regulate abortion from the time of conception forward so long as the regulation does not impose an "undue burden" on the right to abortion. This decision opened a door for the tidal wave of abortion restrictions that took place from the mid-1990s up until the Supreme Court overturned *Roe* and *Casey* in 2022 with the *Dobbs* decision. *Casey* allowed for the proliferation of parental notification laws in addition to restrictions such as mandated waiting times, requirements that patients view an ultrasound of the fetus, requirements that doctors provide medically inaccurate information about the procedure, and restrictions about who could provide abortions and where, among many others.

As this book goes to press, laws in 43 states require a young person under 18 (or in some states, 17, 16, or 15) to involve a parent or legal guardian in their decision to have an abortion.[10] In some states, a young person only needs to notify one parent or guardian, in others they may need the consent of both, and in still others a relative other than a parent may give consent. Some states have imposed additional barriers, such as requiring the parent's proof of identification or parenthood. If a young person does not want to or cannot involve their parent or guardian in their abortion decision, or if the parent or guardian will not give permission, the young person can go to a court to obtain a judicial bypass. The laws and process vary from state to state, but basically the young person attends a hearing in which the judge asks a series of questions to determine if they are "mature" enough to make the decision and that no one else is influencing their decision. Many states also provide legal support for minors seeking judicial bypass, including pro bono (free) attorneys who can accompany them to the hearing. The following section of this chapter details what we know from research on the effects of parental involvement laws on young people's access to abortion.

Parental involvement laws are not the only way that youth are prevented from obtaining the abortion care they need. First, the Hyde Amendment, enacted in 1976 and reauthorized several times since then, bars federal money from being used to pay for abortion care. This means that low-income people who have government-based insurance such as Medicaid or receive care through the Indian Health Services (IHS) or the military cannot get their abortion covered by their health insurance (unless they live in one of the few states that use state money to fund Medicaid abortions). The Hyde Amendment disproportionately affects low-income people and has significant effects on youth and people of color because they are more likely to have health care coverage though Medicaid. Second, the "gag rule," first implemented under President Ronald Reagan in 1988, prevents health care clinics that receive money through the Title X family planning program from counseling patients about abortion. Under the gag rule, health care providers cannot provide abortion information or referrals to patients, even if a patient requests it.[11] Over the years, whenever a Democrat has been in the White

House, the gag rule has been revoked, but when a Republication has been in office it has been reinstated. What this means is that certain health care providers can or cannot refer patients to abortion care depending on who the president is at the time. Finally, abortion restrictions that apply regardless of age are even more burdensome for youth. Even a young person who has parental permission or has obtained a judicial bypass may be unable to afford to get an abortion if they must travel hundreds of miles or schedule multiple clinic visits, particularly if they can't risk missing school or being away from home for so long. Because young people usually have health insurance through their parents, they are unlikely to use it to pay for their abortion without alerting their parents (some states, such as Massachusetts, have taken steps to allow minors to bill insurance for an abortion procedure without their parents' knowledge). And because youth generally do not have consistent incomes—or any income at all—paying hundreds of dollars for a procedure plus transportation and hotel may be completely out of reach.

For the most part, state laws affirm young people's right to consent to reproductive and sexual health care other than abortion, such as contraception, STI (sexually transmitted infection) screening and treatment, and prenatal care. That youth can consent to all these other services, but not abortion, undermines the rationales for forcing parents or judges to get involved in a clinically safe and effective health care service. Medical and public health professional organizations such as the American Public Health Association, the American Medical Association, and the American Academy of Pediatrics all oppose forced parental involvement in a youth's decision to have an abortion. These professional organizations instead emphasize the importance of protecting young people's confidentiality and the risks

ORGANIZING 101: PRINCIPLES OF YOUTH
ORGANIZING

Although their names are sometimes used interchangeably,
there are often big differences between approaches to youth
engagement for social justice. For example, at one end of the
continuum, the *youth services* approach views young people
as clients and provides individual services aimed at prevention and treatment of various educational, health, or legal
issues. Somewhere in the middle of the continuum is *youth
development*, also sometimes called *positive youth development*. This approach sees young people as participants, pro-
motes social emotional learning, and sometimes supports
leadership development. At the other end of the continuum,
youth organizing is the process of young people and their
adult accomplices coming together to build collective power.
It may involve elements of positive youth development or
even youth services, but youth organizing views young people as active change makers in challenging power structures and making concrete difference in their communities.

FIERCE (Fabulous Independent Educated Radicals for
Community Empowerment), a membership-based youth
development organization for and by LGBTQ youth of color in
New York City, offers five key principles of youth organizing.
First, youth organizing starts with building a large, strong
base of youth members. Base building includes outreach,
recruitment, and retention of youth most affected by the
issues at hand. Second, developing youth leadership and
political consciousness is key. This development ranges
from training workshops to political education through social
media. Third, youth organizing involves youth exercising
power through direct action campaigns, like the ones

detailed in this book. Youth identify issues in their communities and put pressure on the people in power to meet their demands. Fourth, youth organizing works to challenge and dismantle interlocking systems of oppression. Rather than viewing struggles for liberation as separate and distinct, youth organizing sees them through the lens of collective power. Finally, youth organizing is youth led, meaning that youth make decisions at all steps of the process and are involved in all levels of leadership. Adults may support youth, but youth have the self-determination to identify issues, choose strategies, and build power on their own terms.

of delaying abortion access.[12] As the American Academy of Pediatrics explains, "Adolescents should not be required to involve parents in the decision to obtain an abortion because legal abortion therapies are safe and most adolescents are capable of medical decision-making."[13]

WHAT DOES RESEARCH TELL US ABOUT THE EFFECTS OF ABORTION RESTRICTIONS ON YOUTH?

Many of my college students are eighteen to twenty-four years old, an age group with higher rates of unintended pregnancy and abortion. Their life stage likely colors their perception that rates of youth pregnancy, birth, and abortion are at an all-time high, or at least increasing from previous generations. They are often surprised to learn that the rates of pregnancy, birth, and abortion among youth in the United States have, in fact, been consistently falling for the past several decades. It's difficult to pinpoint the exact reasons for these declines, but researchers generally attribute them to increased access to contraception, changes in norms around safer sex, and economic and cultural shifts.[14] The years immediately following *Roe v. Wade* in 1973 saw a bump in the rate of abortion for all age groups—understandable given that the procedure became more widely available. In the 1980s, abortion rates for youth ages 15 to 19 years old plateaued, and in the 1990s they began to decline. In 2017, the rate of abortion (both medication and procedure abortion, sometimes called "surgical") among women[15] of reproductive age (15 to 44 years old) was the lowest since abortion became legal. In 1973, the rate was 16.3 abortions per 1,000 among women aged 15 to 44. It peaked in 1980 at 29.3 per 1,000 and by 2017 had declined to 13.5 per 1,000. Teenagers make up a minority of the people who have abortions. For instance, in 2017 youth under 15 years old accounted for only about 0.3 percent of the abortions in the United States. Teens ages 15–19 accounted for about 9 percent of all abortions. However, 18–19 year olds (who are legally adults) had abortions at a rate more than twice that of 17–18 year olds. Young people ages 20–24 made up 29 percent of all abortions in 2017, the largest proportion of any age group.[16]

Most young people accessing abortion care voluntarily involve their parents or another trusted adult. Studies across several decades have found that about two-thirds of minors voluntarily involve at least one parent, often their mother, in their abortion decision. A large 1992 study found that 61 percent of minors in states without parental involvement laws informed at least one parent about their decision to access abortion. In a more recent study, researchers found that 64 percent of people under age 18 reported that their mother was aware of their decision, and 93 percent reported that their mothers were supportive. Studies have also found that youth aged 15 and younger are more likely to notify their parents than 16- and 17-year-olds.[17] Young people offer a variety of reasons for choosing to involve a parent in their abortion decision. Some youth already have a close relationship with their parent and anticipate their support. Some assume that their parents will inevitably find out anyway, and others involve parents because they need practical support, such as financial assistance or a ride to the clinic.[18] Young people who do not want to involve one or more of their parents in their abortion decision have good reason not to. They may suspect that their parents will not support their decision and interfere with their ability to access care. Youth may worry that their decision would negatively affect their relationship with their parent, or they may simply want to have a sense of privacy and personal autonomy. Some may wish to shield a parent under stress from some other cause (e.g., the parents' own health issues) from yet another thing to deal with. Other youth have serious concerns about experiencing conflict with or coercion or violence from family members. Conversely, youth may just be unable to obtain consent from a parent if they are involved in the foster care system, if the parent is incarcerated, or if the parent lives outside the United States.

Youth who cannot involve their parents in their abortion decision must obtain a judicial bypass, travel out of state, or continue the pregnancy. The judicial bypass process poses a serious emotional and logistical burden on the young person, who must navigate the legal system and share intimate details about their lives and bodies in a courtroom—and the judge might not even permit the abortion![19] Youth have described judicial bypass as a humiliating and scary process in which judges shame them and question their maturity.[20] To cite just one example of many, a story that went viral in January 2022 revealed that a Florida judge had denied a judicial bypass for a 17-year-old on the grounds that her low grade point average at school indicated that her "lack of intelligence" meant that she was not mature enough to make the decision to have an abortion.[21] Even the attorneys who assist minors through the process experience shame and stigma from judges, court personnel, and other attorneys.[22] Finally, the harms of the judicial bypass system are not evenly distributed. Minors who seek a judicial bypass for abortion are more likely than those obtaining parental consent to be people of color or economically marginalized, or both. Youth who are homeless, undocumented, or estranged from their parents are also disproportionately harmed by these barriers to access.[23]

Estimating the effects of state laws that mandate parental involvement in a minor's abortion is complicated. Although some studies have found a decline in minors' abortion rate following mandated parental involvement, this research may not account for minors who leave the state for their abortions. Studies that do include data on minors who travel out of state have found no effect of parental involvement laws on the abortion rate. Unsurprisingly, like the experience I share at the beginning of this chapter, research suggests that forcing youth to involve their parents in their abortion decision simply leads them to travel to states without parental involvement laws. The average distance that a minor had to travel to access an abortion increased from 55 miles in 1992 to 454 miles in 2015.[24] Obtaining a judicial bypass adds an additional trip, and youth may have to travel long distances to courthouses. An Illinois study found that minors traveled an average of 48 miles round trip to attend their judicial bypass hearing.[25] The reality that youth must travel long distances to obtain an abortion has become so commonplace that the "abortion road trip" has become a popular novel and film plot.[26]

Although parental involvement laws do not necessarily decrease the youth abortion rate, they *do* increase the risks of delayed procedures (which are more expensive and potentially riskier), unsafe self-managed procedures, and family violence.[27] One study in Massachusetts found that minors who obtained abortions after securing a judicial bypass experienced significantly greater delays than those who had parental consent. Youth who had to go through the judicial bypass process also had higher odds of becoming ineligible for medication abortion due to the delay.[28] Although self-managed abortion (when a person chooses to induce their own abortion outside a medical setting) can be safely completed with medication, parental involvement laws lead some youth to purchase pills from disreputable internet sites or avoid seeking medical care when there are complications.[29] As one young person from Illinois explained, the burden of parental involvement may lead young people to "do some other crazy stuff to get rid of [the pregnancy]."[30] A research study with young people experiencing homelessness found that self-induced abortions were common in that population. Youth reported buying herbs, inserting sharp objects into the vagina, planning physical violence, and consuming extreme amounts of drugs or alcohol or both in order to end the pregnancy.[31] Although advocates of parental involvement laws argue that they promote family communication, no evidence indicates that forcing youth to involve their parents leads to improved family relationships, and it can instead lead to physical and emotional harm.[32]

YOUTH MOBILIZING FOR ABORTION

Data show that young people in the United States overwhelmingly support access to legal abortion, and this viewpoint can be a motivating force to get out and vote. Indeed, many politicians lean into their support for abortion to build their base of young voters.[33] Undoubtedly, public policies, law, and the courts are essential components of mobilizing to protect youth access to abortion. In line with this book's broad focus on youth organizing, however, this section highlights grassroots efforts to challenge abortion stigma and provide financial, logistical, and practical support to young people seeking abortion care. Youth have fiercely reimagined abortion access outside the highly restricted legal sphere and through the full spectrum of reproduction and the politics of mutual aid. The following subsections highlight youth involvement in the full-spectrum doula movement, abortion activism in the digital realm, and abortion mutual aid.

Building Young People's Involvement in the Fight for Reproductive Freedom

Student activism has a rich history in the United States. The 1960s and '70s saw a groundswell of mobilization on college campuses as young people organized around civil rights and against the wars in Vietnam and Cambodia. The Student Nonviolent Coordinating Committee (SNCC) formed in the early 1960s out of lunch counter protests against racial segregation in North Carolina and Tennessee and later organized around voting rights. Students at San Francisco State University went on strike from November 1968 to March 1969 (the longest student strike in US history) to expose white supremacy in higher education and demand support for students of color. This strike resulted in the formation of the school's Black studies and ethnic studies departments and ignited a wave of similar actions across the country. Colleges and universities were also sites for organizing the emerging queer liberation movement, such as the 1970 sit-ins at New York University against the administration's repression of queer social events on campus.[34] Since the HIV/AIDS crisis arose, colleges and universities have been sites of peer health education and mobilization against government neglect of the pandemic. In 2024, students across the United States borrowed a tactic from the 1960s and 70s and began occupying university buildings and lawns to demand an immediate ceasefire in the war on Palestine, an end to the genocide of the Palestinian people, and university divestment from companies that profit from the violence and occupation.[35]

In 1981, Hampshire College, a small liberal arts institution in rural western Massachusetts, formed the first campus-based organization in support of the reproductive rights movement. What was then called the Civil Liberties and Public Policy (CLPP, pronounced "clip") program has since mobilized and supported countless young people in the fight for reproductive health, rights, and justice. As it was for so many other young people, CLPP was responsible for bolstering my involvement in the RJ movement and for expanding my understanding of reproductive freedom beyond just access to abortion. For more than forty years, what is now called Collective Power for Reproductive Justice has been a driving force in leadership development, political education, and movement building. Many of the people and projects detailed in this book have connections to the program. Key among CLPP/Collective Power's work over the years has been its annual activist conference, first held in June 1984. Titled "Reproductive Rights: A Student Issue" and attended by about thirty people, the sessions focused on legislative updates, networking across difference, and organizing workshops. By 1987 the conference was renamed "The Fight for Reproductive Freedom" and refocused the goals of bringing together student activists to learn from one another, build solidarity, and illustrate the broad array of issues that fell under "reproductive rights." Although the term *reproductive justice* wouldn't be coined for another decade, CLPP/Collective Power for RJ was foreshadowing the approach by including racial, disability, environmental, youth, disability, and LGBTQ rights alongside abortion rights. For example, the 1987 conference featured workshops including access to reproductive health care for women of color, disability and reproductive rights, AIDS and the Black community, safer sex, and gay and lesbian parenting. This broad approach was reflected in the 1988 conference title, "The Fight for Abortion Rights and Reproductive Freedom: A Conference for Student Activists and Community Activists." By 2002 the conference title reflected CLPP/Collective Power's role in social justice movement building in and beyond reproduction: "From Abortion Rights to Social Justice: Building the Movement for Reproductive Freedom."

The conference weekend usually begins with an abortion speak-out, where attendees, many of them young people, share their abortion story as a practice of speaking against stigma. Throughout the weekend, well-known reproductive justice activists like Loretta Ross make keynote speeches, and workshop topics range from how to talk with legislators to activist self-care. Dance parties and other social events take place in the evenings, and there are always food and conference goodies like T-shirts, tote bags, stickers, and buttons. I first attended the CLPP conference in 2005, when I was a twenty-three-year-old college student and a single parent to a preschooler. It was actually the first time I attended *any* conference: CLPP was free to attend and offered free on-site childcare, making it possible for me to attend (an example of the connections between economic and reproductive justice). Having an abortion was the first thing that politicized me about reproduction, but it was getting pregnant as a teenager and having a baby as a young, low-income single parent that really lit that fire. From my vantage point, I could easily see how the politics of abortion, childbirth, and parenting were connected, but the CLPP conference expanded that even further. At that first conference I learned about what birth doula programs did inside prisons, how the United States was complicit in promoting sterilization of women in the Global South, and how disability rights were connected to reproductive rights, among many other things. In other words, I began to understand the reproductive justice vision. This is not to say that CLPP was always perfect at rooting out white supremacy or transphobia in its work,[36] but rather that its influence in mobilizing young people in the RJ movement has been extraordinary.

CLPP/Collective Power's leadership development programs and annual conference have helped mobilize young activists through its prescient articulation of reproductive justice and its intersectional framework. The winter 1988 issue of the organization's newsletter, *The Fight for Reproductive Freedom*, reprinted a speech from an event held on the fifteenth anniversary of the *Roe v. Wade* decision. The speaker declared, "Choice shouldn't mean the right to choose a legal abortion—real choice is having social and economic conditions that allow people to live full and productive free lives."[37] Similarly, CLPP/Collective Power for RJ has long articulated the limitations inherent in a narrow focus on white cisgender women's access to legal abortion as the main issue of reproductive rights. A 1994 speech at the Hampshire College Day of Action (later reprinted in the newsletter) by a student named Sarita Gupta named the exclusion that young women of color often faced in the mainstream pro-choice movement:

> Traditionally, the reproductive rights movement has been a white women's movement. But, for many years now, women of color have also been involved in this movement. Some of us have formed our own women of color organizations, and others have worked within the traditional white women's organizations. As young women of color, no matter which way we choose to be involved in this issue, it is very important that we remain active, stay visible, and make our voices heard.[38]

During the Fight for Abortion Rights and Reproductive Freedom Conference earlier that year, eighteen-year-old Afro-Latina activist Noemi Belis pointed out in a speech that, "while mainstream women may worry about political equality, I might worry about economic survival. While mainly white educated women gather to protect the right to abortion, an educated poor woman may worry about childcare."[39] This statement echoes Audre Lorde in her classic 1984 essay "Age, Race, Class, and Sex: Women Redefining Difference": "Some problems we share as women, some we do not. You fear your children will grow up to join the patriarchy and testify against you; we fear our children will be dragged from a car and shot down in the street, and you will turn your backs on the reasons they are dying."[40] Lorde and Belis alike call attention to how race and class privilege shape a person's relationship to reproductive injustices.

CLPP/Collective Power for Reproductive Justice was also at the forefront of incorporating transgender issues in the reproductive freedom movement. The 2002 conference included the organization's first workshop on transgender issues and was one of the first reproductive rights conferences to address trans issues at all. So many conference goers attended that first workshop that the room overflowed and people had to sit in the hallway. Later that year, the newsletter articulated the many connections between trans issues and the reproductive rights movement. "If reproductive rights are the rights to make choices about your body freely without the threat of violence and with the assurance of access to healthcare and support," wrote Ryn Gluckman and Mina Trudeau, "then transgender issues are most definitely reproductive rights issues."[41] In the same issue, Sadie Crabtree, a trans woman known for her work against the exclusion of trans women from the Michigan Womyn's Music Festival, echoed this vision of a transfeminist approach to reproductive freedom: "One of the most fundamental principles to both pro-trans and pro-choice movements is the right to control our own bodies. Trans issues are choice issues, access issues, and feminist issues."[42]

Full-Spectrum Doula Movement

Youth have been at the forefront of the full-spectrum doula movement since its inception in the late 2000s—and CLPP/Collective Power for Reproductive Justice was part of how it all came together. The word *doula* loosely translates as "servant" or "helper" and has historically referred to women who provide emotional and physical support and advocacy to people during labor and delivery.[43] Birth doulas grew in popularity during the 1990s and 2000s, and the term quickly became a household word, although the practice itself has been around for most of human history. In the context of increasingly medicalized birthing experiences, doulas help create the conditions for a more empowering and lower-intervention birthing experience. Birth doulas exist in many communities, but the high costs of training to be,

ORGANIZATION SPOTLIGHT: BUCKLE BUNNIES

When the COVID pandemic led to stay-at-home orders in March 2020, some politicians saw an opportunity to further restrict abortion access. Because only "essential services" like health care clinics, grocery stores, and pharmacies were allowed to stay open, officeholders like Texas governor Greg Abbott declared abortion services "nonessential" and therefore temporarily shut them down. Fortunately, litigation helped return abortion services to the state in April.

The temporary halting of abortions inspired then-twenty-year-old Makayla Montoya Frazier to found Buckle Bunnies, an abortion mutual aid organization. Montoya Frazier, a queer former sex worker from San Antonio, had had multiple abortions as a teenager, including experiences using abortion funds and having a self-managed abortion. She saw a clear connection between the criminalization of abortion and the criminalization of sex work.[a] Congress had stepped up the latter when it passed and President Donald Trump signed into law FOSTA-SESTA, or the Allow States and Victims to Fight Online Sex Trafficking Act and the Stop Enabling Sex Traffickers Act, in 2018. Although the legislation's proponents said that it would help curb sex trafficking, in reality it made sex work more dangerous by eliminating safe venues for workers to screen and meet potential clients.

Montoya Frazier notes that the dual criminalization of abortion and sex work can make accessing abortion especially complicated for sex workers, particularly those facing multiple vulnerabilities. Along with a group of other young queer folks, who were passionate about reproductive justice, Buckle Bunnies began raising money to fund Texans' abortions at a time when the pandemic was greatly increasing economic insecurity.[b] When Senate Bill 8 was passed in May 2021, effectively banning abortion in the state of Texas, Buckle Bunnies shifted to doing more practical support work, like distributing safer sex supplies, Narcan and fentanyl test strips, and abortion care kits. They also helped Texans navigate the ever-changing abortion access landscape by providing information and resources, such as which clinics were providing abortions that week based on the pending legal challenges to SB8, or where to get emergency contraception and pregnancy tests. Through their social media presence, Buckle Bunnies also shared political education materials connecting queer justice and sex worker justice to reproductive justice. Since the fall of *Roe v. Wade* in 2022, they have continued to provide information, resources, and practical support kits to people in San Antonio and Corpus Christi.

Follow Buckle Bunnies online at https://www.bucklebunnies.org/ or on Instagram at @bucklebunniesfundtx.

a. Vásquez 2021.
b. Vásquez 2021.

or obtaining the services of, a doula has resulted in doulas being associated with white, middle-class cisgender women. Indeed, research has shown that the rise of doula care in the United States has largely benefited women with racial and economic privilege.[44] However, many younger birth doulas see their work as inherently political and connected to the reproductive justice goals of ensuring that all people can decide if, when, and how to have children.[45] It was from this radical side of the doula movement that the practice branched out from pregnancy, birth, and the postpartum period to providing support during abortion. From there, it transformed into what is now called "full-spectrum doula" work. Miriam Zoila Pérez, the author of the *Radical Doula Guide,* describes full-spectrum doulas as those who provide support to people during the whole experience of pregnancy from birth to abortion to miscarriage to adoption.[46] Full-spectrum doulas understand what they do as not merely providing care but also as political work. As Mary Mahoney and Lauren Mitchell explain, this politics comes from the conviction that "anyone who becomes pregnant deserves bodily autonomy, meaningful support, and full access to quality health services."[47]

Zoila Pérez notes the phenomenon of young people without children themselves who enter doula work because of their politicization around reproduction and their desire to get involved through direct service or direct action.[48] That was how Mahoney, Mitchell, and Zoila Pérez (who later left the project to pursue other opportunities) came to cofound the Abortion Doula Project—later renamed the Doula Project—and helped spark the full-spectrum doula movement. The CLPP conference brought together young activists interested in both abortion work and doula care and was one of the events that brought the cofounders together and helped catalyze the project.[49] At the time, although young activists were increasingly seeing how abortion justice and birthing justice were both integral to reproductive justice, there was a gap in the broader doula community. Some older birth doulas were staunchly anti-abortion and pushed back against the Doula Project. Others criticized the project because the concept of an abortion doula reinforced the idea that having an abortion is emotionally damaging—a tactic often used by anti-abortion activists.

Young reproductive justice activists, however, were undeterred. Despite many false starts and "no thanks" responses from providers and clinics, Mahoney and Mitchell launched the first abortion doula program in New York City in 2007. Before the advent of abortion doulas, clinics usually did not allow any support people to accompany patients for an abortion procedure. With the support of another young person involved in the CLPP internship program, Mahoney and Mitchell connected with a clinic that served medically or financially complicated abortion cases. Abortion is a stigmatized procedure that many people don't have accurate information about. Patients face many barriers even to getting to the clinic and then often face a barrage of protesters shouting at them at the door. The shortage of abortion providers means that clinics are busy and hectic places; staff are not always able to provide the emotional support or advocacy patients need. Abortion doulas filled that role by offering free-of-cost, nonjudgmental, compassionate support before, during, and after the abortion. This could involve taking the time to explain the procedure, grabbing warm blankets, helping to manage pain, and holding space for complicated emotions. The Doula Project began as a clinic-based project, meaning the doulas worked at the clinic and served patients who happened to come in each day; nowadays there are dozens of abortion and full-spectrum doula projects and many doulas who work independently of a clinic. By 2008 the Doula Project began offering abortion doula trainings, and over the following decade it served thousands of patients and trained hundreds of full-spectrum doulas. Although there is no systematic data collection on community-based doulas and collectives, it is safe to say that youth have been and continue to be at the forefront of this movement. After the fall of *Roe*, this work took on new significance as full-spectrum doulas assumed the work of navigating complex practical needs (e.g., out-of-state transportation) and educating others about self-managed abortion (see the organizational spotlight on Buckle Bunnies).

Abortion Funds and Practical Support Networks

Youth have also been active in abortion mutual aid. According to activist and legal scholar Dean Spade, mutual aid is "collective coordination to meet each other's needs, usually [starting] from an awareness that the systems we have in place are not going to meet them."[50] Mutual aid has a long history in social movements, including the Black Panther Party's food and health care programs, which provided free breakfasts and medical treatment.[51] In terms of abortion, mutual aid projects fill the massive gap between abortion that is legal on paper and abortion that can actually be accessed. Abortion funds are a type of mutual aid that helps people pay for the cost of their abortions. Practical support networks are mutual aid projects that provide people with logistical support like transportation, lodging, childcare, and language interpretation; some projects do both financial and logistical support. The National Network of Abortion Funds (NNAF) serves as an umbrella organization for more than eighty autonomous abortion funds across the United States. NNAF builds power with its member funds by "centering people who have had abortions and organizing at the intersections of racial, economic, and reproductive justice."[52] Similarly, Apiary for Practical Support provides operational and programmatic assistance to practical support organizations to stabilize, scale, and grow their work.[53] Because of the considerable financial and logistical barriers that young people face in accessing abortion, funds and support networks serve large numbers of youth, especially in areas of the country where abortion has long been inaccessible.[54]

Abortion mutual aid can take place informally, such as when a young person helps a friend navigate a judicial bypass or abortion aftercare. There are also projects that support and connect mutual aid work, such as the Advocates for Youth (AFY) Abortion Support Collective (YouthASC). The collective includes more than 280 young people who are committed to supporting other youth in their communities through forms of practical and emotional support in order to gain access to abortion. YouthASC coordinates abortion support training for youth ages fourteen to twenty-four that is focused on tools, resources, and skills related to state and federal abortion policy, digital security, and financial management. The collective also provides political education and connects youth to one another through a nationwide directory. In a YouthASC training on mutual aid, Cathy Torres, also a member of AFY's Young Womxn of Color Leadership Council, explained that mutual aid is "extremely necessary because we're unable to rely on *Roe v. Wade's* bare minimum approach to abortion access" (and this was before the US Supreme Court overturned *Roe* in June 2022). YouthASC sees abortion mutual aid as collective liberation because it connects so many intersecting struggles. For instance, Torres says that economic and reproductive justice are intimately linked because "financial barriers are purposely placed to keep low-income people from accessing abortion in an attempt to fuel a nasty, twisted, anti-choice classist and white supremacist agenda. Mutual aid efforts work to dismantle these financial barriers so people can make their own conscious decisions about their own lives." Khefri, of the Portland, Oregon, Cascades Abortion Support Collective, notes that mutual aid "has always been a way of responding to state violence and police brutality" and draws many its tactics from movements to abolish white supremacy.[55]

As in the full-spectrum doula movement, youth in the abortion mutual aid movement also connect reproductive justice to queer and trans liberation, as Noor ZK, one of the cofounders of the North Texas–based Cicada Collective, explains: "Mutual aid for abortion access arose in my community because I specifically work among queer and trans people of color, and so when I helped start [the Cicada Collective], it was us as a group of young queer and trans people who were dissatisfied with the ways that we were just not represented or misrepresented and the narrative around reproductivity that did not include us and we wanted a way to amplify and support others who shared our identities."[56] The collective started as an abortion doula training project and then shifted to more practical support work when members recognized a major need for transportation access in the area. In addition to its mutual aid work, the collective also explicitly advocates for a cultural shift in the reproductive justice movement to center queer and trans people of color.[57]

Digital Activism

Adults often comment—sometimes derisively—about the amount of time young people spend on social media and call their internet-based activism "slacktivism." This adultist view overlooks how youth have effectively mobilized through digital media, including around abortion. The "slacktivism" critique also reproduces ableism in that the tactics critics most often lament as "lazy" are the ones most accessible to sick and disabled people who may be otherwise excluded from nondigital forms

YOUTH ACTIVIST SPOTLIGHT: DIANA (LOS ANGELES)

Diana (age twenty-three) had long identified as "pro-choice," but it was the experience of having an abortion that made them "completely, unapologetically pro-abortion." Their abortion is something they love and celebrate, and the experience inspired their pathway into activism. Diana was an early advocate for sex education and used any opportunity to center its importance in the lives of young people. While completing a bachelor's degree in public health, Diana stumbled on a curriculum developed by Advocates for Youth (AFY). Getting involved with the organization joyously enabled them to connect with "so many people that are pro-abortion and love abortion."

Diana is a member of the AFY campaign "Abortion Out Loud," which "harnesses the power of storytelling, grassroots organizing, leadership development, and policy advocacy to end abortion stigma and strengthen support for young people's access to abortion."[a] The skills Diana has built through Abortion Out Loud have been instrumental in supporting their growth and empowerment as a young activist. They are also an abortion storyteller who shares their story with pretty much any person they meet and plans to expand this work to social media and beyond. In addition, Diana is an abortion doula with the Los Angeles Abortion Support Collective, a volunteer-led and -run group that provides physical and emotional abortion support services, both in person and virtually, grounded in the principles of reproductive justice.

Diana framed their work as an abortion doula as part of the practice of building community care: "I'm part of something so special where someone's doing the best thing for themselves and then getting community support because that's what we are for each other, a community that is there and cares. That's why I do it."

Being nonbinary and having had an abortion that they celebrate and love so much, Diana has struggled with meeting people who believe abortion access is only an issue for cisgender women. "Abortions are sought out by individuals who don't identify as women," they explain. "Abortions are part of essential health care for our youth, women, trans men, and nonbinary people. It should be a collective effort to make abortion accessible for everyone regardless of how they identify. Abortions are an act of self-love and self-sovereignty." This collective effort is part of Diana's vision of reproductive justice as "not only a dream but a possibility that everyone deserves."

a. Advocates for Youth 2023.

of activism.[58] Many highly visible social movements in the 2000s have harnessed the power of digital activism. The Black Lives Matter (BLM) movement is a key example of grassroots organizing that can harness the power of digital activism, and research indicates that broader public support of BLM has been made possible through social media, including influencing offline participation in the movement and increasing its visibility.[59] Social media was also integral to organizing the 2011 uprisings collectively referred to as the Arab Spring, which led to massive political upheaval in countries including Tunisia, Egypt, Yemen, and Syria.[60] Activists have also used social media to share crucial organizing information across borders. For instance, in 2014

Palestinians took to Twitter to offer advice to protesters in Ferguson, Missouri, following the police killing of Michael Brown on how to deal with tear gas used to disrupt street protest. As they noted, like the canisters used against protesters in occupied Palestine, those used in Ferguson were manufactured by the same companies.[61] This example illustrates the transnational interconnectedness of our struggles for liberation.[62] The digital influence in social movements cuts across issues and communities, but youth have been especially active in using social media as a tool of resistance.[63]

Digital abortion activism in the United States takes its cue from abortion movements in Latin America where youth have been active in street-based and digital activism against femicide (gender-based violence against women and girls). With the hashtag #NiUnaMenos ("Not One Less") the movement emerged in Argentina in 2015 and quickly expanded to include other issues such as intimate-partner violence, workplace sexism, and abortion rights. Known as the *marea verde* (green wave) because of the green handkerchiefs protesters wore,[64] the movement has spread across Latin America and led to the decriminalization or legalization of abortion in Argentina, Mexico, Colombia, and Chile.[65] US-based digital activism around abortion has taken a variety of forms, including anti-stigma storytelling, fundraising, exposing clinic protesters, and engaging in political education.

This work became especially notable as a series of draconian abortion restrictions were enacted in the lead-up to the *Dobbs* ruling. For instance, in May 2021 Texas passed SB8, a "heartbeat bill" that banned abortion after fetal cardiac activity can be detected, at around six weeks' gestation. This bill effectively banned *all* abortions because pregnancy is rarely confirmed before the six-week mark. The law also included a "bounty hunter" provision that enabled members of the public to sue anyone, for a minimum of $10,000, for performing or facilitating an abortion. The anti-abortion organization Texas Right to Life set up a "whistleblower" website for people to submit anonymous tips about anyone who aided and abetted an abortion, and young people were quick to react. Olivia Julianna, an eighteen-year-old queer Latina from Houston, encouraged her TikTok followers to submit so many fake tips that the website crashed. As she explained to a reporter, "My generation, we grew up on the internet and if they're going to use that to come at us and take our rights away from them then we're going to use our knowledge of it to fight back against them."[66] Julianna also made national headlines after she used Twitter to call out Florida representative Matt Gaetz after his public remarks that overweight or unattractive women likely wouldn't get pregnant and therefore didn't need to worry about abortion access. Gaetz attempted to shame and ridicule Julianna on Twitter, but it backfired big time. Julianna turned the clash into a viral abortion fundraising opportunity and raised $2 million dollars in just a week, which was distributed to abortion funds across the country.

TikTok is one of the most popular social media platforms for young people, with about 60 percent of its users falling into Generation Z (people born after 1996).[67] In addition to using TikTok to organize protests or to share resources, youth have also used it as a playful and humorous form of resistance. For instance, young people refuse to give into abortion stigma by joking about "fetus deletus" or "yeetus the fetus" in their videos; they also unapologetically share their abortion stories with candor and wit. Others troll anti-abortion users and dismantle their arguments. As journalist Rachel Charlene Lewis puts it in an article for *Bitch Media,* "Whether their videos are meant to educate or to troll, teens are using TikTok to reshape abortion culture for themselves."[68] One attention-generating form of abortion resistance on TikTok involves videos of young people pushing back against anti-abortion protesters, often in front of abortion clinics. A group of young clinic defenders in Charlotte, North Carolina, went viral several times for videos documenting their taunting of protesters. In a video viewed more than 2 million times, a young woman wearing a Black Lives Matter face mask calmly (but loudly) reads the raunchy lyrics to Meghan Thee Stallion and Cardi B's hit song "WAP" to drown out a bible reading by an evangelical minister (and convicted harasser of abortion providers).[69] In another viral video, the same young person provokes a clinic protester by blasting the 1990s hit "Short Dick Man" at him through booming speakers.[70] Not everyone appreciates the in-your-face approach young people are using on TikTok, however, and a group of older board members at a Charlotte pro-choice organization resigned in response to the confrontational tactics.[71]

LOOKING FORWARD

I was in the middle of writing this book when the US Supreme Court delivered the anticipated yet no less devasting decision in *Dobbs v. Jackson Women's Health,* ending the constitutional right to abortion. Like most people connected to the reproductive justice movement (or who care at all about bodily autonomy), I spent the next few weeks grieving. That abortion had been essentially banned in many parts of the country for years, or that we had known for a long time that a post-*Roe* world was coming, somehow did not soften the blow. Some people on social media expressed shock and disbelief that abortion was recriminalized, while others pointed out that it was quite a privileged position to wonder how a country built on settler colonialism, white supremacy, and class exploitation could so easily annihilate a taken-for-granted right. In the weeks prior to the decision, activists had, in their anger, been pointing fingers and blaming others for the impending fall of *Roe,* some even going so far as to claim that inclusive language such as "pregnant people" had watered down the movement.[72] Amid all of this, I tried to focus on the wisdom of celebrated abolitionist organizer Mariame Kaba. When the world seems to be hopeless, Kaba urges, we must view hope as a discipline, one that we have to practice every day.[73] The summer that *Roe* fell, I practiced hope by focusing on the resistance—so much of it led by young people—that would carry us forward.

CHAPTER TWO

The Fight for Accurate, Affirming, and Liberatory Sexuality Education

When I teach about sexuality education in my college courses, the conversation inevitably turns to the 2004 hit movie *Mean Girls*. Specifically, my students often invoke a memorable scene from the high school drama to sum up their experiences with school-based sexuality education. In the scene, the characters are subjected to a sexual health lecture by Coach Carr, the gym teacher at North Shore High School. Wearing a blue tracksuit with a whistle hanging from his neck, Coach Carr stands in front of a large chalkboard stationed in the school gymnasium while the uninterested students watch from the bleachers. His lesson is simple: "Don't have sex," he implores the audience. "Because you will get pregnant. And die." In a later lesson, he repeats his basic lesson by telling the students, "At your age, you're going to have a lot of urges. You're going to want to take off your clothes and touch each other. But if you do touch each other, you *will* get chlamydia ... and die." Although *Mean Girls* is a fictional comedy, many of my students find that it perfectly illustrates their own experiences with sexuality education. A gym teacher, usually a cisgender man much older than them, who is not trained to be a health educator, inflates the dangers of sex (a chlamydia infection is *extremely* unlikely to result in death) and delivers only one piece of specific preventive advice: don't do it.

Using a smart phone app, I also ask students to name one word that summarizes their experience with sexuality education in middle or high school. I then display a word cloud that shows the responses, with words mentioned multiple times appearing in larger type sizes. The words that tend to appear the largest are "heteronormative," "garbage," "awkward," and "abstinence." In the past fifteen or so years that I have been teaching undergraduate college students, little has changed about what they report, and their experiences vary surprisingly little across age, gender, sexuality, race, ethnicity, where they grew up, family religiosity, and so forth. The students I have taught over the years are unwaveringly captivated by talking about their experiences with school-based sexuality education. It is a perennial topic of interest and one that many students are passionate and politicized about. In particular, queer and trans students emphasize their erasure in sexuality education, and women of color describe how it frames their bodies, sexuality, and reproduction as "problems" in need of solving. That student experiences have so much in common, and that sex ed is a sure-fire way to energize a class discussion, has a lot to teach us about how unanimously bad sexuality education both harms *and* ignites young people.

No discussion of youth reproductive justice is complete without an examination of the abysmal state of sexuality education in the United States. Youth cannot experience reproductive freedom without accurate and affirming sexuality education, which the vast majority of youth do not experience through school-based instruction. Although sexuality education takes place in many other sites besides schools—for example, among peers or through the internet—school is generally the most memorable and impactful. Some advocates and scholars frame school-based sexuality education (SBSE) for young people in instrumental terms; that is, they argue that sexuality education is important because it helps prevent undesirable outcomes like unintended pregnancy or sexually transmitted infections. This frame justifies sexuality education in terms of what it can prevent, rather than what it might promote. In other words, the argument is that we need to increase access to and quality of sexuality education because it can lower rates of "bad" outcomes like STIs. Still, even when rejecting an abstinence-only framework, SBSE isn't necessarily anti-racist, LGBTQ inclusive, or sex positive.

This chapter applies the reproductive justice framework to make a different sort of argument: sexuality education is one part of a much larger strategy to promote sexual and reproductive freedom for youth. Sexuality education has the potential to support young people in deciding if, when, and how to make a family. It has the capacity to promote pleasurable, affirming, and stigma-free intimate experiences while reducing the risk of undesired outcomes such as pregnancy. Moreover, sexuality education has been a site of a great deal of youth-led activism. It has much to teach us about youth resistance and organizing across issues connected by a shared marginal relationship to power. After exploring the various meanings of "sexuality education," this chapter reviews research on the outcomes of such education, outlines a reproductive justice approach, and highlights youth organizing.

DEFINING SEXUALITY EDUCATION

Hearing the term *sex ed* likely calls to mind the awkward, ineffective middle or high school lessons delivered by your version of Coach Carr—that's if you even had sex education in school at all! Most people think about sex ed as something that takes place only in schools and is geared only toward young people. A closer look, though, reveals that sexuality education is a lot more varied. I use the term *sexuality education* both to signal a broader understanding of what sex ed is and what it does, and to trouble assumptions about the relationships between sex, learning, and teaching. If "sex ed" is the awkward and useless one day session with a high school gym teacher, then "sexuality education" is an expansive and harder-to-pin-down enterprise that might include a TikTok video on the difference between internal and external condoms, a pleasure workshop in a community center for elders, or a children's picture book about gender diversity. "Sexuality education" isn't just about preventing STIs or pregnancy; it's also about promoting well-being, bodily autonomy, and pleasure. Sexuality education isn't just something that young people learn in schools; it's something that takes place throughout the life course in a wide variety of places and formats. Sexuality education is for children, adolescents, young adults, and elders; it takes place in schools but also churches, community-based organizations, group homes, the internet, family settings, peer gatherings, and so on. Sexuality education can be *formal,* such as the curricula that are developed and used in schools or community-based organizations, or *informal,* such as the ways that young people share information via social media. There are many intentional lessons in sexuality education—for example, the proper way to use a condom—but there are also many *hidden lessons*, like the idea that using condoms every single time you have sex makes you a good sexual citizen, and *evaded lessons*, like the fact that most safer-sex barriers are designed for cisgender bodies and don't work as well for trans bodies.

Scholars and activists have troubled easy definitions of sexuality education and "sexual health" more broadly. Questions about what it means to be "sexually healthy" or what sexuality education should look like are questions about the politics of knowledge. Whose knowledge about sexuality counts as real and valid? Who is qualified to know? Sociologist Stephen Epstein argues that attaching *health* to *sexual* is a strategy to legitimize and sanitize sexuality.[1] Sex is often culturally taboo and stigmatized, so it can be challenging to advocate in favor of something so fraught. On the other hand, it's easy to get behind promoting "health." As Epstein and others caution us, however, the strategy of justifying policies or programs related to sexuality by adding the word *health* can have unintended consequences. It makes sex and sexuality seem neat, tidy, and apolitical, when in reality they can be messy, unruly, and are always political. It can also lead to mobilizing "sexual health" for purposes that are quite different than the goals of youth activists who connect sex ed to social justice.[2] Epstein and fellow sociologist Laura Mamo analyzed thousands of academic journal articles, newspaper articles, and websites to identity how "sexual health" is framed as a social problem.[3] Some frames understand sexual health through a deficit approach in which sex is a risky practice. These frames focus on action plans to contain the threats of sexual behavior, such as promoting "responsibility" through sex education to stop the spread of STIs. In these frames, "health" mostly means the absence of disease. In other frames, "sexual health" is about solving injustices related to sexual rights or promoting sexual self-expression. These frames focus on social change or the pursuit of pleasure; here "health" includes legislative protection of rights and individual self-actualization. Across all these frames, sexual health is a strategy to professionalize and legitimize sexuality in order to make it a socially acceptable topic in schools, the media, and policy making.

We can also trouble what it means to learn and teach about sexuality or sexual health. What are the purposes or goals of sexuality education? How is learning about sexuality similar or distinct from other kinds of learning? Is sexuality a topic that belongs only in the sex ed classroom, or should it be throughout the curriculum? Education scholars Jessica Fields, Jen Gilbert, and Michelle Miller write that "'sexuality education' is an awkward soldering together of theories of sexuality with theories of teaching and learning."[4] It often rests on assumptions of human rationality and the promises of science. In other words, sex ed understands knowledge in really limited ways: there is one way of being "sexually healthy." Conversely, as Gilbert argues, "not knowing and feeling confused [might become] the basis of learning about sexuality" and not something to be corrected.[5] Because so much sexuality education relies on a deficit framing of sexual health, its lessons tend to be instrumentalist in nature because they are focused just on the end result and not how you get there. In practice, this can look like education that uses shame and stigma to change individual behaviors while ignoring the social conditions in which they take place. For instance, an enduringly popular class activity in sex education includes using colored water (candies are another variation) to demonstrate the spread of STIs. The teacher distributes cups of water to the students, but only one cup has an agent (such as citric acid) that will change color in the presence of another agent, like a litmus paper. Students are instructed to mix water with one another (having sex), and then the teacher uses the litmus paper to reveal whose cup of water has the color change agent (the STI), thus marking some students as infected and others uninfected. This activity might visually demonstrate how an infection can move through a population, but it also reinforces the idea that people with STIs are "unclean" and communicates that STI transmission is inevitable and that "having an STI" equals "sexually *un*healthy." It also ignores the ways young people's STI risk is structured by factors like stigma and discrimination and that all STIs are treatable (and most are curable).

Sexuality education has changed a lot over time, but along the way there have been many similar themes. Before describing sexuality education through a reproductive justice framework and discussing how youth have mobilized around sexuality education, the following sections provide a short history of sex education and what research tells us about its outcomes.

FORMAL SEX ED THEN AND NOW

Sexuality education in the United States—and around the world—has a troubling history. Educating people about sex has long been a response to real and imagined social problems such as changing sexual norms, sex outside marriage, sex work, declining birthrates among white people, poverty, and crime. Through all these historical changes run many common threads as to how the government, schools, and parents view sexuality education for young people. The anxiety that adults hold about youth sexuality and the idea that young people having sex is always risky and dangerous tie these threads together. Efforts to

ORGANIZING 101: BASE BUILDING

Base building refers to the ongoing work of recruitment and mobilization that occurs in social movements. It takes place through both organizations and grassroots networks. Base building involves and looks like a lot of different activities that have the common goal of building collective power. *Base* generally refers to the people who are directly involved in the work or will be in the future. *Constituency* refers to people directly impacted by the issues at hand. For instance, in the youth-organizing examples at the end of this chapter, the base is the youth working on the campaigns for sex ed justice in their schools, while the constituency comprises all the students who stand to benefit from better sexuality education.

Base building begins with cultivating membership and identifying constituencies. As you read the examples in this book, notice the various ways that youth achieved these steps, such as determining membership structure (e.g., a collective or a core team of leaders) or deciding on how to frame the constituency (e.g., youth of a particular social identity or geographic area or of a shared marginal relationship to power). Youth might employ a variety of strategies to cultivate membership or identify a constituency, including promoting the work by word of mouth, building a social media presence, and holding events.

Leadership development is another key component of base building that helps people develop the skills and acquire the knowledge necessary to sustain movements over time. Leadership development isn't just about promoting or worshipping a single charismatic leader who serves as the face of the movement. Instead, it's about meeting people where they're at and supporting their growth. Leadership skills include such varied things as building a political analysis, running a meeting, talking to people in power, engaging with the media, and organizing direct actions. Sometimes adults organize leadership development training sessions for youth, but youth also do peer-to-peer leadership development.

Check out these resources to learn more:

Youth Leadership Institute, https://yli.org/

School of Unity and Liberation (SOUL), https://www.schoolofunityandliberation.org/

Midwest Academy, http://www.midwestacademy.com/

teach about sex have long emphasized purity and morality, linking abstinence and the absence of disease to being a good citizen. Similarly, sex education has often been justified as a strategy to maintain heterosexuality, whiteness, and normative family structures. Curricula and educators have tended to use an adultist, deficit-based approach to youth sexuality that views young people as inferior and incapable of making healthy decisions for their own bodies. Historically and contemporarily, sexuality education has framed the sexuality of people of color as dangerous, ignored or pathologized LGBTQ people, erased pleasure and desire, and reproduced heteronormativity.[6]

One of the early incarnations of educating the public about sex was the social hygiene movement of the early 1900s. This movement evolved out of the eugenics movement, or the idea that the human race could be improved if only certain types of people (that is, white, middle- and upper-class, able-bodied) reproduced.[7] Medical and public health authorities held deep anxieties about declining marriage and birth rates among white people and about increasing rates of sexually transmitted infections among middle-class white men. Sex education during this era took place in union halls and YMCAs, where young white men would view grotesque slide shows depicting the physical symptoms of later-stage syphilis.[8] This tactic is still used in high school and college classrooms today (only now instructors use PowerPoint).[9] Epstein argues that the social hygiene movement focused on sexually transmitted infections because they were "perceived as a threat to the white American mainstream brought by various outsiders, and as a risk to the country's moral fiber and military readiness."[10] During World War I, the US military educated servicemen about what was then called "venereal disease." The goal behind this programming was to reduce rates of STIs among men stationed overseas who engaged the services of (mostly nonwhite) sex workers. The military viewed sexually transmitted infections as a threat to their missions and to the purity of soldiers' wives back home.[11] To them, sex education was important because it supported robust military interventions, US imperialism, and the sexual virtue of white women.

When sexuality education first entered public schools at mid-century, educators framed it as a strategy to discourage premarital sex and prepare students for eventual heterosexual marriage. This "family life education" (FLE) was also a strategy to promote family normativity and thereby ease economic anxieties about preserving upward mobility in the postwar period. FLE moved beyond previous approaches that had focused specifically on disease prevention in order to incorporate a broader set of sexual and social concerns into a framework of "family and personal living." Sociologist Kristin Luker describes FLE programs as "part preparation for marriage, part an attempt to discourage premarital sex, and part training for 'responsible parenting.'" FLE programs included lessons on activities such as planning a wedding and shopping for crystal tableware.[12] Essentially, because sex was only supposed to take place within the context of marriage, FLE skipped lessons about sex itself and went directly to content aimed at promoting properly gendered, heterosexual, middle-class, procreative forms of sexuality.

During the 1960s and '70s, the "sexual revolution" in the United States ignited rapid changes in American sexual life, with rates of reported sex outside marriage increasing and access to contraception and abortion altering the risks of heterosexual sex. Simultaneously, the gay and queer liberation movements, the women's movement, decolonial movements for independence, the Black Power movement, and many others brought attention to deep injustices in the country. These social movements politicized health and spurred peer-to-peer sexual and reproductive health education in such programs as the Black Panther's community health initiative and the Boston Women's Health Collective book *Our Bodies, Ourselves.* In the 1980s, when a new sexually transmitted illness began disproportionately killing gay cisgender men and injection drug users, a grassroots movement of politicized peer-to-peer sexuality education developed as a "community under siege organized to protect itself."[13] HIV/AIDS education took place through community-designed and -distributed pamphlets, comics, videos, and workshops that connected gay liberation to keeping one another healthy. Once HIV/AIDS came to be seen as affecting the "general population," that is, heterosexual people, sex education in schools gained renewed traction and became more common.[14]

In the 1990s, fears about teenage pregnancy and government dependency further bolstered support for sex education in schools. Policy makers framed teen childbearing and family poverty as social problems that could be fixed through school-based sex education. The 1990s saw the rise of "abstinence-only until marriage" (AOUM) instruction, and by the 2000s AOUM and the "comprehensive, scientifically based" approach to sex education (discussed below) were a deep point of contention among policy makers, researchers, and the public at large.[15] A great deal of scholarship, debate, and activism has focused on the differences between these two approaches.[16] Although AOUM initially gained attention and funding during the George W. Bush administration, it was first federally funded as part of the 1996 Personal Responsibility and Work Opportunity Reconciliation Act, heralded by Bill Clinton and more commonly known as welfare reform. This legislation significantly eroded the social safety net for economically marginalized women, children, and families in the United States. It drew on the idea of "welfare queens," women of color who just kept having babies in order to remain dependent on government assistance. As part of instituting dire restrictions on recipients of public benefits, the act included over $100 million a year for funding AOUM in schools; the idea was that if young people were just told to wait to have sex, there would be less need for the government to support vulnerable people. At the time, AOUM programs' official pedagogy included teaching young people that "abstinence from sexual activity is the only certain way to avoid out-of-wedlock pregnancy, sexually transmitted diseases, and other associated health problems" and that "a mutually faithful monogamous relationship in the context of marriage is the expected standard of sexual activity."[17] AOUM programs, both then and now, do not include information on contraception or the prevention of sexually transmitted infections.

In contrast, *comprehensive sexuality education* refers to programs that include age-appropriate, medically accurate information on a range of topics related to sexuality, including human development, relationships, decision making, abstinence, contraception, and STI prevention. Comprehensive, school-based sex education (SBSE) curricula are considered scientifically based because rigorous evaluation research has found evidence of statistically relevant outcomes such as increasing condom use or delaying "sexual debut" (the age at which a young person first has penetrative sex).[18] Comprehensive curricula can range from abstinence promotion that also discusses contraception all the way to LGBTQ-inclusive, consent-focused material. During the Obama administration, millions of dollars in federal funding were made available for "medically accurate and age-appropriate" programs designed to reduce teen pregnancy. For the most part, these scientifically based curricula positioned teenage sex as inherently risky by focusing on the "consequences of sex," which they framed as disease and pregnancy. These curricula implicitly understood "sex" as heterosexual, penetrative vaginal sex and made many value-laden assumptions about teenagers' irresponsible sexual behavior.[19] In 2011, advocates for comprehensive sexuality education authored a set of federal standards for sex education in K–12 schools, titled the "Future of Sex Education." Updated and rereleased in 2020, the standards have as their goal to "provide clear, consistent, and straightforward guidance on the essential, minimum, core content and skills needed for sex education that is age-appropriate for students in grades K–12 to be effective."[20] The standards map out an approach to SBSE that includes topics such as consent and healthy relationships, sexual orientation and identity, and sexual health. However, as sexuality researchers Jamie O'Quinn and Jessica Fields argue, despite their laudable goals, the standards' emphasis on science, rationality, and a linear path to a sexually healthy future leave little room for the messy, queer ambiguities of learning, sexuality, and time.[21] What's more, meeting the standards is almost entirely voluntary, and a 2016 study found that only about 40 percent of US school districts had adopted them.[22]

Throughout the 2000s and 2010s, school districts, parents, policy makers, and researchers clashed over whether abstinence or comprehensive sex education should be taught in schools. These two camps often saw each other as complete opposites, with AOUM supporters accusing comprehensive supporters of corrupting children, and comprehensive supports accusing AOUM supporters of ignoring youth safety and well-being. Fields's research in North Carolina during this period illustrates how advocates used the racialized rhetoric of "children having children" to persuade school committees to vote in favor comprehensive sex education. In their view, the school needed to step in and "save" young women of color from health inequalities.[23] Similar debates have taken place in school districts throughout the United States, from areas urban and progressive to rural and conservative. Even in my home state of Massachusetts—often viewed as a politically left place—has been trying unsuccessfully for more than a decade to pass a statewide comprehensive school-based sex education bill. As recently as 2021, sex education tensions flared in the city of Worcester, with opponents of the comprehensive approach distributing yard signs that read "Opt Out of Pornographic Sex Education."[24]

Although feminist, queer, and anti-racist scholars of sexuality education have shown us that the approaches actually overlap in many ways, advocates for abstinence-only and comprehensive-based sex education frame each other as fundamentally different. Comprehensive approaches still usually stress abstinence, even though they do also include information on condoms and other forms of contraception. Both frame teen sexuality as something dangerous and risky and, therefore, profoundly worrisome to adults. Whether they view the solution as abstinence or comprehensive, sexuality education is a necessary, rational, and corrective response to that danger, risk, and worry.[25] Moreover, for the most part, both approaches do not meaningfully include queer and transgender youth, do not emphasize consent or pleasure, and do not understand the potential "risks" of sexual activity in terms of the social systems like white supremacy, transphobia, and capitalism that harm young people.[26] In addition, both abstinence and comprehensive approaches rely on *sexual ableism* to determine whose sexual behavior is "normal" and whose is risky. As disability scholar Michael Gill explains, dominant forms of sexuality education are structured by sexual ableism, which he defines as a "system of imbuing sexuality with determinations of qualifications to be sexual based on criteria of ability, intellect, morality, physicality, appearance, age, race, social acceptability, and gender conformity."[27]

In the new millennium US policies regarding school-based sexuality education have varied widely. School-based sexuality education in public schools is funded by federal and state governments, and its content is regulated by school districts and boards. In contrast, private schools have much more flexibility in their funding and content because they can rely on tuition to fund their programs. This disparity has the effect of reproducing race, class, and gender inequalities in access to sexuality education and what kind of sexuality education young people receive.[28] Generally, schools can receive federal money to run their programs only if they adopt an approved curriculum, and which programs are eligible for funding differ depending on who the president is and whether Democrats or Republicans control Congress. Laws in a little over half the states mandate sexuality education in schools, and those laws vary considerably. At the time of this writing, only 3 states require comprehensive sex education to be taught in all schools; 30 states require that schools emphasize abstinence, and 16 provide abstinence-only content. Only 18 states mandate that content be "medically accurate," meaning that it is technically legal, say, to teach young people in a Massachusetts sex ed class that you can become pregnant by sitting on a public toilet seat, or that only gay men get HIV. Although 11 states and the District of Columbia require that content include LGBQ people, 6 states require only *negative* information about homosexuality or a positive emphasis on heterosexuality, or both. Although most states require provision of content on teen dating violence, only 10 require content on the importance of sexual consent. Twenty-one states offer training for teachers delivering healthy-relationships content, but just 10 require teachers to attend such training and a meager 3 states require a certificate for or expertise in teaching the content.[29]

Although considerable policy making, research, and activism have focused on formal SBSE, cultural and technological changes have created a huge growth in informal content. Unsurprisingly, many youth today report getting their sexual education from peers and from the internet.[30] Peer education can take place through formal programs, often nonprofit organizations where youth are trained in content and pedagogy. The idea behind these programs is that youth peer education can disrupt the hierarchal and ineffective structure of school-based instruction through the affinities of teacher and learner both being young persons.[31] More commonly, young people informally turn to each other and to social media for information about sex and sexuality. Of course, this is not entirely new: most of what I learned about sex as a young person was from the health columns in fashion magazines or pilfered VHS porn tapes. What is new is the seemingly endless amount and different forms of content. Sexuality education content can be found on TikTok, Facebook, YouTube, Instagram, and other social media; it can range from personal narratives about living with STI stigma, to vibrator reviews, to instruction on how to use a dental dam.[32] Much of this content is youth produced, but professional sex educators and organizations also maintain a social media presence and produce content. Scholars have argued that this social media–based sexuality education can shift power dynamics, build community, and spark social movements.[33] LGBTQ youth and youth of color are especially likely to turn to the internet for health-related information, so online sex education has considerable potential to reach and mobilize multiply marginalized youth.[34]

WHAT DOES THE RESEARCH ON SEXUALITY EDUCATION FOR YOUTH TELL US?

There is such an enormous body of research about sexuality education for youth that it is nearly impossible to review even a fraction of it here. However, for thinking about the relationship between sexuality education and reproductive justice, it's useful to review some of what we know about youth sexual health, educational outcomes, and inequalities. First, research has dem-

ORGANIZATION SPOTLIGHT: THE NATIVE YOUTH
SEXUAL HEALTH NETWORK

The Native Youth Sexual Health Network (NYSHN) was created in 2008 by a group of Indigenous youth who identified a
need for "by us, for us" sexual and reproductive health education. Now a grassroots network of Indigenous youth leaders across Turtle Island (what settlers call "North America"),
NYSHN works across issues of sexual and reproductive
health, rights, and justice. With a collaborative, nonhierar-
chical structure, the organization does not have an executive director, core funding, or a nonprofit tax status. Instead,
NYSHN is composed of a core group of youth organizers and
leaders supported by aunties and mentors. Indigenous
youth under thirty work as peer educators within regional
teams to facilitate workshops and conduct advocacy, outreach, and community-based research.

NYSHN distinguishes itself from mainstream public
health initiatives through core values of youth leadership
and empowerment and intergenerational organizing for
future generations. In practice, this involves working against
deficit framings of Indigenous youth as "at risk" and instead
naming how racism and colonialism cause harm. NYSHN's
core values mean that reducing the harm of colonialism,
racism, homophobia, and transphobia is a way of life and a
practice that Indigenous people have held for a long time.
The core values also involve working for sexual and reproductive justice through the connections linking bodies, the
environment, and communities; working against shame and
stigma; cultivating self-determination that honors interde-
pendence and the diversity of Indigenous people; and engaging in multimedia arts justice.

Past projects include creating a mental health peer support manual for Indigiqueer, Two Spirit, LGBTQ, and gender nonconforming Indigenous youth; working in solidarity with ongoing environmental work which resists resource extraction that harms sexual and reproductive health; reenvisioning the harm reduction model through an Indigenous lens; creating Indigenous feminist condom cases and beaded condoms; and creating a toolkit for holding a Sexy Health Carnival.

You can download toolkits, view safer-sex memes, and learn more about NYSHN's work at https://www.nativeyouthsex ualhealth.com/ or by following the group on social media.

onstrated that young people in the United States today are *less* likely than they were in the mid-1990s to receive adequate school-based sex education on topics like how to use a condom or where to get birth control.[35] From 2015 to 2019, only about half of US adolescents received sex education that met the minimum standards set out in the Centers for Disease Control and Prevention public health planning document Healthy People 2030 (these are much more minimal standards than those of the Future of Sex Education Initiative, or FoSE).[36] Research also shows significant inequities in who receives sex education and what they learn. Youth of color are less likely to receive comprehensive sex education than are their white peers. For instance, public health researchers Laura Lindberg and Leslie Kantor found that from 2015 to 2019 Black and Latinx (assumed but not stated to be cisgender) youth were less likely than their white counterparts to receive education on a variety of topics such as methods of birth control, where to get birth control, and condom skills. Youth from families living above 200 percent of the federal poverty line were more likely to get sex education than those who came from families living below.[37] Research has also found that LGBTQ youth are far less likely than cisgender, heterosexual youth to receive sex education that is inclusive and affirming of their identities, bodies, and sexual practices; this is especially the case for LGBTQ youth of color.[38] Only 8.2 percent of students surveyed in the 2019 Gay, Lesbian, and Straight Education Network's (GLSEN) National School Climate Survey reported receiving LGBTQ-inclusive sex education.[39]

Even though there is much to critique about school-based sex education, these inequities are troubling because we know marginalized youth in the United States are disproportionately likely to experience unintended pregnancies, sexually transmitted infections, and interpersonal violence. Youth who are multiply marginalized along the axes of race, class, gender, sexuality, and so on are especially likely to bear the brunt of sexual health inequalities. Young people ages fifteen to twenty-four account for nearly half of new STI diagnoses in the United States.[40] Because interlocking systems of oppression, including racism, sexism, and classism, structure access to education and health care, youth of color are disproportionately likely to experience STIs and unintended pregnancies.[41] Somewhat ironically, queer and transgender youth may be *more* likely than their heterosexual and cisgender peers to become unintentionally pregnant or contribute to an unintentional pregnancy, likely because contraception promotion is not tailored to them.[42] Young gay, queer, or bisexual cisgender men of color and young transgender women of color are disproportionally likely to become HIV-positive, but are less likely to know about how to get on PrEP (pre-exposure prophylaxis), a medication that reduces the risk of HIV infection by about 99 percent.[43]

Like many other critical scholars of sexuality education, I am dubious about the liberatory potential of school-based instruction.[44] As described above, there is much to critique about SBSE and its limitations for promoting sexual wellness and sexual freedom. Much of the research on the efficacy of comprehensive sex education narrowly understands "success" as merely behavior change, such as delaying the age at first intercourse or increasing condom and contraceptive use and preventing "bad" outcomes like unintended pregnancy or sexually transmitted infections.[45] Like Jessica Fields, I want to imagine what sexuality education can *promote*, not just what it can *prevent*.[46] At the same time, research shows that, compared to abstinence-only and sexual risk avoidance programs, comprehensive school-based sex education can lower rates of unintended pregnancies, STIs, and homophobic-related bullying; increase student understanding of gender and sexuality; and improve knowledge and skills that contribute to healthier intimate-partner relationships.[47] Looking beyond these instrumental outcomes, a reproductive justice framework and the work of youth activists have much to teach us about the possibilities of an emancipatory sexuality education.

A REPRODUCTIVE JUSTICE APPROACH TO SEXUALITY EDUCATION FOR YOUTH

Sexual and reproductive liberation are at the center of a reproductive justice approach to sexuality education. RJ sex ed extends a "comprehensive" approach to include naming and dismantling how adultism, white supremacy, transphobia, and other systems of oppression show up in sex education. Working against interlocking systems of oppression in sexuality education means critically interrogating its framing, content, and pedagogy. This work goes beyond simply teaching young people the symptoms of chlamydia or where to access contraception. Instead, it reimagines sex education as a worldmaking project focused on bodily autonomy and collective liberation. As Jessica Pinckney, director of the California-based organization ACCESS Reproductive Justice, explains, "A world where everyone received comprehensive sexuality education would mean we were one step closer to our goal of reproductive justice for all women, girls, and femmes.... Comprehensive sexuality education gives young people of color—particularly Black, queer, and trans folks—autonomy and the agency to explore the formation of healthy relationships with others as well as themselves."[48] Similarly, the Chicago Women's Health Center, a feminist collective that provides sexuality education in the Chicago Public Schools, "offers an explicitly feminist, body-positive, queer-inclusive, and gender-expansive program that uses a harm reduction model to promote healthy-decision making."[49] As the center explains, "Feminist and abolitionist sexual health care and education are central tools for proactively creating relationships built on safety through community-based health education, access to health care regardless of ability to pay, and the belief that individuals know enough and are best positioned to make decisions about their bodies and relationships."[50] A reproductive justice approach to sexuality education thus embraces a vision of what sex ed could be, a framework for how to do it, and a social movement for building collective power. The RJ approach is also intersectional, anti-racist, queer and trans inclusive, and youth led.[51] Women of color feminisms and queer of color critique offer tools to help us imagine an RJ approach to sexuality education:

1. FOCUS ON POWER. The Chicago Women's Health Center writes: "Comprehensive sexual health education must help young people understand what power is and how it works within interpersonal relationships, communities, and institutions."[52] Queer of color critique helps to make that connection in order to, as Martin Manalansan puts it, "understand how certain bodies matter and certain bodies are located on the wayside."[53] It's not an accident that queer and trans youth have been mostly left out of sex education, nor is it a coincidence that sex ed has pathologized youth of color as dangerous or dirty. An RJ approach to sexuality education must be attuned to the ways that power moves around policy, curriculum, and instruction. Attention to power enables us to name and dismantle deficit framings, white supremacy, hetero- and cissexism, ableism, and other systems of power and oppression.

2. CENTER THE MOST IMPACTED. The authors of the Combahee River Collective Statement wrote: "If Black women were free, it would mean that everyone else would have to be free since our freedom would necessitate the destruction of all the systems of oppression."[54] Centering the youth most impacted by the interlocking systems of oppression that operate in sex education benefits *all* youth. For example, centering the most impacted could involve highlighting the sexual health needs of queer and trans youth in a way that benefits all youth. Using gender-inclusive, youth-preferred anatomical language affirms trans, nonbinary, intersex, and cisgender youth simultaneously. Similarly, analyzing how sexual health promotion has pathologized

youth of color enables students to make connections between racial health inequities and white supremacy in education and health care.

3. CONNECT DISPARATE TOPICS BASED ON SHARED MARGINAL RELATIONSHIP TO POWER. Women of color feminisms and queer of color critique teach us to connect seemingly disparate issues or groups of people based on their shared marginal relationship to power. In sex ed, this could mean connecting topics that may seem out of place in a health classroom, such as the prison industrial complex. As the Chicago Women's Health Center reminds us, "Sex education classes are spaces where it is possible to acknowledge and challenge the power dynamics in our relationships and institutions."[55] Sex ed is a space where young people can learn about the politics of abolition feminism (see chapter 5) and transformative justice approaches to repairing harm through topics like negotiating sexual consent and destigmatizing STIs.

4. EMPHASIZE PLEASURE. Much has been written about the lack of pleasure-focused sex education.[56] An RJ approach to sex ed doesn't just refuse to exclude the fact that sex is pleasurable; it emphasizes the transformational power of pleasure, including the pleasure of learning.[57] RJ-focused sex education includes content *about* pleasure but also makes the experience of learning pleasurable itself. As Audre Lorde wrote in her celebrated 1978 essay, "The Uses of the Erotic: The Erotic as Power," the erotic isn't just about *what* we do: "it is a question of *how* acutely and fully we can feel in the doing" (emphasis added). When we are in touch with the erotic, we become less willing to accept powerlessness, resignation, despair, and self-denial.[58]

YOUTH ORGANIZING FOR SEXUALITY EDUCATION

With this vision in mind, this section highlights youth organizing for sexuality education that draws on elements of the reproductive justice framework. Youth-led movements for sex education justice have focused on school-based instruction, grassroots organizing, and policy change, among other issues (of course, these are not mutually exclusive). A great deal of youth organizing has focused on school-based sex education. As much research has illustrated, and my undergraduate students have recounted, young people know that their school sex ed was awkward, abstinence-focused, heteronormative trash. They know they deserve much better. In 2012, high school students in Oakland, California, collaborated with the reproductive justice organization Forward Together to conduct a youth participatory action research (YPAR) project titled "Sex Ed the City: More than Just Protection." Their goals were to identify the state of sex education in the district and what students actually wanted it to look like. YPAR is a research methodology in which young people are the primary researchers in all stages of the process—from identifying an issue and selecting data collection methods to collecting and analyzing data and disseminating results.[59] Adults may be involved in a YPAR project as co-conspirators, but youth are in the driver's seat. Critical education scholars Patricia Krueger-Henney and Jessica Ruglis describe participatory action research as a "collective act of reimagining the world" through which practitioners can "piece together and combine social imaginations of worlds not yet actualized, possible, and urgently needed."[60] In Sex Ed the City, youth imagined a comprehensive sexuality education program for their schools that was grounded in collective liberation.

In addition to designing and facilitating a workshop about sex education justice and student rights under the state's sex education policy, youth collected survey and focus group data about students' experiences with sex education. Through this research, they learned that most students reported not having spent any time in a sex ed class in the current school year. Students believed that comprehensive sex education was important for their lives and wanted their schools to spend more time on it. They also identified big gaps between what the existing curriculum covered and what students wanted to learn. For example, students indicated that sex ed should spend less time urging delay of sexual activity and more time discussing sexual orientation and gender identity, peer pressure, and bullying and harassment. They also noted that existing instruction was not inclusive of LGBTQ students, English-language-learning students, or students with disabilities.[61] The research team assembled and delivered a report calling for a set of policies based on their findings, including recommendations that the district follow state guidelines for sex education, adopt a more inclusive curriculum, train teachers better, work against stigma, and support a culture of sex ed justice. In addition to public presentations of their report and extensive media coverage, youth in the project successfully lobbied the US senators from California, Diane Feinstein and Barbara Boxer, to support the federal legislation "Real Education and Access for Healthy Youth."[62] In 2016, the state legislature passed the California Healthy Youth Act, which strengthened and updated existing state law to expand the provision of sex ed in middle and high school with a focus on healthy relationships and LGBTQ inclusivity.[63] Today, the Oakland Unified School District delivers comprehensive sex education in fifth through ninth grades that includes content on the effects of homophobia and transphobia on health, strategies for negotiating sexual consent, and using a teen-focused app to locate accessible sexual health clinics.[64] The current state of sex education in the district may not perfectly align with Sex Ed the City's vision of sex ed and social justice, but the project undoubtedly mobilized significant shifts in the city's schools.

The uprisings in the summer of 2020 following the police murder of George Floyd in Minneapolis brought attention to how policing and criminalization affect a host of issues, including reproductive justice and sexuality education. Since then, the national capacity-building organization Advocates for Youth (AFY) has supported youth organizing to persuade governments and their agencies to divest from policing and invest in reproductive and sexual health, rights, and justice.[65] In 2021, in collaboration with AFY, the campaign "Schools on Fire" released a tool kit documenting its work in pressuring Miami–Dade County Public Schools to divest from policing and reinvest resources in programs that promote students' well-being, such as comprehensive sexuality education.[66] The campaign is led by the organization Power U Center for Social Change, which focuses on youth organizing for safe and supportive schools and "developing the leadership of Black and Brown youth and Black women in South Florida so that they may help lead the struggle to liberate all oppressed people."[67] As part of its larger campaign centered on problems in the district, Schools on Fire connects defunding the police to reproductive justice because both movements are focused on bodily autonomy and self-determination.[68] They pinpoint how white supremacy and state violence threaten young people's health by criminalizing youth of color and fail to invest in their well-being. Shifting federal, state, and local

SAMAR (VIRGINIA) AND HANAN (WISCONSIN), OF THE MUSLIM YOUTH LEADERSHIP COUNCIL

Although they both got interested in reproductive justice through survivor-led violence prevention and consent education, it was Advocates for Youth's Muslim Youth Leadership Council (MyLC) that brought Hanan and Samar together. "The sexual violence survivor movement tends to be so white woman focused," Samar (age twenty) explains. "For nonwhite people, for queer people, there's so many different identities that just affect your experience so deeply, and it affects what you need on such a different level." The MyLC is a space where young Muslims working on issues of sexual and reproductive justice can find community, because, as Hanan (twenty-three) describes it, "community-building is one of the foundations of reproductive justice." The council focuses on countering Islamophobia and anti-Muslim hate, strengthening sexual health and reproductive rights for young Muslims, promoting LGBTQ rights and supporting queer Muslims, working toward racial justice, and countering anti-Blackness in their communities. One strategy that the MyLC employs in this work is to create and distribute resources for youth in its communities who may not have access to spaces that affirm all aspects of their lives. The zines *I'm Muslim and I Might Not Be Straight* and *I'm Muslim and My Gender Doesn't Fit Me* (available in print and online) are among their biggest projects.

For Samar, reproductive justice, whether it concerns health care or policing, falls at the intersection of bodily autonomy and social inequality, an intersection that her work in survivor-led organizing has vividly illustrated. Hanan agrees, adding that reproductive justice organizing can encompass everything from distributing menstrual supplies and providing labor and birth support to fighting for parental leave or sexuality education. In response to suggestions from their mother that they should just focus on their work as a doula and abortion facilitator, Hanan argues that "what is so important about reproductive justice is that you can't just focus on *x*, *y*, or *z*," because you can't work on abortion without also working on birth equity without also working against racism—it's all connected. "The more you get into the work," Samar believes, the more "it's about finding that balance between taking on systemic inequality and oppression while also focusing on the individual person that you're working with." According to Hanan, "You have to know yourself; you have to know what limits you have, and you have to have people to fall back on, who support you."

Among their various pathways and work in the movement, Samar and Hanan view the interconnectedness of reproductive justice struggles as a key movement strategy. Referencing the links between banning abortion and attempts to regulate the lives of queer and trans youth, Samar explains that "doing the work has really made me realize that the big issue is that people in power just get to pick and choose who they view as human." Although abortion is often at the forefront for Hanan, they acknowledge how the fall of *Roe v. Wade* is about so much more, from access to contraception and fertility treatment to the right to have gay sex in the privacy of your own home. As Samar puts it, the work isn't just about abortion or even reproductive health; it's about "who you believe is human and should have access to bodily autonomy."

For more on the council, see "Muslim Youth Leadership Council (MyLC)," Advocates for Youth, accessed June 22, 2024, https://www.advocatesforyouth.org/about/our-programs/muslim-youth-leadership-council-mylc/.

funding away from policing in schools—which disproportionately harms youth of color, queer and trans youth, and disabled youth—and toward investing in sexuality education can help young people decide if, when, and how they decide to make a family. Schools on Fire mobilizes the worldmaking capacities of Black and brown youth to at once dismantle systems of oppression and imagine another world into possibility.

The sex education campaign began by building a team of those most impacted: young people in the Miami–Dade County school system. Power U recruited youth activists and provided trainings on reproductive justice, the school-to-prison pipeline, organizing strategies, and how sex education supports self-determination. A core group of youth organizers developed out of this training and began to build relationships with stakeholders (parents, teachers, faith leaders, health professionals, etc.) and recruit and train new youth leaders. They identified the district superintendent as their main target and began to put pressure on the superintendent and other decision makers during school board meetings and budget hearings. Organizers also built community support for the campaign through billboards, banner drops, classroom presentations, and social media. The tool kit they created explains their strategies for other youth organizers who want to replicate their work, including how to work with adult allies and confronting opposition from supporters of school policing and opponents of sex education. As a result of the campaign's work, in 2019 Miami–Dade County Public Schools signed a contract to institutionalize sex education and implement a comprehensive curriculum. The district refused to cut funding for school policing, but the campaign knows that undoing ongoing state violence and white supremacy and their effects is a long-term struggle.[69]

CONCLUSION

As a practice of imagining reproductive justice–oriented sexuality education for youth, let's return to the Coach Carr version, which you might have experienced in school. Let's reimagine the whole scene. It's not an older, white, presumably heterosexual, cisgender gym teacher awkwardly telling you that you'll die from chlamydia. Instead, let's say a collective of youth organizers worked collaboratively with a team of adult accomplices to design a peer-to-peer curriculum based on what students want to learn. Sessions take place throughout the school year and are experiential, rather than lecture based. The overarching goals are to promote bodily autonomy and self-determination so that young people can decide if, when, and how they have sex or build a family. The curriculum starts with an analysis of power—how it structures health inequities but also how it shows up in the classroom. Through naming and interrogating how power shows up through both structural violence and interpersonal relationships, students experience and practice the concept of bodily autonomy and self-determination. This strategy helps to connect the macro to the micro—how, for instance, racism and sexism structure access to health care but also the dynamics of negotiating safer sex. It also enables young people to make connections between sexuality, sexual health, and other issues that affect them, such as police in schools and the criminalization of abortion. This reimagined experience is something you later describe not as "awkward garbage" but rather as a time when you laid the foundations for sexual and reproductive self-determination, pleasure, and joy.

CHAPTER THREE

Depathologizing Teen Parenting and Abolishing Teen Pregnancy Prevention

In the spring of 2008, news outlets around the United States began to report on an unusual story out of Gloucester, Massachusetts. A small, working-class fishing town of primarily white residents on the North Shore of Boston, Gloucester was about to be famous for a group of young women who formed a "pregnancy pact." The Gloucester High School principal claimed that eighteen students had become pregnant over the school year—four times as many as usual—and that the students had formed a pact to become pregnant together. Some news reports even suggested that they had sought out the assistance of a young homeless man in order to conceive. As the media circus exploded, many people focused on the lack of sex education in the Gloucester school system, or on the perception that the heavily Catholic community did not approve of contraception. For the most part, media coverage characterized the so-called pact as a scandal and a tragedy, brought on by the "romanticization" of teen pregnancy in shows like MTV's *16 and Pregnant* and *Teen Mom.*

A rather different story emerged once the young women had an opportunity to tell their side of things. According to them, there was no pact or agreement to get pregnant at the same time. Instead, it was a coincidence that several of them happened to be pregnant all at once. As one young woman, Lindsey Oliver, told the audience when she appeared on *Good Morning America*: "There was definitely no pact. There was a group of girls already pregnant that decided they were going to help one another to finish school and raise their kids together."[1] An article that appeared on *Salon* at the time pointed out that this was actually a *great* idea: a group of moms supporting one another get through their education and raise their children. One adult staffer shared that the young women in Gloucester were doing something that she had often fantasized about with her friends: "I have thought several times about how this story resembles the plan my single urban working girlfriends and I have openly fantasized about: We'll have kids on our own but together. We can share childcare responsibilities, help each other have lives while raising kids. I'm not saying it's a good idea, but it definitely struck me as a plan that didn't sound unfamiliar in another context."[2] Notice how she points out that she's not saying a pregnancy pact is a "good idea" but that the plan sounded pretty appealing to her as a thirty-something white woman with a middle-class job and income.

Most media coverage, however, did not point out this double standard. In general, like academic research and public policy making, both news and popular media portrayals of youth pregnancy and parenting rely on tropes of pathology and danger. They have long constructed teen pregnancy as a dire social problem, though, as this chapter shows, this idea is not based in robust evidence. The belief that teen pregnancy is unequivocally "bad" is deeply entrenched in our minds: teen pregnancy is an epidemic that ruins lives, is bad for children, and costs taxpayers millions. Teen pregnancy and parenting are also deeply racialized. What was unusual about the Gloucester pregnancy pact was that the youth at the center of the story were white. Generally, media coverage about teen pregnancy has used pregnancy among Black and Latina youth as the scapegoat for everything that's wrong about youth childbearing.[3] Likewise, social policy discourses in the United States have long relied on racialized teen mothers, specifically in the figure of the anti-Black "welfare queen," to promote policies that diminish the social safety net.[4] Consequently, "teen pregnancy" is always a racialized category.[5] This does not mean that white teen moms are literally seen as people of color, but rather that the deep, deep racialization of teen childbearing means that teen parents are always cast in the shadow of white supremacy.

A core component of the RJ vision is reframing the focus on white, economically privileged women's access to contraception and abortion toward the struggles of women of color, queer and transgender people, and disabled people to have the children they want and to parent them with dignity and support. This vision must include supporting pregnant and parenting youth and abolishing teen pregnancy prevention. This vision does not mean that youth should not have access to the knowledge and tools to prevent pregnancy if they want to. Instead, abolishing teen pregnancy prevention involves framing contraceptive access or sexuality education as tools to promote young people's bodily autonomy and self-determination, rather than simply preventing pregnancy. It means honoring and supporting *all* of young people's reproductive choices, whether they choose to parent or not.

Abolishing teen pregnancy prevention as we know is part of a reproductive justice vision for a number of reasons. Policy makers, researchers, and the media have long pathologized teen childbearing, a tactic that does not improve the well-being of young parents or their children. In fact, it does quite the opposite, as shame and stigma are never good for your health! Similarly, these groups have framed reducing the teen pregnancy rate as a means to the end of reducing the taxpayer burden or curtailing the presumed sexual deviance of youth. Even some feminist scholars and activists have over the years positioned reducing teen pregnancy rates as a feminist goal, thereby tacitly or even explicitly stigmatizing pregnant and parenting teens. As a result of these widespread discourses, pregnant and parenting teens are often scapegoated for a host of social problems ranging from poverty to school dropout.

This chapter analyzes the pathologization of youth childbearing in terms of broader, racialized ideas about sexual and reproductive deviance. The analysis of youth childbearing connects to the themes of the other chapters by highlighting the coalitional possibilities of organizing around a shared marginal relationship to power held by people whose reproduction does not conform to dominant social ideals. Following from the book's overarching theoretical frameworks, this chapter argues that teen childbearing is threatening precisely because it disrupts white, middle-class, able-bodied, heteronormative ideas about sexuality and reproduction. First, I describe how a closer look at research on the causes and consequences of youth childbearing tells a much different story than the media and government portray. Next, I describe how queer of color critique and abolition feminism provide tools for incorporating youth childbearing into the reproductive justice framework, vision, and social movement. Finally, I describe how teen and young parents have advocated fiercely for mutual support of one another and for abolishing the shame and stigma of early childbearing. Readers should note that this chapter uses both the terms *teen* and *youth*. Adultism contributes to the pathologization of teen childbearing by using the phrase "children having children." I use the term *teen* to signal that I am engaging with the circulating discourses that construct early childbearing as a social problem. Because adultist, infantilizing language is often used to harm young people, I generally use the phrase "pregnant and parenting youth," though, as the chapter illustrates, some activists have reclaimed the language around teen motherhood. And who is even considered a "teen" or "young" mom is very much up for debate.

CREATING THE TEEN PREGNANCY "PROBLEM"

As with deciding who is a "youth," who is considered a "teen" parent is not readily agreed upon. Generally, "pregnant or parenting teen" refers to someone under twenty years of age, but changes in broader fertility patterns and growing concern over the "appropriate" age to have children have pushed the construction of "early" or "youth" childbearing later and later into a person's twenties. For instance, in 2005 the organization founded in 1996 as the National Campaign to Prevent Teen Pregnancy renamed itself the National Campaign to Prevent Teen Pregnancy and Unplanned Pregnancy and expanded its mission to include the prevention of pregnancies among young people up to age 29. In 2017, the organization changed its name again to simply Power to Decide but kept its focus on, as rhetoric scholars Jenna Vinson and Clare Daniel note, "surveilling and changing individual women's reproductive behaviors rather than the systemic inequalities that shape women's lives."[6] The age at first birth *has* been steadily inching higher in the United States: in 1990 the median age was 27, and in 2019 it was 30—and birthrates have been rising the most among the age group 35–44.[7] There are many variations in the age at first birth across race and ethnicity, geography, marital status, and level of education, but the overall aging of first-time parents contributes to the meaning of "young" shifting younger and younger. In addition, when epidemiologists and policy makers report on the rate of teen births, they generally use the age range 15–19. This data obscure the reality that most "teen" births occur to 18- and 19-year-olds—that is, legal adults.[8]

The fact that the age at which someone is considered a "young" or "teen" parent has changed over time or differs from community to community is evidence that "teen pregnancy" is a socially constructed concept. Whose childbearing is considered "young" is always relative to the norms among people in your racial, ethnic, and social class group and where you live. Prior to the 1970s, there was no such thing as "teen pregnancy" in the United States. That is, many people married and had their first children in their late teens and early twenties—that was just normal and didn't merit the qualifier "teen." On the other hand, unmarried motherhood was deeply stigmatized. Women of any age who became pregnant while unmarried were often shunned by their families and communities. In this era, white, economically privileged women would be sent to "maternity homes," where they would carry their pregnancies to term in secrecy and then place their infants for adoption with a respectable, two-parent family. In 1976, a report from the sexual and reproductive health think tank the Guttmacher Institute heralded the beginning of teen pregnancy as a social and health problem. Titled "11 Million Teenagers: What Can Be Done about the Epidemic of Adolescent Pregnancies in the United States," the report brought teen pregnancy to the attention of researchers, policy makers, and the general public. Notably, naming teen pregnancy as an "epidemic" coincided with the understanding that it was a phenomenon affecting "our girls," in other words, respectable young white women.[9] As education scholar Wanda Pillow points out, during this time the prevention of teen pregnancy became a public policy objective in part to rescue young white women from the stigma of unintended pregnancies and their association with Blackness and brownness.[10]

The overall birth rate among all ages in the United States has been steadily falling since 2007, but the teen birth rate has declined even more dramatically. From 2010 to 2020, the birth rate among 15- to 19-year-olds declined 54 percent to the lowest rate it has ever been.[11] It is difficult to pin down exactly what contributed to the decline, but researchers speculate that increased contraceptive access under the Affordable Care Act, a declining national economy, and easy access to sexual health information via the internet are all factors at play.[12] Even though teen birth rates have been on the decline for many years, teen pregnancy has retained its status as a social problem in the minds of most policy makers, researchers, health care providers, journalists, and the public at large. As teen birth rates plummeted in the early 2010s, the government and nonprofit organizations continued to funnel millions of dollars into preventing it.[13] It does not seem that the rates of teen childbearing can ever fall low enough for it *not* to be a problem. That's the point: it's not the numbers alone that construct youth childbearing as a problem; it's the social anxiety that surrounds youth sexuality, the reproduction of people of color, and the perceived threat to normative family making.

It's important to note that not every young person in the United States has the same likelihood of becoming a teen parent. The annual *rates* of teen birth are higher among Black and Latinx youth than they are among white youth. However, the *number* of youth who have babies tells a different story. In 2020, white, non-Hispanic people accounted for approximately 34 percent of the births to teens 15–19, which was not much different than percentage of Black youth (37 percent), but higher than the percentage of "Hispanic" youth (26 percent).[14] That is, young women of color are more likely to become young parents, but the actual numbers of white teen parents and Black teen parents are close, and there are fewer Latinx teen parents than there are white. Nevertheless, because early childbearing is so deeply racialized, young women of color are often the face of teen pregnancy in media and policy. Rates of teen birth also vary dramatically by geography, from a low of 6.1 per 1,000 in Massachusetts to a high of 27.9 per 1,000 in Mississippi.[15] As a whole, the United States consistently has higher rates of teen childbearing compared to other resource-rich nations in the Global North. Researchers, the media, and policy makers frequently compare the rates of teen pregnancy in the United States to countries like the Netherlands, where the rates are about 80 percent lower. However, the European countries with these very low rates also have universal health care and robust social welfare policies, both of which contribute to the accessibility of contraception and also mitigate the potential negative effects of unintended or early pregnancies.

The idea that teen pregnancy is an urgent social, health, and economic problem is so deeply entrenched in our minds that it is often hard to imagine otherwise. As scholars of social problems show us, phenomena like teen pregnancy are viewed as problems not because of objective standards but because people believe they are problems.[16] The 1976 Guttmacher report helped to establish teen childbearing as a social problem, a conclusion buttressed over the next several decades by policy makers, the media, and academic research. In the 1990s, President Bill Clinton declared teen pregnancy "our most serious social problem." His related promise to "end welfare as we knew it" demonized poor women and families and pathologized teen parents. As a subset of the racialized "welfare queens"—a term that legal scholar Ian Haney López calls an anti-Black dog whistle—who were content to keep having babies on the government's dime, pregnant teens were central to the 1996 welfare reform bill that gutted the social safety net in the United States.[17] Disability scholar Jina B. Kim contends that the welfare queen was framed as an infectious threat to the health of society. Proponents of welfare reform ultimately painted "poor Black mothers as disabling to the nation writ large" and therefore sought to cure that disablement through punitive public policy.[18] The end of welfare introduced new regulations into the lives of economically marginalized mothers, such as "family caps" that prohibited meager benefit increases if a recipient had another child. It also provided $50 million per year in funding for teen pregnancy prevention in the form of ineffective and stigmatizing abstinence-only education. Countless studies have demonstrated that welfare reform did indeed reduce the number of welfare recipients; it did so by kicking families off cash assistance and in turn increasing child poverty.[19] Likewise, research has overwhelmingly demonstrated that abstinence-based sex education does not improve youth sexual health outcomes.[20]

Throughout the 1990s and 2000s, social science research came to focus on documenting the supposed perils of teen pregnancy. The edited volume *Kids Having Kids: Economic Costs and Social Consequences of Teen Pregnancy*, for example, published in 1997 and updated in 2008, was pivotal in establishing teen pregnancy as a problem of concern for social scientists. The infantilizing rhetoric of "kids having kids" proved highly sticky and remains a commonly used idiom to describe teen childbearing. Scholars who contributed to the book, including Rebecca Maynard, Saul Hoffman, and Frank Furstenberg—to the best of my knowledge, all white people with social class privilege—focused their research on identifying the "costs and consequences" of teen pregnancy. According to this genre of research, teen childbearing costs billions of dollars per year in public assistance expenditures, and therefore preventing it could save a lot of money. The research has also tended to paint youth as "bad" parents who are more likely to neglect or abuse their children, who in turn are more likely to be incarcerated and less likely to be academically successful in school. Overall, the research has positioned teen parents and their children as doomed to an intergenerational cycle of poverty and suffering.

In the 2000s, social panic about the rapid growth of the Latinx population in the United States, the ongoing controversy about immigration, and the discourse of Latinas as "hyperfertile" increasingly positioned young Latinas as the target of teen pregnancy prevention.[21] Alongside this shifting racialization of the teen pregnancy problem erupted a media obsession with teen parents through MTV's reality programs *16 and Pregnant* and *Teen Mom*. Developed in collaboration with what was then called the National Campaign to Prevent Teen Pregnancy, the programs were designed specifically to dissuade young people from early parenthood. The shows actively contributed to the shaming and stigmatization of teen parents, who critiqued the unrealistic and problematic depiction of their lives.[22]

By the 2010s, the growing popularity of the language of "social determinants of health" (the economic, educational, and environmental conditions that affect our health), helped shift research on teen childbearing away from the "pathology" approach and toward a "reform" approach. This newer body of research mostly eschewed the hyperbolic rhetoric of the past but still framed teen pregnancy as a problem.[23] In this era, research did shift somewhat toward determining the social structural conditions, such as poverty, that contributed to higher rates of teen pregnancy and potential negative outcomes for young parents and their children. Instead of focusing on punitive polices like denying public assistance benefits, this research promoted solutions like comprehensive sex education and provider-controlled long-acting reversible contraceptives (LARCs) such as the implant and the IUD to reduce teen pregnancy rates.[24] As much reproductive scholarship and activism have demonstrated, these technologies have long been linked to the reproductive oppression of women of color and disabled people deemed "unfit" to parent.[25] However, neither sexuality education nor long-acting contraception can solve the disabling conditions of ableism and racial capitalism: these are still individual-level solutions for structural-level social problems. The reform approach still expects marginalized parents to regulate their sexual and reproductive behavior by not having children in order to "fix" social problem they did not create.

ORGANIZING 101: CAMPAIGN DEVELOPMENT

When you hear the word *campaign*, you might think of a politician working to get elected by holding press conferences, running television ads, and leading voter registration efforts. Maybe you think of a time when you were a kid and you and your siblings campaigned to convince your parent to let you get a pet by trying to persuade them how responsible you were. When people involved in social movements use the word *campaign*, they are referring to something similar: an organized struggle that uses various tactics to convince a decision maker to do something you want (or not do something you don't want them to do).

A social movement campaign begins when a group of people come together and identify a problem they wish to solve or mitigate. They might come together via the internet, a school or workplace, or the neighborhood they all live in. A *problem* is a social condition like poor-quality schooling or police brutality. These conditions have *root causes* in interlocking systems of oppression such as white supremacy, class exploitation, transphobia, and ableism. It's important to identify and work to change the root causes of the problems that social movements wish to address: if you don't address the root causes, the problems will just continue.

Once people have come together and identified a problem, they need to determine their *target*: the person or people who have the power to do (or not do) what they want. The target is where you direct your *demand*, the specific change you want to occur for the campaign to succeed. It's important to identify the target(s); otherwise your campaign will be limited. For example, if your demand is that a school stop using stigmatizing teen pregnancy prevention messages, you need to identify who has the power to make that change. It would not be effective to target the school principal if the school board has the final say on school policy. Likewise, it's important to be clear and specific about what your demands are. Demanding that the administration stop stigmatizing young parents is less concrete than demanding that they take down stigmatizing posters and form an advisory council composed of pregnant and parenting students.

A campaign develops an overall *strategy* for achieving demands. For example, your strategy might be to convince the school health office of the harm of using stigma to promote health. A campaign achieves this strategy through the use of *tactics*, which are discussed in the boxed feature "Organizing 101: Movement Tactics" in chapter 4.

HOW DO WE KNOW WHAT WE KNOW ABOUT TEEN PREGNANCY AND PARENTING?

Other scholars, or even just random people I end up engaging in small talk, often challenge my critical take on youth pregnancy and parenting by invoking the belief that research demonstrates how it's "bad" for young people, their children, and society at large. Research on teen pregnancy is useful for illustrating the *politics of knowledge*, or how power is related to how we know what we know. How is knowledge about teen pregnancy created and distributed? Whose knowledge is considered "real" and valid? What forms of knowledge are considered most persuasive, and why? How does knowledge about teen pregnancy conform to preconceived notions about social problems, themselves inflected with race, class, and gender bias? How we know what we know is very much influenced by power relations. The struggles of people of color, women, disabled people, LGBTQ people, and many others to name and challenge the politics of knowledge have much to teach us.

Take for example the ideas that teen childbearing is always already bad; women of color are hyperfertile; poor people are lazy, unproductive, and dependent; young people are irresponsible; and women who want or enjoy sex should be ashamed. Many people are so conditioned to see teen childbearing as terrible that they cannot view it in any other way. Researchers call this "confirmation bias," or how our methods and results tend to confirm dominant social views. To be sure, as someone who was both a pregnant teenager and who has spent many years talking about it in my professional capacity as a researcher, I am well accustomed to students, colleagues, and acquaintances insisting, "But we know that teen pregnancy is so bad for the moms and their kids!" no matter what data I share with them.

When we take a closer look at the research on the causes and consequences of teen pregnancy, we discover that what we know is actually quite equivocal. The hyperbolic claims made by advocacy organizations, politicians, and the media are not supported by the research. The negative outcomes associated with teen childbearing are the result of interlocking systems of oppression, but research blames pregnant and parenting youth for the consequences of structural inequality. Much of the research on teen childbearing positions the *age* of the mother as the causal factor in negative social, economic, or educational outcomes. From this perspective, if a young person simply waited to have children, they would be happily married in a healthy relationship, have plentiful social support, a reliable income and job security, and a postsecondary degree. However, this perspective overlooks the ways racism, classism, sexism, ableism, homophobia, xenophobia, and so on affect life chances. Are the sons of young mothers more likely to be incarcerated because of inadequate parenting or because they are more likely to live in heavily policed communities? Are young mothers more likely to be reported for child abuse and neglect because they are bad parents or because social workers, teachers, and health care providers are more likely to already believe them to be bad parents? These are all examples of how social inequality, not age, may be a more relevant causal factor in negative outcomes for young parents and their children.

For racialized and economically marginalized young people living in disinvested communities, waiting a few more years to have children does not suddenly make quality, affordable health care, education, employment, or housing suddenly available. The young mothers I discuss in my book *Distributing Condoms and Hope* lived in a community where the majority of jobs were minimum wage with no opportunity for advancement. The soaring costs of housing had prompted white middle-class outsiders to increasingly purchase property in the city, thus pushing out the people who had lived there for decades. The state had taken over the public school system for underperforming on standardized tests, and students did not have the kind of preparation to be admitted to the nearby elite colleges—which were all predominately white institutions with extraordinarily high tuition. Waiting a few years to have a baby wouldn't have changed any of that.

When carefully designed studies make adequate comparisons between young people of similar socioeconomic backgrounds, they find that it is the existing social conditions—not the age of the mother—that are the prime causal factors in negative outcomes.[26] Epidemiologist Arline Geronimus has argued that having children earlier in life can be an adaptive strategy to cope with the effects of structural inequality, such as economic uncertainly or shorter lifespans.[27] As the organization Bold Futures (formerly Young Women United) puts it: "Why postpone parenting when opportunities for socioeconomic advancement are few whether or not childbearing is delayed? Why wait to have children when it may be a sound strategy for a young person to parent while they and the members of their support system are in (relatively) optimal health?"[28] If policy makers actually wanted to improve the lives of young families, investing in housing, education, and health care would be much more effective strategies than trying to stop them from having children in the first place.

In addition to misattributing the causal factor for negative outcomes to age, many of the negative outcomes associated with early childbearing that we regularly hear are quite exaggerated. Even researchers whose work is included the book *Kids Having Kids* found that the negative effects on educational attainment and economic security were minimal and short-lived. In fact, for economically marginalized young women, having children earlier in life can result in *greater* lifetime earnings than if they had delayed childbearing a few years.[29] Similarly, research such as that produced by the National Campaign's project "Counting It Up" has used dubious and problematic estimation methods to make the exaggerated claim that that teen childbearing in the United States costs more than $9 billion per year. In this research, the "costs" of teen pregnancy include health and welfare programs like Medicaid, housing assistance, and childcare vouchers that can help improve the well-being of marginalized families. Programs like these compose a tiny fraction of the amount that the government spends each year on costs like the military or subsidies to private corporations. Nevertheless, teen pregnancy is widely framed as something that "costs" society a lot (read: white, middle-class people with normative fertility patterns). In this view, social programs to support pregnant and parenting youth are a zero-sum game in which supporting the lives of vulnerable families harms honest, hardworking, sexually respectable taxpayers.

The research that has been used to paint a dire picture of teen pregnancy and parenting is largely *quantitative* (analyzing whole populations using statistics) rather than *qualitative* (studying individuals and groups in their social context through interviews or participant observation). Recall how people in Gloucester observed a higher than usual number of pregnant teens and jumped to conclusions, but a very different story emerged when the young women were actually interviewed. Paying attention to the specific, contextual, lived details of pregnant and parenting young people's experiences tells much more than reducing them to numbers ever can. It can also help create policies and programs that support, rather than shame. For example, ethnographic, participatory, and arts-based research with pregnant and parenting youth demonstrates how shame and stigma harms their self-esteem, how hostile schools limit their educational success, and how punitive public policies limit their socioeconomic mobility.[30] These approaches can help us understand how pregnant and parenting youth are "both resistant to and inscribed upon by discourse," or how they navigate the ways that society pathologizes their bodies, lives, and families.[31]

The negative portrayal of teen childbearing in research, the media, and policy making has real, negative effects on young people's lives. Shaming and stigmatizing people for their reproductive decisions or family structures does not improve their life chances. It doesn't help them finish high school or college. It doesn't put nutritious food on the table, support healthy relationships, or create meaningful jobs that pay a living wage. It does lead to punitive public policies like welfare reform and slashing the budgets of public programs that support young parents, and to the hyperpromotion of provider-controlled contraceptives like IUDs. The pathologization of pregnant and parenting teens is key to what I call the teen pregnancy prevention industrial complex (TPPIC), or the webs and relationships of organizations, service providers, programs, and funding through which people with social, racial, and economic privilege control the sexual and reproductive lives of marginalized young people. The TPPIC in the United States has resulted in decades of research, policy making, and health promotion aimed at regulating the sexual and reproductive behavior of economically marginalized young women of color. Preventing teen pregnancy has overshadowed the issues that young people define as problems in their communities, such as intimate partner violence, hyperpolicing, poor-quality schooling, and a lack of economic opportunities.[32] Understanding teen pregnancy prevention "as a set of relationships, practices, and technologies that constrain liberatory possibilities allows us to see how health promotion can reify inequalities and serve the interests of those in power, rather than those targeted by its apparatus."[33] Critically examining the TPPIC also illustrates how research, the media, and policy making promote individual behavior change (don't have babies until you graduate college and have a middle-class income) as a solution to structural inequality (costs of higher education have skyrocketed while living wage jobs disappear while racial discrimination in employment remains rampant).

Young parents are a group of people that "everyone loves to hate" across political divides: conservatives and progressives alike have framed teen childbearing as a social problem, albeit in different ways. Both have used pathologizing and stigmatizing rhetoric to talk about teen pregnancy. Preventing teen pregnancy has been a key objective of Democratic administrations, including those of Presidents Bill Clinton and Barak Obama. Whereas Clinton used teen pregnancy as a justification to end the social safety net, Obama used it to justify spending millions of dollars in "evidenced-based" school sex education that included abstinence promotion, excluded LGBTQ youth, and ignored agency and pleasure.[34] Indeed, liberals, progressives, and conservatives alike use teen pregnancy rates as a justification for increasing school-based sex education or hyperpromoting long-acting reversible contraceptives to young people, low-income people, and people of color.

Issues that unite people across sharp political divides have much to teach us, as when feminists or progressives unite with conservatives to regulate the lives of pregnant and parenting youth, sex workers, or transgender people. For instance, sociologist Elizabeth Bernstein demonstrates how anti–sex trafficking activism brings feminists together with evangelicals, political conservatives, and other groups generally hostile to feminist politics. Bernstein rejects the idea that feminists and conservatives working together on trafficking and other issues related to sex work are merely strange bedfellows. Rather, the substantial overlap between their interests and objectives in the form of a "social strategy for regulating race and class others ... [is] part of a neoliberal gender strategy that securitizes the family and lends moral primacy to marriage."[35] Anti–sex trafficking activism and teen pregnancy prevention unite people across sharp political divides precisely because these positions benefit dominant social groups. It also helps these groups to position their own sexuality and reproduction as normal and normative. Much of the activist response to sex trafficking has taken place through the framework of what Bernstein terms *carceral feminism,* in which "previous generations' struggles for gender justice and sexual liberation are recast in terms of criminal justice (often via social actors and institutions that do not necessarily identify as feminist but have explicitly declared their allegiance to the empowerment of women and girls)."[36] Similar to policies and programs that shame and regulate pregnant and parenting youth, the carceral approach to sex trafficking has done little to help the lives of people who have been sex trafficked. Instead, it creates more surveillance and policing, which have resulted in less safe working conditions and more violence toward sex workers.[37] In the same way, stigmatizing teen pregnancy does not improve the lives of pregnant and parenting youth and their children. Instead, it harms their self-efficacy and hinders access to supportive services and solidarity with other marginalized young people.

REPRODUCTIVE JUSTICE DEMANDS COALITIONAL POLITICS AND THE ABOLITION OF TEEN PREGNANCY PREVENTION

As I've argued elsewhere, queer of color critique "allows us to consider how the figure of the racialized teen mother, lacking in respectability, normative heterosexuality, and socioeconomic progress, becomes the embodiment of a public health problem in which there is little room to understand teen motherhood outside a binary of pathology or romanticization."[38] This framework provides tools for analyzing how youth pregnancy and parenting are reproductive justice issues. In "Punks, Bulldaggers, and Welfare Queens: The Radical Potential of Queer Politics," a germinal essay and early explication of queer of color critique, political scientist Cathy Cohen took to task whitedominated queer politics and activism for their reliance on shared identity as a source of political unity. Instead, she argued for a coalitional politics organized around a shared marginal relationship to power held by people whose sexuality and reproduction does not conform to dominant social ideals. Cohen suggested that the "process of movement building be rooted not in our shared history or identity, but in our shared marginal relationship to dominant power which normalizes, legitimizes, and privileges."[39] Youth pregnancy and parenting are threatening because they disrupt white, middle-class, heteronormative ideas about sexuality and reproduction. Therefore, coalitional political frameworks, visions, and social movements enable us to identify and disrupt the systems of power that regulate, pathologize, and harm youth, whether they are young parents, youth seeking abortion services, or criminalized youth.

A teen pregnancy prevention campaign that was implemented in Milwaukee and Chicago in the 2010s using digitally altered images of pregnant cisgender boys demonstrates the need for coalitional politics around youth childbearing. Posters and billboards in each city depicted these "pregnant boys" shirtless with big bellies and solemn, downturned faces. The campaigns used slogans such as "It shouldn't be any less disturbing when it's a girl. Teen pregnancy: stop ignoring it." and "Unexpected? Most teen pregnancies are." As sociologist Deborah Lupton explains, campaigns like these are intended to evoke impossibility and disgust by sending the message "Look at these gross pregnant boys—you should be just as grossed out when you see a pregnant girl!"[40] The campaigns led to substantial media coverage and public debate over whether the approach was warranted given the high rates of teen pregnancy in Milwaukee and Chicago, particularly among young women of color.[41] Many trans people and their allies were outraged over the images' implicit transphobia. The notion that pregnant boys are "disturbing" and "unexpected" results from the way cissexism positions pregnant men and boys as disgusting impossibilities. This position denies the reality that trans men and boys do indeed carry pregnancies, and that they often experience bias, mistreatment, violence, or outright denial of care when seeking reproductive health services. As trans studies scholar Toby Beauchamp has argued, the campaign images invite the viewer "to feel disturbed by a visibly non-normative body that is read as such not only through gender, but through the racialized and classed tropes of the welfare mother and pregnant teen."[42] Aside from Beauchamp, however, few commentators have made the connection that pathologizing racialized teen parents is just as problematic as denying the existence of pregnant trans men and boys. Indeed, I remember seeing multiple online rants along the lines of "Teen pregnancy is bad and needs to be stopped, but don't throw trans folks under the bus to do it."

The response among some trans people to the campaign is what I refer to as an #IntersectionalFail. In attempting to call out how power positioned only one marginalized group of young people (trans boys) as disgusting and out of control, critiques of the campaign overlooked the shared marginal relationship to power held by trans youth *and* racialized pregnant and parenting youth. Thinking about youth reproduction through coalitional politics is a way to remedy this fail. Pregnant and parenting cisgender youth and transgender youth are both pathologized and regulated by the same interlocking systems of adultism, racism, and cis-heterosexism. What would it have looked like to call out the ways the campaign stigmatized and otherized multiple groups of marginalized youth at the same time? What would it have looked like to link demands to stop the campaigns to demands for the safety of trans youth, especially given that the 2013 Chicago version of this campaign corresponded with the explosive rise in media attention directed at trans youth?

Like the carceral feminist approach to sex trafficking, teen pregnancy prevention campaigns such as these, as well as programming for young parents, largely focus on punishment and exclusion.[43] Prevention efforts are generally meant to persuade young people to avoid sex or use provider-controlled long-acting contraceptives. Programming for young parents focuses on preventing second pregnancies and reducing public assistance "dependence." As part of a coalitional political vision, abolition feminism provides an antidote to carceral feminism and offers a framework for building a reproductive justice approach to youth childbearing with the goal of abolishing not only shame and stigma but also teen pregnancy prevention as we know it. Abolition feminism is a politics and a practice that rejects criminalization, policing, surveillance, and punishment as strategies for solving social problems such as gender-based violence.[44] For example, locking up the individual perpetrators of intimate-partner violence does nothing to change the social conditions that foster violence, such as white supremacy, patriarchy, or social disinvestment in marginalized communities. Likewise, preventing individual young people from getting pregnant and raising their families with dignity and support does nothing to change the social conditions that produce poor outcomes for young parents and their children. Abolitionist feminism also believes that no one is disposable and that the strategies we use to achieve justice are just as important as the ends. In other words, we cannot scapegoat pregnant and parenting youth as a health promotion strategy.

A reproductive justice approach to youth childbearing must have as its goal the abolition of teen pregnancy prevention. As scholar-activists Angela Y. Davis, Gina Dent, Erica R. Meiners, and Beth E. Richie note in their book *Abolition. Feminism. Now.*, abolitionist politics is often misunderstood and criticized for a perceived narrow focus on what it wants to dismantle rather than what it wants to build. To say that we must abolish teen pregnancy prevention is *not* to say that youth shouldn't have access to the knowledge and tools that prevent pregnancy. Rather, a coalitional feminist abolitionist approach to youth childbearing understands goals like increasing contraceptive access or sex education in terms of their potential to promote young people's social, economic, and political power, not merely to prevent pregnancy. The goal is to help young people decide if, when, and how to have children—the core of the reproductive justice vision. As Young Women United (now Bold Futures), a New Mexico–based reproductive justice organization, argued in its critical 2016 report "Dismantling Teen Pregnancy Prevention," teen pregnancy prevention "is designed to influence the reproductive decisions and outcomes of an entire segment of a population, simply [based] on their age.... [We take an] explicit stance against efforts that seek to control, coerce or manage the reproductive agency of any person."[45] The goal of teen

ORGANIZATION SPOTLIGHT: CALIFORNIA
LATINAS FOR REPRODUCTIVE JUSTICE,
JUSTICE FOR YOUNG PARENTS

California Latinas for Reproductive Justice was formed in 2005 and, as of this writing, is the only statewide advocacy organization in California that focuses on Latinas and reproductive justice. The organization combines policy advocacy, community-engaged research, community mobilization, leadership development, and movement building to cultivate Latina/x power and leadership. In 2012, the group launched the Justice for Young Families (J4YF) initiative to "challenge the dominant frame, account for the inequities experienced by Latina/o youth and address the root causes to ensure Latina/o youth who are pregnant and/or parenting can thrive."[a] J4YF recognizes that policy and media discourses frame Latina/o/x/e teen pregnancy as an inherent problem—instead of naming the systemic social and economic conditions that prevent young Latinas/os/xs/es from deciding if, when, and how they make a family. Images of Latinas as "hot" and "spicy" hypersexual young women and young Latino men as "irresponsible" fathers and partners support punitive public policies and a lack of support for young families. J4YF fomented a cultural shift concerning these harmful misrepresentations by promoting the health, equity, and dignity of young parents through policy advocacy and youth development.

J4YF began this work by releasing a series of issue briefs based on interviews with pregnant and parenting young Latines aimed at dismantling shame and stigma. In 2016, the California legislature approved a resolution mobilized by J4YF and NoTeenShame activists to establish August 25 as

"California Young Parents Day." The resolution named young parents as part of the fabric of vibrant communities across the state and acknowledged that shame and stigma, combined with systemic inequalities, worked to limit their success. In 2021, J4YF commemorated the day by creating a digital exhibit titled "Celebrating YOUng Parents & Families" with the goal of uplifting all young parents and families of color in celebration of Young Parents Day of Recognition in California and New Mexico (the only other state that officially celebrates the day, which was initiated by the RJ organization Bold Futures in 2012). The exhibit featured photos, stories, and poetry by young parents celebrating the full range of their lived experiences, including their resilience, joy, and struggles. In 2022, J4YF launched the Young Parent Leadership Council. This paid opportunity for Los Angeles–area parents between the ages of fourteen and twenty-one offers young people an opportunity to build leadership skills and community with other young parents.

See "Justice for Young Families," California Latinas for Reproductive Justice, accessed June 26, 2024, https:// californialatinas.org/our-work/justice-for-young-families/.

a. Franco 2012.

pregnancy prevention is to control, manage, exclude, and punish nonnormative reproduction. A coalitional, abolitionist reproductive justice approach rejects this goal. The following section highlights the work of pregnant and parenting youth who have organized to abolish the idea that teen pregnancy is a social pathology that must be prevented.

ORGANIZING TO ABOLISH SHAME, STIGMA, AND
TEEN PREGNANCY PREVENTION AS WE KNOW IT

The young women in Gloucester were definitely not the first
teens to support one another during pregnancy, birth, and
parenting. In fact, young people have a rich history in organizing
to abolish the pathologization of youth childbearing while sharing resources and support. I vividly remember being nineteen,
pregnant, isolated, and scared, and accessing the internet via the
loud screech of dial-up and finding the support and community
I wasn't getting in the "real world." It was 2001, and I found Girl-
Mom.com, an unapologetically feminist site whose purpose was
to "support young mothers, of all backgrounds, in their struggles
for reproductive freedom and social support."[46] Girl-Mom.com
greatly influenced how I became politicized around issues surrounding reproduction, gender, race, class, and sexuality; without it I probably wouldn't have written this book. The site had
been founded earlier that year by a California-based teen mom
named Alli Crews. In the early 2000s, the George W. Bush
administration's "compassionate conservatism" was laser focused
on dismantling what was left of welfare benefits in favor of
spending millions of dollars on marriage promotion initiatives. It
was also in 2001 that the National Campaign to Prevent Teen
Pregnancy launched its notorious, controversial print campaign
"Sex Has Consequences," which featured posters of young
women of color with words like REJECT, DIRTY, and CHEAP
stamped across their bodies. Girl-Mom.com grew out of this
political climate and the 1990s feminist zine and DIY (do it yourself) cultures.[47] This was a transitional era in which activist print
media culture like zines was morphing into grassroots digital
organizing. Feminist activists were beginning to use the internet

as an organizing tool, many years before Facebook or Twitter radically transformed social movement work. In the 1990s and early 2000s, zines brought people with radical politics together through DIY printing and distribution, but the growth of electronic communication drastically changed this landscape.

Girl-Mom.com featured personal narratives and political articles, but the heart of the site was its message boards. This is what I found after dialing onto the internet on a massive beige desktop computer: forums where users shared advice and experiences and commiserated while also developing a vision of reproductive justice for young mothers. The message boards were organized in forums such as "Pregnancy and Birth," "School and Work," and "Social Justice." It was there that I found a community of other marginalized young parents who were pushing back against the pathologization of their lives, bodies, and families—all while trying to figure out how to go to school, make ends meet, have a social life, and so on. The forums generated numerous lifelong IRL (in the real world) friends, semiannual regional get-togethers, a few romantic couples, and of course, political organizing.[48]

It was through the forums that the idea for the National Day to Empower Teen Parents (NDETP) was born in 2003. The year prior, the National Campaign to Prevent Teen Pregnancy had launched the first National Day to Prevent Teen Pregnancy, which included national, state, and local events aimed at encouraging teens to make "a personal commitment to avoid becoming teen parents." The NDETP was created in response. As our mission statement read:

> Teen parents are routinely vilified in our society, and their rights as parents are stripped away. "Babies having babies" we are told, over and over again, without any reasons given as to WHY

teenagers are told that they are unilaterally unable to parent effectively. Our society has not been able to collectively realize that the more you tell any person or group of people that they will fail, the more likely it is that they will do just that. Fail.

Using the forums, we planned a National Day of Action for October 11, 2003, and put together a print zine. Users pitched topics for the zine, and the site's editors assembled the resulting articles into *EMPOWER: A Young Mama's Guide to Taking Control.* At seventy pages, it was a thick zine that contained essays on such topics as accessing reproductive health care, leaving an abusive relationship, and going to college. The zine existed only in hard copy. Organizers mailed a packet containing a flat copy of the publication along with suggestions for planning a local day of action to any interested young mom. About a hundred packets were mailed to young people across the United States and Canada, who would photocopy the zine, distribute it locally, and plan speak-out events. Events occurred in Austin, New York City, Boston, Minneapolis, San Diego, and Edmonton, Alberta. I had just started college that fall, and I remember being outraged that the campus activity email administrator would not allow info about the NDETP to be included on grounds that they did not distribute "anything too political."

EMPOWER and the NDETP spoke back to the ways that the media, government, and society at large tend to blame young parents for all of society's problems. The problem isn't that, say, wages haven't kept up with inflation while the costs of housing, health care, and education have soared—the problem is pregnant teenagers. In articulating a vision of reproductive justice that necessarily included supporting pregnant and parenting youth and abolishing teen pregnancy prevention as we knew it, we reframed the problem from our lives, bodies, and children to the problem of the way society treated us. "If all parents were equally supported and respected," the NDETP mission statement read, "many of the problems that are typically associated with teen pregnancy would dissipate. We do not claim that teen parenting is an easy path to choose. Rather, we recognize the intense difficulty that comes with teen pregnancy and we are working to ease some of that burden for teen parents everywhere, so that they are freer to be the best possible parents."[49] The zine was boldly pro-abortion *and* pro-parenting, as one author explained: "The writings here are based on the rock-solid belief that women have the right to control their reproduction, whether by becoming mothers in their teens, or by having abortions when they become pregnant." Girl-Mom.com, the *EMPOWER* zine, and the National Day to Empower Teen Parents held the vision of a world where teen parents and their children are valued and cared for. This vision is an essential part of the reproductive vision in which all people have the bodily autonomy to have children or not have children, and to parent the children we have in safe and sustainable communities.

Girl-Mom.com was not the first or the last group of young people to bring issues surrounding teen pregnancy and parenting into the reproductive justice movement. I highlight it here not only because of my personal connection but also because the print-to-digital transition during which it emerged means that much of the organizing has been lost to history. The early days of digital organizing were much different than today because a lot of our work left few traces online and the internet was not our main mode of communication and community. Some of Girl-Mom's legacy can be found in internet archives like the WayBack Machine, but much of it lives on in yellowed zines and blurry 35 mm film photos stored in shoeboxes, as in my home.

The work of Girl-Mom.com undoubtedly paved the way for the social media–based teen parent activism and organizing of the 2010s, such as #NoTeenShame. In April 2013, nearly ten years after the National Day to Empower Teen Parents, young parents began using the hashtag on Tumblr, Twitter, and Instagram in response to pathologizing teen pregnancy prevention discourses. Much in the way that forum participants used Girl-Mom.com in the early 2000s, the cross-platform use of #NoTeenShame enabled young parents to counter the prevailing images of youth pregnancy and parenting found in the dominant media. It quickly became more than a hashtag, as a group of seven young mothers came together to harness the power of #NoTeenShame into a "movement illuminating the need for shame-free LGBTQ-inclusive comprehensive sexuality education and equitable access to resources and support for young families."[50] The founders, Natasha Vianna, Gloria Malone, Marylouise Kuti, Lisette Engel, Consuela Greene, Christina Martinez, and Jasmin Colon lived in different cities across the United States but used their social media savvy to build a new movement online. As they later explained:

> As young mothers, especially young mothers of color, we have historically been silenced, ignored, and erased from important decisions that impact our family's futures. This is also true for our labor within movements. Between policymaking and public health interventions, it was necessary for there to be a voice at the table to help decision-makers understand our reality and needs as industrious members of society. We knew a social, public, and visible movement wouldn't just give us seats at the table, but it would open up seats for young parents across the nation.[51]

As the founders point out, not only have young parents have been vilified in the media, research, and policy making, but social movement organizations have also excluded their voices and concerns. #NoTeenShame went on to make critical interventions in all of these arenas.

#NoTeenShame engaged with many of the same issues that young parent activists had dealt with in the early 2000s, including the shaming of teen moms as a teen pregnancy prevention strategy and an overall lack of support and resources. The political context surrounding teen childbearing had changed little: teen pregnancy was still highly stigmatized and blamed as the cause of all sorts of social problems. Notably, a 2013 prevention campaign created by the New York Human Resources Administration echoed the notorious 2001 National Campaign to Prevent Teen Pregnancy's "Sex Has Consequences" images. Plastered across New York City buses and subways, images of crying babies (most of whom were Black or brown) were paired with tag lines such as the deeply sexist "Honestly Mom ... chances are he won't stay with you. What happens to me?" and the dubious "If you finish high school, get a job, and get married before having children, you have a 98% chance of not being in poverty."[52] The political and technological climate did change, however, between the 2000s and the 2010s in ways that supported the emergence and success of the movement. The moment in which #NoTeenShame metamorphosed from a hashtag to a broader movement included a growing conversation about the failures of abstinence-only-until-marriage sex education in the United States. Moreover, the emergence of social media enabled marginalized people to respond to media images in new ways.

The hashtag NoTeenShame had initially arisen in response to a deeply shaming teen pregnancy prevention campaign launched by Candie's Foundation in 2013. Formed as a nonprofit arm of the Candie's fashion brand, the foundation's goal was to bring attention to the "devasting consequences of teenage pregnancy and parenthood."[53] Its initial campaign featured an image of pop star Carly Rae Jepsen along with the text, "You're supposed to be changing the world ... not changing diapers. Nearly 750,000 teenage girls will become pregnant each year. Change it! #NoTeenPreg." #NoTeenShame was a direct indictment of and counter to this campaign that illustrated not only its stigmatizing rhetoric but also its absurdity. Young people changing the world *and* changing diapers are obviously not mutually exclusive! Indeed, #NoTeenShame's group of seven core organizers was already involved in social movement work around youth pregnancy and parenting both in and out of organizations.[54] In response to the Candie's ad, #NoTeenShame organized a Change.org petition calling on the foundation to take down the ads and for its CEO to meet with the organizers (he refused). After the Candie's actions, #NoTeenShame organized a cross-platform social media campaign in which hashtag users shared images and stories to counter the notion that having children precludes changing the world. The petition and campaign were supported by national reproductive justice organizations such as the National Latina Institute for Reproductive Health (now the National Latina Institute for Reproductive Justice) and garnered a wide range of press coverage, including news outlets such as the *New York Times* and National Public Radio.

Contrary to the notion that digital activism using hashtags is mere "slacktivism," media scholars Sarah J. Jackson, Moya Bailey, and Brooke Foucault Welles argue that marginalized groups use hashtag activism as a counterpublic strategy to build "diverse networks of dissent and shape the cultural and political knowledge fundamental to contemporary identity-based social movements."[55] This was certainly the case with #NoTeenShame, as young parents used the tag to highlight their experiences with teachers who told them they'd never graduate, health care providers who shamed their reproductive decisions, and strangers at the park who criticized their parenting. In this work, users spoke back to what Black feminist sociologist Patricia Hill Collins calls the "controlling images" of young parents as stupid, lazy, and irresponsible.[56] As rhetoric scholar Jenna Vinson explains, resisting controlling images can secure "visibility, allies, and potentially an audience for young women's own messages if young mothering women are able to seize opportunities to interrupt the discourses that pathologize them."[57] Organizers also facilitated Twitter chats on youth parenting and reproductive justice, created guides for media and nonprofit organizations for talking about pregnant and parenting youth, and organized pregnant and parenting youth to post pictures and stories about the impact of shame on their lives. Over the following several years, #NoTeenShame generated a significant public presence through social media activity, press coverage, and speaking engagements, such as the annual CLPP (Civil Liberties and Public Policy, now Collective Power for Reproductive Justice) conference.

In addition to their work elevating counternarratives on youth pregnancy and parenting, #NoTeenShame also helped shift the discourse on teen pregnancy prevention. In 2019, SIECUS: Sex Ed for Social Justice, along with its partners Advocates for Youth, Healthy Teen Network, Planned Parenthood, and Power to Decide, rebranded the month of May from "Teen Pregnancy Prevention Month" to "Sex Ed for All Month." They directly referenced #NoTeenShame's work to "change policies, messages, and attitudes around the autonomy of young people" as having laid the groundwork for the initiative.[58] A joint statement made by #NoTeenShame cofounder Natasha Vianna and

SIECUS's president and CEO, Christine Soyong Harley, identified the racist and classist roots of teen pregnancy prevention and the harms caused by the pathologizing and stigmatizing rhetoric typically used in prevention campaigns. They called on policy makers and service providers "to support young people whether they choose to postpone pregnancy or become parents, and to provide them with the sexual health information and resources they need to live healthy and fulfilling lives." As they explained, "It was imperative to NoTeenShame that the field of sex education eradicate language that shames young people who experience pregnancy and/or parenthood."[59] More than 180 organizations working in reproductive and sexual health, rights, and justice signed on to the call for action.

This was undoubtedly an important victory, though not without limitations. Vianna publicly critiqued some national organizations for taking advantage of their unpaid labor and using their content without attribution. In an interview with Repro Jobs, a project dedicated to improving worker conditions in the reproductive justice movement, Vianna shared that she'd "never forget the pain of being a youth-led, unpaid movement and learning that well-funded organizations were replicating our content to fundraise, never including us in the process or even hiring any young moms to be leaders in their own space. To them, we were invisible, and it was just Twitter and Tumblr content."[60] Scholars Daniel and Vinson argue the activism around #NoTeenShame was one of the forces that prompted the National Campaign to Prevent Teen and Unplanned Pregnancy to rebrand as Power to Decide—but this was a change in name only, as the campaign kept the same frames of neoliberal logic and teen pregnancy as pathology. In addition, as many scholars and activists have argued, even comprehensive sexuality education leaves much to

YOUTH ACTIVIST PROFILE: VIVIANA (CALIFORNIA)

As a young mom, Viviana (age twenty-five) received support services from a community-based organization focused on empowering young parents with the skills and resources they need to thrive. Through this experience, Viviana discovered her love of public speaking and went on to become an ambassador for the program. "If one of my daughters or my son decide to become a young parent," she says, "I don't ever want them to feel that they're wrong for choosing that path or that they're set up for failure. I want to create a world where we normalize that and in normalizing that we also create the resources that they need to thrive."

Advocating for policies and programs that enable young moms to thrive—and not merely survive—is at the heart of Viviana's work. Along with her collaborators in a youth participatory action research (YPAR) project, she created a list of policy recommendations that the local county could implement to ensure that young moms thrive. The recommendations, including universal basic income, access to affordable childcare, and mandatory stigma-free training for service providers working with young parents between the ages of twelve and twenty-six, were based on research findings that existing systems were both stigmatizing young moms *and* failing to meet their needs.

A challenge Viviana has experienced in her work is how to sort out which level of policy making to target. Recognizing the need to work at multiple levels simultaneously, in addition to her local advocacy, she works at the national level to advance a vision of reproductive justice for young moms. As part of *IMPACT: Invincible Mamas Pushing Action and Change Together*, Viviana traveled to Washington, DC, and spoke to policy makers on Capitol Hill about policies designed to support pregnant and parenting youth. She has observed that marginalized folks are often brought into policy-making spaces like these to talk about the barriers they face, but aren't included in the decision making about the solutions. During the event in DC, the audience clapped and snapped their fingers in response to her assertation that young moms need living wage jobs. "But," Viviana says, "who's gonna implement it? We can list all the barriers and I can go on for days, but at the end of the day, if we're not willing to implement the change that we actually need to get rid of those barriers, then there's no reason for me to keep listing them." She shared her dream that schools could change so as to welcome and support young parents by offering, among other services, access to condoms and birth control and abortion information without judgment, counseling services that support young people in the whole spectrum of pregnancy decisions, and onsite childcare and housing.

be desired. For instance, the organizers of Sex Ed for All Month endorse and promote the Future of Sex Education Standards (FoSE) discussed in Chapter 2, which, despite their laudable approach, are still limited and have not been widely adopted.[61] The fight against shame and stigma continues.

CONCLUSION

In the summer of 2017, the Trump administration quietly defunded grantees who had been awarded millions of dollars for programming under the federal Office of Adolescent Health's

Teen Pregnancy Prevention Program (TPPP). Congress had created the program in a 2010 appropriations bill and mandated that initiatives be medically accurate and age appropriate and discuss abstinence *and* contraception. The Trump administration had decided to end grantees' funding in 2018, rather than 2020, as originally scheduled.[62] This move met with much ire from the media and activists, with even the usually radical *Teen Vogue* pointing out that although teen pregnancy rates were at a historical low, the defunding of prevention programs meant that the "trend could be in danger of reversing," implying that teen pregnancy is in itself a problem.[63] After a series of lawsuits brought by the organizations that were poised to lose their funding, in the spring of 2018 the US Department of Health and Human Services announced it would continue funding recipients for the following year. Nevertheless, the federal government also began directing money toward abstinence-only sex education, now rebranded as "sexual risk avoidance."

This series of events was a minor blip in what was otherwise an era of decreasing attention to youth pregnancy and parenting. It's difficult to say exactly why attention to teen pregnancy among policy makers, researchers, and the general public has declined. As research demonstrates, declines in teen pregnancy rates aren't necessarily enough to reduce the emphasis on it as a major social problem, though it is still true that the teen pregnancy rate continues to drop in the United States.[64] As Vinson and Daniels argue, the influence of activism such as #NoTeen-Shame also likely contributed to reducing the pathological focus on teen pregnancy and parenting.[65] Too, the political chaos of the Trump years—including the president's emboldening of white supremacists, forced child separation along the Mexico-US border, and efforts to prevent people from Muslim-majority countries from entering the country—left activists and policy makers at all points along the political spectrum struggling to keep up. At the tail end of this chaos, the COVID-19 pandemic further distracted us all from teen pregnancy as a major policy focus even as some people speculated that disruptions to school-based sex education would lead to increased rates of teen pregnancy. In the United States, this prediction did not come to pass, as rates continued their historical downward trajectory.[66]

Pregnant and parenting youth have long been scapegoats for broader endemic social problems such as poverty, but it is more difficult to blame teen parents for acute issues like border security or the COVID pandemic. As the number of pregnant and parenting youth in the United States continues to decline, increasing numbers of youth who identify as queer or transgender or both have become a popular new scapegoat for the Right, which is the subject of the following chapter. Yet, given historical patterns of social anxiety over young people's sexuality and reproduction, it would be far too premature to declare the end of labeling teen pregnancy a social problem.

CHAPTER FOUR

Transgender Youth, Family Making, and the Livability of Trans Lives

Just a few miles from my home, a small group of protesters (and about twenty times as many counterprotesters) assembled outside the Boston Children's Hospital on a sunny day in the early fall of 2022. About ten protesters held signs with anti-trans slogans such as "No child is born in the wrong body" and "Children cannot consent to puberty blockers." About two hundred counterprotesters carried signs stating "We love our trans kids" and "Trans people belong." The protesters were there to demonstrate their objection to the life-saving care of the hospital's Gender Multispecialty Service (GeMS). Established in 2007, GeMS was one of the first major programs in the United States to provide coordinated gender-affirming care to trans youth. This care can include medications like puberty blockers that temporally halt the physical effects of puberty (such as body hair, body fat distribution, and voice changes), as well as gender-affirming hormones and referrals for gender-affirming surgery for older youth. The efficacy and safety of this medical care are confirmed by countless studies and are supported by all major medical associations, including the American Academy of Pediatrics and the American Medical Association.

None of this mattered to the protesters, whose action was part of a wave of increasing harassment and violence against providers of health care for transgender youth that began to escalate in in the mid-2010s. Just a month before the protest, a woman had been charged for calling in a bomb threat to Boston Children's, one of dozens of threats the GeMS clinic had received by that time. This was in addition to targeted harassment of the hospital's clinical providers both on- and offline. Shortly after the summer bomb threat the clinic had removed all of the provider information from its website. Although an important step to protect staff safety, this move also makes it harder for patients and their families to access information about their services.

As transgender people and trans issues rapidly gained social visibility in the early 2010s, trans youth became both a cultural obsession *and* the focus of conservative political efforts to restrict their access to safe, affirming health care and education—or really just to exist at all. Initially anti-trans policy focused on so-called "bathroom bills," which restrict trans people's access to a public bathroom that best fits their identity, in addition to bills that prevent trans youth from participating in sports. The protesters at the 2022 action in Boston were part of an increasingly vocal (and violent) group of people who view gender-affirming care for trans youth as "child abuse" or "experimental medicine." Rather than a fringe position, the notion that gender-affirming care is a harmful, coercive practice that must be stopped gained considerable support in the early 2020s as politicians increasingly worked to limit or criminalize health care for trans youth and adults. At the time of the Boston

Children's protest, over twenty-two US states had proposed legislation to restrict transgender youth's access to health care that year alone. Three states already had laws on the books restricting trans youth's access to health care. Other states employed procedural moves to limit access, as when Texas governor Greg Abbott ordered the Texas Department of Family and Protective Services in March 2022 to investigate parents whose children received gender-affirming care for child abuse, and when the Florida Board of Medicine approved a rule in early 2023 that barred all minors in the state from receiving this care. This period also a saw dramatic rise in the number of bills that censor discussions of sexuality and gender in schools, such as the Florida law known as "Don't Say Gay," along with increased protests against and attacks on youth-centered LGBTQ events, such as drag queen story hours. By the time this book was going to press, twenty-four states banned best-practice medical and surgical care for trans youth, though some bans were not in effect because of legal challenges.[1]

Efforts to criminalize trans youth health care must be understood as reproductive justice issues tied to systems of social control that limit self-determination and bodily autonomy. We must understand these efforts in the context of broader attempts to regulate nonnormative sexual and reproductive bodies, such as the forced treatment of intersex babies or the hyperpromotion of long-acting contraceptives among Black and brown youth. The RJ movement has increasingly recognized the connections between reproductive justice and trans justice and the need to build a movement inclusive of trans people, but there has certainly been some stumbling along the way. This chapter first provides an overview of trans inclusion in the reproductive justice movement and makes a case for understanding the interconnectedness of both struggles. It then analyzes gender-affirming care for trans youth through the reproductive justice vision and highlights how attempts to criminalize it are connected to the criminalization of marginalized bodies more generally. Trans youth organizing as reproductive justice organizing works for the livability of trans lives, or what advocates refer to as "giving them their roses while they're still here." After describing how the legendary trans activists Sylvia Rivera and Marsha P. Johnson fought for the livability of unhoused trans youth, the chapter profiles contemporary activism by and for trans youth and their co-conspirators.

TRANS JUSTICE IS REPRODUCTIVE JUSTICE AND REPRODUCTIVE JUSTICE IS TRANS JUSTICE

The transgender political movements that coalesced in the United States during the 1990s recognized that reproductive justice was central to trans justice—even if that wasn't the exact language they used. Activists called attention to the fact that transgender parents were more likely than cisgender parents to lose custody of their children during a bitter breakup, that lack of access to affirming health care limited the ability to get pregnant or to carry a pregnancy to term, and that laws governing legal sex or gender change could require surgical sterilization.

Beyond the ability to choose or not choose pregnancy, abortion, birth, or parenting, trans people cannot exercise reproductive autonomy if they are *not alive*. Trans people have long been the target of state violence and neglect by the health care system, the carceral system, and the law. The oft-repeated statistics on the number of trans women of color murdered each year, the high rates of health inequalities in trans populations, and the disproportionate criminalization of trans people are all reproductive justice issues: a trans person cannot decide if, when, and how to make a family when their lives are subject to extreme precarity. Trans people cannot access health care, choose whether or not to parent, or raise a family with dignity and support if they can't also be free from violence, economic marginalization, and oppressive gender norms. The case of Nex Benedict, an Indigenous, nonbinary sixteen-year-old from Oklahoma, illustrates this point. In 2024 Nex died shortly after a group of peers assaulted them in a school bathroom. Oklahoma had passed a bill in 2022 that forbids students from using the bathroom that best fits their gender identity, and Nex began getting bullied at school shortly thereafter. Despite the assault, the state medical examiner's office ruled that they died by suicide—a finding that most trans people and their allies rejected.[2] Whether Nex died by suicide or homicide, it was clear that structural and interpersonal transphobia cut their life short.

In earlier chapters I note that the annual CLPP conference was one of the first places I learned about transgender issues in tandem with reproductive rights issues. As Ryn Gluckman and Mina Trudeau wrote in a 2002 CLPP newsletter, "Trans issues bring to the table the possibility that all genders are affected by reproductive rights issues and that feminism in its truest form must include the liberation of all genders from oppressive social roles and regulations." These activists understood that trans issues were integral to the RJ movement, and they also recognized that this inclusion was on a learning edge for many cisgender women in the movement. "Ultimately," they wrote, through intergenerational conversations "we need a new reproductive rights movement that, rather than dividing on the basis of a rigid idea of gender, is willing to expand ever outward to explore those ideas."[3]

More than twenty years later, much has changed and there is still much work to be done. Activists and organizations increasingly use gender-inclusive language such as "pregnant people" to talk about abortion and birth—indeed, all of the youth-led projects described in this book use this inclusive language. Leading reproductive justice organizations like Pregnancy Justice (formerly National Advocates for Pregnant Women) have changed their names to reflect the reality that not all people who have the capacity to carry a pregnancy are women. We can turn to the work of groups like URGE: Unite for Reproductive and Gender Equity for examples of youth organizing that seamlessly interweaves trans justice and reproductive justice.[4] We can turn on the news and watch prominent RJ scholars like law professor and anthropologist Khiara Bridges calling out Republican US senators for their erasure of trans people's need for abortion access.[5] Yet, at the same time, some activists and scholars have doubled down on decentering trans people in RJ. They argue that the use of inclusive language is hurting the movement by distracting from the interlocking systems of racism and misogyny that drive the criminalization of abortion or, absurdly, by distracting from addressing transphobia in health care.[6] And even as trans men and nonbinary people assigned female at birth have become nominally included in the reproductive justice framework, many scholars and activists fail to see how trans women's bodies and reproduction are affected by the same sexist, racist, and classist systems that harm cisgender women—or even to see trans women *as women*.[7]

"THERE IS NO SUCH THING AS A TRANSGENDER CHILD"

The 2010s witnessed an explosion of attention to transgender people and transgender issues, and trans children occupied a particularly notable corner of this fascination. In 2014 *Time* Magazine declared the "trans tipping point" of increased media representation and a new civil rights movement that was "poised to challenge long-held cultural norms and beliefs."[8] The following year saw the debut on TLC of the reality documentary show *I Am Jazz*, chronicling the life of a teen trans girl named Jazz Jennings. In 2017 *National Geographic* Magazine dedicated an entire issue to gender and trans youth. The cover featured a portrait of Avery Jackson, a white nine-year-old girl from Kansas City, and the article quoted her: "The best thing about being a girl is, now I don't have to pretend to be a boy." The cover and the issue as a whole were both celebrated and condemned in the press and on social media, prompting the magazine's editor to publish a number of articles to answer the question, "Why we put a transgender girl on the cover of *National Geographic*."[9] In sum, she wrote that a "gender revolution" is afoot and that "beliefs about gender are shifting rapidly and radically."[10] Conversely, opponents of the issue insisted that *National Geographic* was supporting child abuse and trying to brainwash young people.[11]

Scholars have critiqued claims of a trans tipping point, the portrayal of transgender people as a "new" phenomenon, and the notion that greater social visibility is an entirely good thing for trans youth and adults.[12] As Tourmaline, Eric Stanley, and Johanna Burton have argued, increased visibility for some trans people exists alongside increased violence, poor health, and social marginalization for others: not everyone reaps the potential "benefits" of visibility, and in fact many suffer because of it.[13] Critics call this the "trap" of representation, the idea that visibility is the primary way that trans people can hope to access livable lives.[14] Indeed, media representation of trans people tends to follow the same logics as the broader media, which center whiteness, gender normativity, sexual respectability, wealth accumulation, and celebrity culture.[15] In other words, the main beneficiaries of the "gender revolution" and the "trans tipping point" are the trans people with the most racial, gender, and economic privilege.

According to historian Jules Gill-Peterson, transgender children are powerful and flexible symbols of the future. "Sanitized, innocent, and always highly medicalized," she writes, "they are domesticated figures, either reassuring that the so-called trans tipping point heralds a new generation of liberal progress and acceptance or, to the transphobic agitators involved in political campaigns focusing on bathrooms and schools, acting as proof that trans life deserves to be repressed . . . for the threat to the social order that its future would represent."[16] Representing trans youth as a "new" phenomenon drives the activism of both camps. But as Gill-Peterson argues, the notion that trans youth are new or lack a history neglects evidence of the existence of trans children much earlier than contemporary narratives like *I Am Jazz* or *National Geographic* acknowledge. Moreover, it hides how medical discourse produces the category of trans youth, a category that has long been tied to whiteness. For example, during the advent of medical gender affirmation for trans youth in the mid-twentieth century, doctors and researchers tended to reject the idea that Black and trans youth of color's gendered embodiment was malleable. The notion that gender transition was possible was reserved for white kids, who were the vast majority of young people, then as now, able to access medical gender affirmation. Black trans youth were more likely to be criminalized or institutionalized for their gender transgressions, whereas white youth were more likely to be medicalized and receive treatment (which itself was often administered through rigid and pathological clinical guidelines). Likewise, the same treatments that white trans youth began to access were adapted from the coercive practice of using hormones and surgeries to "correct" the bodies of intersex babies, a practice that continues today.

Consider all of these developments in light of the chant of the organizer at the Boston Children's Hospital protest that "there is no such thing as a transgender child." What inspires a white, presumably heterosexual, cisgender man to stand outside a children's hospital shouting this statement and wearing a sign that proclaims the dictionary definition for "dad" is a "human male who protects his kids from gender ideology"?[17] One of the things that women of color feminisms and queer of color critique teach us is that a focus on shared marginal relationships to power can strengthen solidarity between movements. It is neither a coincidence nor an accident that attempts to criminalize trans health, restrict abortion access, and prohibit schools from teaching about racism intensified at the same time: all are policies that uphold white supremacy, heterosexuality, and normative gender. Efforts to outlaw abortion, criminalize trans youth's access to health care, and suppress education about white supremacy or queerness are attempts to deny marginalized groups bodily autonomy and self-determination. Using coalitional politics to analyze efforts to ban abortion, gender-affirming health care, and teaching about racism helps us make connections between what may appear to be distinct issues. It can also help us fight against them more effectively through collective action and coordinated policy responses.

Proponents of trans youth health care bans claim that their goal is to protect children. However, "protecting children" is always already about protecting white childhood innocence. The same years that witnessed a growth in state-level abortion bans (and eventually the *Dobbs* decision) coincided with attacks on trans youth *and* efforts to restrict teaching about racism and the history of white supremacy in the United States. These include bills and policies forbidding the use of critical race theory; banning the Pulitzer Prize–winning 1619 Project, about the centrality of slavery to American politics; outlawing discussions of the idea that racism is a system of oppression and not merely individual bias; and banning discussions about the existence of white privilege, which opponents believe is "divisive" and harmful. At the time of the Boston Children's Hospital protest, seventeen such bills were on the books in the United States. Likewise, efforts to prevent discussion of sexuality and queerness in schools also escalated during this time: six US states had laws that prohibit discussion of queer and trans topics in schools, such as the "Don't Say Gay" bill, and four states required schools to notify parents of LGBTQ-inclusive curricula and allow them to opt their children out.[18]

When proponents couch policies that ban abortion or trans youth medical care in terms of "protecting" fetuses and vulnerable children, they are referencing those deemed "worthy" of protection under white supremacy. Protection for some lives is pursued through policies that criminalize and punish youth of color, queer, and transgender youth. For instance, during school segregation struggles in the 1950s and '60s, white parents insisted

ORGANIZING 101: MOVEMENT TACTICS

Tactics refers to the tools activists use to achieve campaign demands. Examples of tactics used in social movements include, among many others, direct action (sit ins, boycotts), street theater, postering and visual arts, lobbying for a bill, banner drops, alliance building, and communication (op-eds, blogs, letter writing).

In order to be effective, tactics should be (1) directed to a specific target, (2) understandable to the target, (3) within the experiences of your group, and (4) connected to the overall strategy. For example, say you are working on a campaign to get your state to adopt trans youth sanctuary legislation that protects families traveling from out of state to receive health care that is criminalized elsewhere. (In 2022 California became the first state to enact such a law.) Your tactics must directly address the target (the state legislators) by persuading them to introduce and vote for the legislation. It would not be effective to poster your neighborhood with art illustrating the importance of sanctuary states if none of the decision makers will see it. You might choose to make your case in language that makes sense to the legislators; for example, elected officials might be more likely to be swayed by the financial benefits of becoming a sanctuary state than by the language of health equity.

Various tactics can be used to meet your demands, and tactics may escalate in intensity as a campaign unfolds. For instance, you might start persuading your local school board to adopt a gender-inclusive sports policy by sending letters to the board members. If your demands go unmet, you might shift to staging a sit-in or escalate to a more confrontational action. Likewise, your tactics must fit within your existing skill set or one you wish to build. As the "Stop Arkansas HB 1570" campaign demonstrates, to achieve your demands, you may need the support of people with specialized expertise, such as lawyers. (See the boxed feature "Campaign Spotlight: Stop Arkansas HB 1570" later in this chapter.) Finally, tactics should demonstrate collective power by connecting with similar campaigns and movements in support and solidarity. In the case of trans youth, as this chapter explains, this solidarity building can involve supporting racial or reproductive justice organizing, even if it doesn't seem to connect directly to transgender youth.

that school segregation was necessary to protect their children from being exposed to disease and violence. In this view, Black children were the *cause* of disease and violence in schools and therefore unworthy of protection. More recently, proponents of anti-trans bills that forbid youth from using the bathroom or playing sports are promoted as creating safety for cisgender children. However, research demonstrates that queer and trans youth are the ones much more likely to experience violence in schools.[19] As journalist Sherronda J. Brown points out, these proponents help consolidate political power among white Christian nationalists, who are mobilized by a perceived leftist agenda to make children queer, transgender, and ashamed of their whiteness.[20] Unsurprisingly, anti-transgender and anti-abortion movements also have roots and alliances with white nationalist agendas such as the "great replacement" theory, the idea that the influx of nonwhite immigrants to the United States and other Western countries is "replacing" white people and overpowering their concerns and votes. In this context, trans youth health care poses a threat to white fertility and birth rates, powerfully symbolized by the virulent anti-trans author Abigail Shrier's book *Irreversible Damage: The Transgender Craze Seducing Our Daughters*, whose cover features a young white girl with a gaping hole across her pelvis. Shrier represents trans youth health care as a grave threat to the fertility of (implicitly white) girls; it should come as no surprise, then, that the book's publisher also puts out books by white ethnonationalists such as Richard Spencer and Ann Coulter, or that the book was favorably reviewed by media outlets that regularly espouse white supremacist views.[21] Conservative politicians have capitalized on this racialized transphobia as a political tactic to energize their bases and win elections—with some even going so far as to conduct focus groups to determine which states were more uncomfortable with trans people's existence and therefore more promising for pushing anti-trans legislation.[22]

GENDER-AFFIRMING HEALTH FOR TRANS YOUTH AS A REPRODUCTIVE JUSTICE ISSUE

It's crucial to note that not all transgender people—youth or adults—desire medical gender affirmation, and that taking hormones or having surgery is not what makes someone "really" trans. Moreover, not everyone who desires medical gender affirmation is able to get it, and there are many barriers to access that disproportionately effect economically marginalized and youth of color trans persons. Criminalizing trans youth access to health care, like criminalizing abortion access, disproportionately harms young people and their families who are already subject to state violence through criminalization, incarceration, deportation, and death. It may appear superfluous or disingenuous to focus on medical care that is typically associated with white, class-privileged adolescents in the United States. Yet coalitional politics helps us to analyze how the criminalization of trans youth health care is deeply interwoven with white supremacy, class exploitation, gender normativity, and family regulation—all issues at the heart of reproductive justice.

Criminalizing trans youth health care is tied to a host of other forms of bodily and family criminalization. Black, Indigenous, other people of color, immigrant, and poor and working-class families are already subjected to reproductive and family regulation in a wide range of ways and are therefore less likely to avoid the state surveillance of trans youth health care bans.[23] Criminalizing trans youth means that multiply marginalized families will be disproportionately arrested or have children removed from their care by the state. Criminalizing health care involves increased policing and surveillance to enforce the law, whether through schools, health and human service providers, or increasingly, lateral surveillance in which ordinary citizens are deputized to report abortions or trans identity to authorities (which we've also seen used to enforce abortion bans, as Texas Senate Bill 8 did in 2021). As Interrupting Criminalization, a project led by abolitionist organizers Mariame Kaba and Andrea Ritchie, argues in its tool kit: "Criminalization of gender-affirming care is a direct consequence of funding the prison-industrial complex instead of communities. New criminalization laws are a result of, and lead to more funding for surveillance and policing which leads to more incarceration, and less money for life-affirming efforts."[24] Similarly, scholar-journalist Steven Thrasher, drawing on lessons learned from the criminalization of trans sex workers, poor Black queer people, and HIV-positive people, emphasizes that we must resist the criminalization of the parents of trans kids.[25] Mainstream LGBTQ rights organizations like the Human Rights Campaign (HRC) mobilize queer and trans respectability politics and rely on litigation and legislation to achieve assimilation into mainstream society. Instead, as Interrupting Criminalization and Thrasher argue, we must turn to abolitionist strategies that resist criminalization of difference more broadly, from the clinic to the street.

In addition, just as the RJ framework reframes narrow ideas about preventing pregnancy as liberation (e.g., cisgender women of color pushing back against white women's narrow focus on contraception and abortion), it also demonstrates that access to gender-affirming health care—or any health care, for that matter—can't be the ultimate goal on our path to liberation. The multiple forms of marginalization, exclusion, and violence that trans people face every day cannot be solved with medical care alone. As the poet Morgan Robyn Collado passionately argued in a speech at the 2014 CLPP conference:

> Violence against trans women of color is a reproductive issue. We are unable to build families because of state violence, because we do not have access to transition-related care, because our economic opportunities are limited, because most girls like me are killed before they reach twenty-five. Put simply, if trans women of color cannot reproduce because of the violence we face, then it is a reproductive issue. If we cannot build the network of people and community that constitutes a family because of the transmisogyny we face, then it is a reproductive issue. If we cannot find people who will cherish us and desire us for who we are, then it is reproductive issue. If we cannot survive—if we cannot thrive—then it is a reproductive issue.[26]

With all of this in mind, the chapter now turns to a discussion of how access to gender-affirming health care for trans youth contributes to what scholars and activists call the "livability" of trans lives.[27] Livability and reproductive justice are intimately connected. Achieving the vision of a world where all people can create the families they choose free of state control includes mobilizing the support and resources trans people and their families need to lead livable lives.

THE IMPORTANCE OF GENDER-AFFIRMING HEALTH CARE FOR TRANS YOUTH

The protesters standing outside clinics and the politicians drafting legislation lack an accurate understanding of what it means for a transgender youth to "transition" or to receive gender-affirming health care. First of all, gender-affirming health care is not limited to transgender people. Cisgender people get gender-affirming health care all the time—often the same procedures and medication as trans people—but generally without the massive barriers and scorn that trans people face. Cisgender women take hormonal contraception to prevent pregnancy and clear up acne or get breast implants and butt lifts. Cisgender men take erectile dysfunction medications like Viagra or get hair transplants to reduce a receding hairline. These are all ways of affirming one's gender. Protesters and legislators also misunderstand that when young trans children transition it is mostly about *social* transition, that is, being socially recognized in their gender by wearing certain clothing or hairstyles or asking friends and teachers to use a new name and pronoun. Before a young person begins puberty, there is no specific health care related to being trans except finding providers that support and affirm their gender.

Young people entering the hormonal processes associated with puberty may, with their parents' consent and cooperation, get prescribed gonadotropin-releasing hormone analogues—medications that temporarily pause unwanted effects of puberty. These puberty blockers have long been prescribed to cisgender children for conditions like precocious puberty, when the body begins developing too early (for instance, a seven-year-old girl who begins to menstruate and develop breasts). Puberty blockers are completely reversible—if a young person stops taking them, natural puberty will then occur—and are considered safe, evidence-based medications.[28] Generally, trans youth who desire and have access to medical gender affirmation do not begin taking hormones such as estrogen or testosterone until they are sixteen, at which point they would begin to develop the secondary sex characteristics typically associated with their affirmed gender.[29] (Note also that age sixteen is late for a young person to develop breasts, body hair, or a deeper voice and therefore this care strategy leaves trans youth's bodies in a state of limbo while their peers grow into young adults.) Youth cannot receive any kind of medical gender affirmation until after an extensive process that includes finding and regularly traveling to a provider, a formal diagnosis of "gender dysphoria,"[30] individual and family counseling, medical examinations, and (usually) arguing with health insurance companies to pay for the care or fundraising, or both, to pay for it.[31] Contrary to what opponents think, surgeons are not just performing hysterectomies (removal of the uterus) or vaginoplasties (penile inversion to a vulva-vagina) on children all day long. In fact, it is extraordinarily rare for young trans person to undergo *any* gender-affirming surgery before turning eighteen, and even trans adults face countless barriers and delays in obtaining this care.[32]

Fertility preservation is another facet of health care for trans youth that is deeply relevant to reproductive justice. Because biomedical research has long excluded trans populations, clear evidence is lacking as to the effect of gender-affirming hormones on fertility, and health care providers must practice "uncertain expertise" in counseling their patients.[33] Trans adults have adopted a variety of strategies to navigate the uncertainties surrounding gender-affirming hormones and fertility, such as home sperm analysis and harm reduction approaches to hormone dosing.[34] Because the effect is unknown and could potentially be adverse, trans youth may preserve the ability to someday have biological offspring through gamete (ova or sperm) cryobanking. The majority of trans youth do not access fertility preservation, because of inadequate counseling, high costs, unacceptable preservation methods (e.g., egg retrieval), or the likelihood that completing the preservation process will delay transition—or a combination of these factors.[35] Trans adults frequently name fertility preservation as a desirable option they wished they'd had access to when beginning medical transition.[36] And, of course, trans youth fighting to survive by obtaining basic needs such as housing, food, schooling, freedom from violence, and so on aren't thinking about fertility preservation—they are focused on staying alive.

In 2014, the suicide of Ohio teen Leelah Alcorn, following her parents' refusal to allow her to live as the girl she knew herself to be, brought widespread attention to the heightened risk of suicide among trans youth. In a suicide note she timed to post to her Tumblr account immediately following her death, Alcorn described how, on her sixteenth birthday, her parents denied her request to begin gender-affirming care and she cried herself to sleep. There is well-documented evidence that gender-affirming care greatly improves and even saves the lives of trans people who desire and are able to access it. Transgender youth cannot anticipate a future in which they can create the families they want with dignity and support if they cannot anticipate having a future *at all*. Research has found that trans youth tend to experience worse mental health than their peers. Trans youth report depression and anxiety at rates up to four times that of the general adolescent population.[37] Tragically, rates of suicidal ideation and suicide attempts are considerably higher for trans youth than for either cisgender heterosexual youth or cisgender LGBQ youth. A 2017 study found that 34 percent of transgender youth reported a previous suicide attempt, compared to just 7 percent of cisgender youth.[38] For youth who desire medical transition, access can be a matter of life and death. A landmark 2020 study found that 9 out of 10 trans adults who desired but did not receive pubertal suppression as a young person experienced suicidal ideation at some point during their life. The researchers found that even when taking into account factors like demographics and level of family support, compared to those who wanted pubertal suppression but did not receive it, trans adults who were able to access this care as youth had a lower likelihood of lifetime suicidal ideation.[39] Studies have also found that accessing desired care results in better mental health and body satisfaction for trans youth and adults.[40]

Unfortunately, the significant barriers to receiving this care mean that there are many more trans youth who desire medical affirmation than actually receive it. For instance, the 2020 landmark study mentioned above found that of the adult respondents who had desired puberty suppression as youth, only 2.5 percent were able to obtain it. Unsurprisingly, socioeconomic status and presence of a supportive family were associated with ability to access care, as young people from families with higher household income or with greater support shown for the young person's gender identity were more likely to obtain care. Gender-affirming care for trans adults became (somewhat) more accessible in the 2010s as clinical guidelines (somewhat) shifted away from a pathology-based, gatekeeping approach toward an informed-consent model.[41] However, trans youth have not equally benefited from the move toward informed consent, as gender-affirming care in the United States is not exempt from age of consent laws in the same way as other politicized health care for minors, such as sexual and reproductive health, mental health, and substance use treatment.[42] Youth who lack the consent (allowing them to access care) and cooperation (navigating the maze of providers, insurance companies, protesters, etc.) of one or both parents cannot access care, nor can youth in the foster system or juvenile justice system. Legal scholars have argued that youth should be able to access gender-affirming care under legal precedents such as the mature minor doctrine and through a judicial bypass similar to the procedure for minors seeking an abortion.[43] However, as chapter 1 details, the judicial bypass system is rife with problems. While it might allow some trans youth to access care without their parents' permission, it would still subject young people to an intimidating, infantilizing, and difficult-to-navigate process. Some states have increased youth access to gender-affirming care, as Maine did in 2023 when it became the first state to pass a bill ensuring access to care for sixteen- and seventeen-year-olds whose parents refuse to support treatment.[44] Other states have implemented "shield laws," which protect trans people, their families, and their medical providers from civil or criminal charges when the patient has traveled from a state with a ban in order to receive care in a state where such care is legal.

YOUTH ACTIVIST SPOTLIGHT: JADEN (TENNESSEE)

Jaden (age twenty-three) credits Black women organizers in the South for his entry into reproductive justice organizing: "It was southern Black women that really put in the work to truly educate me when I was coming up." Describing his early organizing work as "a lot of bouncing around," Jaden was the "resident queer person" in high school who did a lot of peer education. He was the trusted person that students would come to when they had questions like "How do two girls have sex?" or "I think I'm pregnant—what can I do"? In college he got involved with Healthy and Free Tennessee, a reproductive justice organization working to build the movement "across race, class, and gender by bringing new people into the movement, developing skills and capacities, and building connections across organizations and sectors."[a] His activist work focuses on his local community and ranges from supporting state senate candidates to getting sponsorships to giving out free chest binders for trans youth.

As a trans man, Jaden has often had the spotlight on him in RJ organizing spaces, both before and after medically transitioning. As he puts it, "We're already here: there's trans men that need abortions; there's nonbinary people that need abortions." Jaden also notes that "there's still transmisogyny in reproductive justice spaces, especially in talking about abortion," and that it took the surge in trans youth health care bans in the 2020s to really get a conversation going about the intersections between reproductive justice and trans justice. Jaden connects legislation banning abortion with that banning trans health care for minors as a strategy to affirm heteronormativity and cisnormativity while feeding white supremacy. "From my point of view as someone who's half white, half Puerto Rican," Jaden explains, "a lot of things tend to root back into white supremacy, from colonization to slavery to thinking there's only two genders."

Centering trans joy amid the weight of living in a transphobic world is also part of Jaden's work. "You know," he says, "in my little RV with my three cats and fiancé, I can be as queer, as trans as I want to be, and I can celebrate all parts of me, being Puerto Rican and being trans and all the things I've gone through to get to a point where I can be happy and love myself." Jaden recalls speaking at a rally against anti-trans legislation the day after the funeral for his college roommate, also a trans man, who died by suicide. At the rally, a young trans person from his hometown approached him and shared that Jaden was the first trans person he had ever met. Through all the "dark and deep depression and suppression," Jaden says, "I was still able to be a role model for this one little kid that made his way down to Nashville for a rally about trans rights." This chance encounter happened years before anti-trans legislation became widespread in the United States. As Jaden says, "Trans kids are still killing themselves, and we're still getting legislation against us."

a. Healthy and Free Tennessee 2023.

GIVING THEM THEIR ROSES

In 2019 a Denver-based tattoo artist name Rio Juniper Wolf designed the image for the popular "Protect Trans Kids" T-shirt. The words appear in a bold gothic font with a knife between "protect" and "trans" and a rose between "trans" and "kids." The message is blunt: protect trans kids by "giving them their roses while they're still here" . . . or else.[45] This common phrase in trans resistance movements calls attention to the need to nurture and celebrate trans *lives,* not just trans deaths (as is done annually during Transgender Day of Remembrance, often as a spectacle in which white trans people elide the structural violence that results in the violence directed at trans women of color).[46] The popular hashtag #ProtectTransKids has become a rallying cry to resist the rise in efforts to regulate, criminalize, and erase transgender youth. On its face, the hashtag can be read as paternalistic, as if trans youth are fragile beings in need of protection. In practice, the phrase is generally used as a way to signal solidarity with trans youth, who are under relentless attack; it also acknowledges the structural vulnerability that many trans youth experience by virtue of their age and their gender (a vulnerability that can be compounded by race, class, disability, and so on). The following subsection profiles resistance and organizing by and for trans youth and their adult co-conspirators focused on "giving them their roses" while they're still here; in other words, sustaining the livability of trans lives. Framing the livability of trans youth within the RJ framework highlights resistance and organizing for access to gender-affirming health care and a livable life.

Marsha and Sylvia's Kids

We can look to legendary trans of color ancestors such as Sylvia Rivera and Marsha P. Johnson for early examples of youth and reproductive justice organizing aimed at giving trans youth their roses. Marsha and Sylvia's activism has become more widely known in recent years, thanks to Tourmaline's archival work and

Micah Bazant's visual art, as well as greater academic attention to their lives.[47] Participants in the 1969 Stonewall uprisings that helped spark the contemporary gay-queer-trans liberation movement, Sylvia and Marsha were highly critical of the assimilationist tendencies in much of the gay liberation movement that centered white, gay, cisgender men. It's a critique that is, regrettably, still relevant today. Their names are often invoked when referencing the ways trans women of color have long been fiercely leading our movements, though, because *transgender* was not a term in use at the time, they generally referred to themselves as "street queens," "drag queens," "transvestites," or simply "gay people."[48] Sylvia and Marsha both left home at a young age, eleven and seventeen, respectively, for the streets of New York City, where they hustled and did sex work to meet their basic needs for food and shelter. Then as now, the streets were one of the only options available to queer and trans youth who were shunned by their families of origin and excluded from safe schools or meaningful employment.[49] Marsha and Sylvia formed Street Transvestite Action Revolutionaries (STAR), a radical activist organization for and by homeless trans and queer youth, in 1970. The group came together following the occupation of a building on the campus of New York University to protest the administration's cancelation of gay dances at the school. As queer of color theorist Rod Ferguson explains, like the Stonewall riots, the NYU action "bore the imprint of anti-racist politics . . . and provided the grammar and the politics for seizing and redirecting institutional and political itineraries."[50] Noting its concurrent focus on homelessness, sex work, and gay, queer, and trans youth, Ferguson characterizes STAR as "the result of an emerging multi-sided understanding of liberation that was shaped by anti-racist and anti-imperialist movements."[51]

As Sylvia explained, "STAR was for the street gay people, the street homeless people and anybody that needed help at that time."[52] She was nineteen and Marsha was twenty-five when the group formed, but they did the labor of mothering other street-based queer and trans youth. STAR House, a refuge for the youth they nurtured, first existed in an abandoned trailer truck in Greenwich Village. It provided some protection from the streets for Marsha, Sylvia, and up to twenty other young trans street youth until someone reclaimed the truck and drove it away with one youth still asleep inside.[53] So they found a vacant building in the East Village and "hustled their asses" off to come up with the down payment to rent the building from a local Mafia guy. It didn't have electricity, toilets that flushed, or heat, but they made it work with do-it-yourself repairs and fund-raising attempts. As Sylvia explained, "Marsha and I just decided it was time to help each other and help our other kids. We fed people and clothed people. We kept the building going. We went out and hustled the streets. We paid the rent. We didn't want the kids out in the streets hustling."[54] STAR House was a not only a place to seek shelter and food but also a site of political education about the multiple forms of structural violence that plagued trans and queer street kids: police harassment and brutality; the criminalization of survival sex work; deplorable conditions at the Riker's Island jail that youth cycled in out of; the mistreatment of trans and queer people at the Bellevue psychiatric hospital; the struggles of drug addiction; and the marginalization of street youth, people of color, and gender-nonconforming people in the broader gay rights movement. Although it never materialized, Sylvia wanted to create a school, on the building's top floor, where youth who had been pushed out of traditional school could learn to read and write. STAR House lasted only about nine months before the youth got evicted. The extreme precarity of the young street-based organizers also thwarted other planned projects, including dance fund-raisers, a new STAR home, a hotline, a recreation center, a bail fund for arrested queens, and a lawyer for queer people in jail.[55]

Jules Gill-Peterson asks why the media obsession with trans youth doesn't recognize street kids like Marsha and Sylvia as proof that trans youth have a past. One reason, she argues, is that "their radical politics would hardly be compatible with the modernizing, progressive narrative of [transgender] medicine and corporate political lobbying."[56] Looking to their histories can teach us a lot about shared marginal relationships to power and coalitional politics. STAR youth demanded "the right to self-determination over the use of [their] bodies; the right to be gay, anytime, anyplace; the right to free physiological change and modification of sex on demand; the right to free dress and adornment."[57] These are demands at the core of the reproductive justice vision. They were also central to Sylvia and Marsha's mothering efforts to, as SisterSong puts it, "parent the children we have in safe and sustainable communities."[58] STAR was about sustaining trans youth life, and not only the socially acceptable ones who would one day grace the cover of *National Geographic*. Though still a teenager herself, Sylvia in particular took on the mother role for other gender-nonconforming street youth so that they "not only could find emotional comfort but could maybe even learn enough skills to start another kind of life."[59] As philosopher Amy Marvin points out, this mothering is fundamentally about fostering the livability of trans youth lives and is a task neglected by mainstream gay rights organizations. Sylvia and Marsha "thus cared in a way that suggests a particular wisdom about the crucial link between dependency and solidarity."[60]

Contemporary Leadership Development and Solidarity

The legacy of STAR lives on in efforts to develop the leadership of trans youth in resistance movements. As this book's introduction explains, however, a lot of this work takes place through nonprofit organizations and government-funded projects that view youth through the lens of victimization. In the case of trans youth, these programs often confirm the "adultist, cisgender perspective that trans youthhood is a pathological phenotype to be repaired or assimilated."[61] For instance, it is unusual to find programming specifically for trans youth that isn't combined with LGBQ youth, and the programming that does exist often takes the form of social support groups focused on coping with minority stress. This subsection profiles efforts to reframe this deficit approach, nurture the next generation of trans youth leaders, and build adult-youth solidarity.

URGE: Unite for Reproductive and Gender Equity is a youth leadership development organization that "envisions a liberated world where we can live with justice, love freely, express our gender and sexuality, and define and create families of our choosing."[62] Its work encompasses a broad range of reproductive and gender justice issues with a geographical focus on the US South and Midwest. URGE believes that "progressive, abortion-positive young people have the power to transform systems and institutions to promote reproductive justice—centering the needs of LGBTQIA+ youth and young people of color."[63] Their program "Our Folks: Voices of LGBTQ+ Youth of Color—A Cohort of Young Creatives" responds to the long-standing neglect of the narratives and expertise of young queer and trans people of color. The goal of the program is to build participants' skills in giving media interviews, writing for blogs and other media outlets, creating engaging digital content, and using social media to amplify their work. Staff support each cohort member in producing written and video content for URGE's social media platforms and external speaking engagements. Youth receive a stipend for their work and at the end of the program will have produced a portfolio of work that demonstrates their analyses and communication skills on a host of reproductive justice issues.

Similarly, the Trans Youth Justice Project (TYJP), a nationwide remote leadership development and political education program for trans youth, is based on the belief that trans youth have the capacity to become leaders in the fight for their collective liberation.[64] The six- to eight-week program meets on Zoom and features content on theories of youth organizing, trans justice history, and campaign strategies and tactics. Through facilitated lessons and hands-on activities, youth foster critical consciousness and leadership skills like organizing a protest, identifying their role(s) in social movements, and navigating conflict without reproducing harm. Although it began as an in-person academic-community collaboration in Milwaukee, the COVID-19 pandemic forced it to go online, but the benefit of that move was that youth from all over the country are able to participate. Like participants in URGE's "Our Folks," those in the TYJP are financially compensated for their time. An evaluation of two cycles of the program found that the participation helped to reduce the effects of gender minority stress and build concrete activism skills. Notably, youth reported that a main benefit of participation was the ability to make connections with other trans youth and with the adult trans facilitators. In this sense, the program works against the isolation and marginalization that limits the livability and joy of trans youth lives. The

CAMPAIGN SPOTLIGHT: STOP ARKANSAS HB 1570

In February 2021, the Arkansas House of Representatives introduced HB 1570, the "Save Adolescents from Experiment (SAFE) Act," which would ban gender-affirming medical care for trans youth under eighteen years of age. The law also sought to prohibit the use of public funds for and prohibit insurance companies from covering care. Health care providers who violate the law could be sued for damages or professionally sanctioned. Both the Arkansas house and senate approved the bill the next month.

Trans youth, families, medical providers, and a number of celebrities spoke out against the harms of the bill through social media and protests at the Arkansas capitol in Little Rock. As a result, Governor Asa Hutchinson vetoed the bill on April 5, 2021, but the legislature overrode his veto the very next day. The American Civil Liberties Union (ACLU) immediately filed a lawsuit in federal district court on behalf of four families of trans youth and two physicians, asking the court to rule the law unconstitutional. In July 2021 the district court issued a preliminary injunction that blocked enforcement of HB 1570's provisions, and in August 2022 the US Eighth Circuit Court of Appeals upheld that injunction. Even though the bill was temporally blocked, medical providers had stopped offering gender-affirming care to youth out of fear that they would be prosecuted, and some families with the economic means to do so had moved out of state.

As Chase Strangio, a transgender lawyer who is deputy director for transgender justice at the ACLU's LGBTQ & HIV Project, explained, HB 1570 was "designed to consolidate power in the hands of the powerful. It is not about protecting children. It is not about protecting ciswomen or any women. It's about controlling people's bodies."[a]

The case went to trial in the fall of 2022, the first time that a ban on trans youth health care in the United States reached this stage of the legal process. On June 20, 2023, US District Judge James Moody issued a permanent injunction, meaning that the bill would not be allowed to go into effect. Judge Moody affirmed what youth, their parents, and their health care providers know to be true: "The State offered no evidence to refute the decades of clinical experience demonstrating the efficacy of gender-affirming medical care."[b]

a. American Civil Liberties Union 2021.
b. Ellis 2023.

program curriculum is open-source and can be freely used and adapted by any group committed to trans justice.[65]

In addition to supporting the next generation of trans youth activists, adults committed to trans youth liberation must invest in meaningful, cross-movement solidarity with trans youth under attack. As evidenced by the crowds of counterprotests at Boston Children's Hospital and the number of people at annual pride events wearing the "Protect Trans Kids" T-shirt, trans and cis adults alike push back against the transphobia that threatens trans youth. As mentioned earlier in this chapter, Interrupting Criminalization released a briefing and toolkit in 2022 connecting the criminalization of trans youth health care to the criminalization of abortion, the emboldening of white nationalism, and the carceral state. "We Must Fight in Solidarity with Trans Youth: Drawing the Connections between Our

Movements" is just one of their many crucial toolkits aimed at ending the criminalization and incarceration of women, girls, trans, and gender-nonconforming people of color. The collaboratively co-authored toolkit highlights the coalitional politics described throughout this chapter. It declares that "it is imperative for us to fight for conditions that enable trans people to live full, dignified and thriving lives.... Conceding ground to attacks on trans people expands opportunities for increased surveillance, policing, and criminalization across the board, and the acceleration of white supremacist agendas. This fight belongs to all of us."[66] To this end, Interrupting Criminalization offers concrete solidarity strategies, including supporting trans youth in making a safety plan in case of forced outing by "concerned adults" and financially supporting trans-led organizations such as the Sylvia Rivera Law Project, the Marsha P. Johnson Institute, and the TransLatin@ Coalition.

TOWARD THE LIVABILITY OF TRANS YOUTH LIVES

What does it look like to "protect trans kids" without falling into an adultist mindset that views trans youth as inherently vulnerable and confused? How can we connect resistance to attacks on trans youth to fights for abortion access or against white supremacy? This chapter provides some entry points and potential roadmaps, but there is certainly much work to be done. One important first step for cisgender people in the reproductive justice movement is to listen to transgender people when they call attention to their exclusion. Making the analytic connections between threats to bodily autonomy and self-determination under racial capitalism is a crucial next step. Likewise, an important step for adult allies or co-conspirators is to resist the media fascination with (often white, middle-class) transgender youth and instead follow the lead of young people and families who will be most harmed by the criminalization of trans youth lives. Let's help them get their roses while they're still here.

CHAPTER FIVE

Criminalized Youth and Abolition Feminisms

By all accounts, Cyntoia Brown's youth was marked by sexual and reproductive injustices. Cyntoia's biological mother was young when she gave birth, struggled with drugs and alcohol, engaged in sex work, and spent time in jail. Like many parents with limited resources, her mother had few options for securing the support she needed to parent, and so a family friend took in Cyntoia when she was less than a year old. Her adoptive mother was loving and supportive, but Cyntoia struggled nonetheless and frequently got into trouble at school. "If everybody thought I was bad already," she later wrote in her memoir, "what was stopping me from doing what everyone thought I was doing?"[1] As a girl and preteen, she became accustomed to having little autonomy over her body, including when she had sex and with whom. She was first expelled from school at age twelve after a school resource officer found caffeine pills in her possession. Soon afterward, she became wrapped up in the juvenile legal system and cycled in and out of alternative schools, psychiatric institutions, and correctional facilities. Research has documented that young people who end up in juvenile detention facilities in the United States are disproportionately likely to be youth of color, have experienced childhood trauma, and have physical or mental health issues—all of which were parts of Cyntoia's experience growing up.[2] After she left home at age fifteen, Cyntoia became involved with the sex trade—what activist Shira Hassan defines as "any way that girls are trading sex or sexuality, for anything like money, gifts, survival needs, documentation, places to stay, [or] drugs."[3] Survival sex work can be one of the only ways a young person can support themselves when they leave home, the foster care system, or detention facilities.

At age sixteen, Cyntoia came to live in a hotel room with a man who went by the name Kut-Throat. He was both her boyfriend and her pimp. He was also physically and sexually abusive to Cyntoia, who had little control over her own body and what happened to it. One night in August 2004, while trying to catch a ride across town to engage in street-based sex work on Kut-Throat's command, she met a forty-three-year-old white man who took her back to his house to engage in paid sex. The man showed her numerous guns, and later, in bed, he became violent with Cyntoia. Fearing for her life, Cyntoia reached into her purse, pulled out a gun, and shot him. Despite her insistence that she was acting in self-defense, prosecutors framed the encounter as a violent robbery and murder. They charged sixteen-year-old Cyntoia as an adult. In 2006, she was convicted of first-degree premediated murder, first-degree felony murder, and aggravated robbery. She was sentenced to life in prison. Then, in 2017, seemingly out of nowhere, her case caught the attention of celebrities including popstar Rihanna and basketball player LeBron James. This media attention exposed the hypocrisy of her incarceration even as it often relied on infantilizing victim tropes that denied

Cyntoia agency and self-determination as a young person caught up in a carceral system.[4] This renewed focus on the case was ultimately successful, and in January 2019, the governor of Tennessee commuted Brown's life sentence to fifteen years plus ten years of supervised parole. She was released from prison later that year.

When activists and scholars use the term *criminalized*, they are referring to the social and political processes through which individuals, groups of people, their bodies, or their behaviors become something to be managed through the tools of the carceral state: exclusion, punishment, and incarceration. Most of the sexual and reproductive criminalization that young people experience does not draw the attention of activists, celebrities, and the media in the way that Cyntoia's did when she fought back against her sexual exploitation. More common is the routine, everyday criminalization young people experience in their schools and communities. This criminalization can take many forms—from young people trying to access abortion across state lines, to resisting zero-tolerance school policies, to merely existing in public spaces. As scholar-activist-lawyer Andrea Ritchie explains it, "Criminalization is a process of sensemaking and placemaking that makes the existence—and violence—of policing and punishment seem both necessary and inevitable."[5] In other words, criminalization isn't just about what the law officially considers to be crimes; it's a social process whereby certain people come to be seen as unworthy of human dignity, resources, and protection from violence.

The reproductive justice movement has illuminated how the child welfare system and the criminal legal system[6] outlaw and regulate the reproduction of adults most impacted by interlocking systems of oppression: women of color, low-income people, disabled people, queer and trans people, sex workers, and others.[7] For example, prosecutors in the United States have used pregnancy loss and self-managed abortion as an excuse to charge women with feticide and child neglect. In 2010, the state of Indiana charged an immigrant named Bei Bei Shuai with murder and attempted feticide after her fetus died following Shuai's suicide attempt. In a similar case in 2013, Indiana charged and convicted Purvi Patel with feticide and child neglect after delivering a stillborn baby in her bathroom. Patel's feticide (but not child neglect) conviction was eventually overturned on appeal, and Shuai eventually pleaded guilty to lesser charges and time served. As Lynn Paltrow, the executive director of Pregnancy Justice (then National Advocates for Pregnant Women), a legal advocacy organization that defends people charged with any pregnancy-related crime, stated when the court overturned Patel's feticide conviction, "The court reached a decision that . . . is in accord with widely held public opinion that women who have or who attempt to have abortions should not be put behind bars."[8] In the aftermath of the *Dobbs* decision, legal experts predict that the criminalization of spontaneous abortion (aka miscarriage) and self-managed abortion will amplify significantly.[9]

Substance use during pregnancy or while parenting is another prominent site of reproductive criminalization and punishment. As legal scholars Jeanne Flavin and Lynn Paltrow argue, punitive measures against people who use drugs while pregnant and parenting are strategies to distract attention from significant social problems such as our lack of universal health care, the dearth of policies to support pregnant and parenting women, the absence of social supports for children, and the overall failure of the drug war.[10] The widespread belief that drug use during pregnancy is always harmful to the fetus or that parents who use drugs cannot be good parents is not supported by robust scientific evidence.[11] Nonetheless, beginning with the hysteria over supposed "crack babies," born to crack cocaine–using Black mothers in the 1980s, the criminal legal and child welfare systems have disregarded a public health approach in favor of a carceral one. More recently, as legal scholar and anthropologist Khiara Bridges argues, responses to the opioid crisis have increased the criminalization of white women who use opioids while pregnant or parenting to the extent that their white privilege provides less and less of a buffer against being prosecuted.[12] Despite the widespread medical and public health consensus that carceral responses to drug and alcohol use during pregnancy—including forced treatment, arrest, incarceration, and child removal—undermine people's ability to seek the care and support they need, these responses remain common in the United States.[13]

Although RJ activists and scholars have brought much-needed attention to the ways adults are criminalized for self-managed abortion, pregnancy loss, or substance use during pregnancy or while parenting, they have focused less attention on youth criminalization as a reproductive justice issue. This chapter extends the book's argument that all youth organizing is reproductive justice organizing by demonstrating the particular effects that reproductive criminalization has on youth—and how youth organize in resistance. The RJ lens is a tool for analyzing issues such as the school-to-prison pipeline and the experiences of youth in the foster care and juvenile punishment systems. Black, brown, Indigenous, economically marginalized, and LGBTQ youth are disproportionately criminalized in ways that deny them bodily autonomy and self-determination. Youth experience reproductive criminalization in many of the same ways that adults do—such as outlawing abortion or policing families through child welfare services—but also in unique ways based on adultism and their structural vulnerability as young people. For instance, youth of color like Cyntoia and LGBTQ youth are overrepresented in the foster care and juvenile punishment systems, sites that expose them to hypersurveillance and regulation of their bodies, sexuality, and reproduction. This chapter argues that we must frame these systems and their impact on youth through the RJ framework, vision, and social movement as well as the framework, vision, and social movement of abolition feminism.

According to Critical Resistance, a national grassroots organization working to end the prison industrial complex, *abolition* refers to a "political vision with the goal of eliminating imprisonment, policing, and surveillance and creating lasting alternatives to punishment and imprisonment."[14] As Angela Y. Davis, Gina Dent, Erica A. Meiners, and Beth E. Richie argue in their book *Abolition. Feminism. Now*, abolition and feminism are deeply interrelated. Abolition feminism is "an insistence that abolitionist theories and practice are most compelling when they are also feminist, and conversely, a feminism that is also abolitionist is the most inclusive and persuasive version of feminism for these times."[15] Bringing an abolitionist feminist lens to the criminalization of youth such as Cyntoia Brown helps us understand how all youth criminalization is ultimately a form of reproductive criminalization that surveils, regulates, condemns, and punishes bodily autonomy and self-determination. Like reproductive justice, abolition feminism is both an organizing tool and a long-term vision of the world we want to live in. Following an overview of the carceral sites through which youth reproductive criminalization takes place, this chapter highlights abolitionist organizing for and by youth. The policing of multiply marginalized youth that occurs through schools and the child welfare system is a project of enforcing the racialized borders of idealized white, heterosexual, middle-class family formation. In other words, whether pushing youth out of school based on their refusal to conform to sexual and reproductive normativity or punishing street-involved youth for crimes of survival, policing youth polices the boundaries of normative race, sexuality, and reproduction.

THE CARCERAL STATE AND YOUTH REPRODUCTIVE JUSTICE

The organization Critical Resistance and scholar-activists Angela Y. Davis, Ruth Wilson Gilmore, Dylan Rodríguez, and others have helped to familiarize the term *prison industrial complex* (PIC). The PIC is more than just the physical institutions of jails, prisons, and detention facilities. The concept helps us to understand how mass incarceration is also a "set of relations [that] makes visible the connections among capitalism, globalization, and corporations" and "the practices of surveillance, policing, screening, profiling, and other technologies to partition people and produce 'populations.'"[16] The PIC isn't just a *place*; it's also a set of carceral relationships that surveil, target, and contain people whose lives exist at the center of multiple systems of oppression. This chapter uses the term *carceral state* to refer to a broad set of institutions and agencies that includes but goes beyond the prison industrial complex. As education scholar Erica R. Meiners defines it, the term *carceral state* "highlight[s] the multiple and intersecting state agencies and institutions (including not-for-profit organizations) that have punishing functions and effectively police poor communities beyond the physical site of the prison: child and family services, welfare/workfare agencies, public education, immigration, health and human services agencies, and more." Similarly, disability scholar Liat Ben-Moshe argues that we must also understand how institutionalization in psychiatric hospitals or group homes for disabled people functions as part of the carceral state. Although institutionalization and hospitalization are not the same as imprisonment in jails and prisons, they share the carceral logics of containment, surveillance, and capital accumulation through the bodies of marginalized people.[17] Similarly, the carceral state weaponizes "care" through therapeutic governance that takes place in schools, child welfare agencies, and juvenile detention facilities.[18] The following subsections detail how each of these sites contributes to youth criminalization and reproductive injustice.

Schools as Sites of Youth Criminalization

In addition to being key sites of race, class, and gender regulation, schools have long been places where young people experience criminalization. Scholars and activists have called attention to the *school-to-prison pipeline* that tracks Black, brown, disabled, poor, and LGBTQ students out of school and into the carceral state though zero-tolerance behavioral policies, harsh disciplinary practices, and the presence of law enforcement officers in schools.[19] More recently, Savannah Shange, Damien Sojoyner, Erica R. Meiners, and other education scholars have pointed to limitations of the pipeline metaphor.[20] As Meiners argues, the pipeline metaphor "erases the historic and ongoing criminalization of many communities, suggests that the solution

ORGANIZING 101: POLITICAL EDUCATION

Education is always about power; therefore, education is always political. However, *political education* refers to the specific work of examining how the world works in order to change it. As the organization Critical Resistance puts it, political education takes a participatory approach to studying and engaging in collective struggle. Critical Resistance views political education as a strategy that helps us "build the collective leadership our organization and communities need for self-determination and collective liberation."[a]

Political education takes place on the streets and on the internet, in classrooms and in living rooms. It can look like a lot of different things, like a social media graphic interpreting data on the school-to-prison nexus, or a training for youth on how to get police out of their schools.

Political education is also an integral part of an organizing campaign. For instance, in the Power U campaign to divest from school policing and invest in sexuality education (described in chapter 2), organizers conducted political education for their fellow youth and for adult stakeholders on the harms of school policing and the connections to sexual and reproductive justice. Similarly, through its writing workshops and know-your-rights trainings, Rise (see the "Organization Spotlight" later in this chapter) supports political education that helps system-impacted parents make connections between their experiences and the structural violence of the family policing system.

For many young people, social media has become a key site of political education. A TikTok video that explains self-managed abortion, an Instagram post that illustrates the US prison population, a retweet of Abolitionist Youth Organizing

Institute's (AYO-NYC!) "Cosmic Possibilities" guide to abolitionist organizing for youth (described later in this chapter)—these are all ways that youth take the means of political education into their own hands.

a. Critical Resistance n.d.

is more education or better discipline practices, and overwhelmingly misses the intertwined centrality of capitalism, heteropatriarchy, colonialism, ableism, and white supremacy to the work of public education."[21] Instead, scholars have coined the phrase "school-to-prison nexus" to emphasize how schooling and the legal system complement each other as symbiotic arms of the carceral state—rather than a pipeline from one space to another, a nexus is a linked site.[22] Movements for school abolition draw on the same analysis as movements to abolish the prison industrial complex in arguing that the existing school system in the United States cannot be reformed. Instead, we need to radically reimagine schooling and, as Black studies scholar David Stovall argues, "end the conditions that sustain and support white supremacy through an endemic system of training rooted in dehumanization and white supremacy."[23]

In 2015, a Black high school student in Columbia, South Carolina, took out her phone during class and refused to hand it over to her teacher; eventually a school police officer was called to the classroom. What happened next could be seen in another student's phone-recorded video that soon went viral: the white, male officer violently flipped the desk over with the student still in it, dragged her to the front of the classroom, and arrested her. This viral video opens the 2019 documentary film *Pushout: The*

Criminalization of Black Girls in Schools as the narrator says, "This video went viral, but it's not unique. Incidents like this can be found in every corner of America, from major cities to small towns." As disability and education scholar Subini Ancy Annamma explains, the carceral function of schooling targets bodies "furthest from the desired norm of white, male, and abled" and therefore causes the most harm to Black, brown, Indigenous, queer, trans, low-income, and disabled students.[24] Policies that funnel youth out of school and into carceral institutions, including removal from class, suspension, and expulsion, are more frequently used against Black students than white students, even for similar or less serious conduct violations.[25] Andrea Ritchie has called attention to how society tends to frame police brutality as affecting Black men and ignores how it affects Black women, girls, and trans people. Similarly, Annamma's research demonstrates how framings of the school-to-prison pipeline obscure the criminalization of Black girls in schools. Compared to white girls, Black girls are subject to excessive school surveillance and punishment for failing or refusing to adhere to white, middle-class norms of femininity.[26]

Researchers have also found that school discipline, peer-to-peer anti-queer violence, and hostile teachers and staff expose queer youth to surveillance, policing, and expulsion for making public displays of affection and violating gender norms.[27] For instance, in research conducted in California, a young woman shared a story about how hugging another female student in the hallway spiraled into accusations of making out in the bathroom and eventually a suspension from school.[28] An adult youth worker in the same study described how young LGBTQ people are penalized for kissing and other displays of affection (which technically goes against school policy), "but they don't enforce that for straight youth."[29] Unsurprisingly, intersections of racism and homo- and transphobia make queer and trans youth of color especially vulnerable to school punishment and exclusion, which envelops them in the carceral state.[30] What's more, transphobic and cissexist environments that, for example, deny gender-appropriate facilities are associated with anti-trans mistreatment by police, and anti-trans victimization or expulsion is associated with subsequent incarceration.[31] For example, in 2021, an eleven-year-old nonbinary student assigned male at birth made national news over their suspension for having a hair length that violated the school district's dress code. The student's mother explained that their child "was able to identify as nonbinary based on being able to present themselves as feminine with long hair." While the student was attending in-school suspension, teachers bullied them to "just cut their hair." After a group of parents sued the school district over the policy, the gendered language on hair length was removed from the dress code, but other harsh penalties remained.[32]

Whether we call it a pipeline or a nexus, the carceral function of schooling in the United States is a form of reproductive injustice. First of all, when schools—where young people spend a great deal of their time—function or even just look like prisons, they are denying youth self-determination and bodily autonomy. Policies like dress codes are intended to prevent gang activity and reduce violence while promoting a professional, disciplined learning environment, but there is little evidence to suggest that the policies actually do any of this.[33] Instead, dress codes police young people's bodies along lines of normative expectations of gender, race, and social class (e.g., banning natural hairstyles, ripped clothing, exposed bra straps). Racist, sexist, and classist school dress codes use the same logic as policies that restrict abortion or trans health care: they essentially tell young people that their bodies do not belong to them. Predictably, research has found that schools target Black students of all genders and LGBTQ youth of all races for dress code violations more frequently than they do white or cisgender, heterosexual students. In addition to policing their bodies and gender expressions, dress code policies heighten the surveillance and discipline of marginalized students and serve as one of many entry points for the school-to-prison nexus.[34]

Forcing students out of school through suspension, expulsion, or arrest also has negative short- and long-term health effects. Lower levels of educational attainment (e.g., a high school diploma, years of high school completed) predict higher incidence of chronic illness, injury, and communicable disease and shorter life spans. Education level is also a social determinant of sexual and reproductive health. For instance, the odds of an STI diagnosis among African American women with a college degree is 73 percent lower than among those who have not completed high school.[35] Infants born to women with fewer than twelve years of formal schooling are more than twice as likely to die in the first year of life than infants born to women with four years of college.[36] To be sure, the social mechanisms through which lower educational attainment is related to poor health are complex, but it is safe to say that getting pushed out of school is not good for your well-being. Relatedly, criminalizing youth out of the classroom and into prisons, detention centers, and other carceral institutions does not set them up to exercise reproductive freedom. As the sections below explain, these sites regulate young people's sexual and reproductive autonomy. Therefore, school policies and practices that target Black, brown, queer, trans, and economically marginalized youth actively contribute to future involvement with carceral systems that constrain sexual and reproductive freedom through sexual violence, lack of access to health services like abortion, and the inability to parent one's children.

The Juvenile Punishment System and Reproductive Injustice

Although the United States constitutes only 5 percent of the world's total population, it holds 25 percent of the world's prison population. The incarceration rate in the United States began to rise dramatically in the 1980s due to policies related to the "war on drugs" and the "war on crime" that disproportionately criminalized Black, Latinx, Indigenous, and low-income people. In 1975, there were 240,593 people locked up in US prisons and jails. That number rose 545 percent to peak at 1,553, 570 people in 2009.[37] There are about five times as many Black incarcerated people in the United States as there are white imprisoned people.[38] As Ava DuVernay's award-winning 2016 documentary *13th* brought to light, although the Thirteenth Amendment to the US Constitution outlawed slavery more than 150 years ago, in practice enslavement has continued through the mass incarceration of Black people. Legal scholar Michelle Alexander has called a related phenomenon the "New Jim Crow": the ways that the explicit racial segregation of the Jim Crow era lives on via the continued subjugation of Black people through mass incarceration. The mechanisms through which this criminalization takes place are multiple and complex and include hyperpolicing in communities of color, racialized sentencing guidelines for crack versus powder cocaine possession and distribution, and the structural disinvestment in particular communities that prompts crimes of survival.

Although the youth incarceration rate in the United States declined dramatically in the first decades of the twenty-first century—by 60 percent between 2000 and 2019—the nation nevertheless incarcerates more youth than any other industrialized country in the world. On any given day, about 48,000 people under eighteen are confined in juvenile detention centers, long-term secure facilities, residential treatment centers, group homes, and adult jails and prisons, and most of them are incarcerated for nonviolent offenses.[39] Racism, sexism, transphobia, and other systems of oppression play out in schools, families, and communities in ways that contribute to stark inequities in the selection of which youth get locked up and why. Nearly two-thirds of youth incarcerated in the United States are Black or Latinx.[40] Similar to the rate for Black versus white adults, the incarceration rate for Black youth of all genders is more than four times higher than the rate for white youth.[41] Youth incarceration also varies significantly by gender and sexuality. African American girls are more than three times as likely to be incarcerated as their white peers, and Native American girls are more than four times as likely. Girls are more likely than boys to be incarcerated for low-level offenses like truancy, curfew violation, and running away from home.[42] LGBTQ youth are overrepresented in the juvenile legal system: about 20 percent of incarcerated youth identify as LGBTQ, compared to 9 percent in the population overall.[43] Family rejection, homelessness, and participation in survival crimes contribute to the overrepresentation of LGBTQ youth in carceral institutions, where they are more likely to experience peer and staff violence and be kept in solitary confinement for their own "safety."[44]

Countless activists and scholars have underscored the harm that incarceration imposes on young people's lives, bodies, minds, and communities. For instance, disability justice activists and scholars argue that carceral institutions are disabling sites that harm the bodies and minds of people caged within their walls.[45] Youth who've experienced incarceration are less likely to finish high school, enroll in college, or earn a living wage as adults; they are more likely to experience physical and mental issues ranging from dental problems to posttraumatic stress disorder.[46] Youth incarceration also deeply constrains reproductive freedom. Incarcerated youth face even higher barriers to quality sexual and reproductive health care, including contraception, abortion, and dignified birthing, than do youth on the outside (who, as previous chapters demonstrate, already face significant barriers). The structural violence, dispossession, and complex trauma that contribute to youth incarceration in the first place are also forces that harm the health of young people even before the carceral state envelopes them. Therefore, youth entering the juvenile legal system who are already likely to have experienced an STI or unintended pregnancy are then faced with further constraints on care. The chaos of living "on the run" or being moved in and out of detention facilities makes it extremely difficult to access any of kind of health care with consistency.[47] What's more, correctional facilities are often out of compliance with standards of care for providing adolescent sexual and reproductive health care.[48]

Incarceration also deeply constrains access to abortion and the ability to parent. Legal scholars argue that incarcerated people have a right to abortion care while in custody, but in practice this right exists only on paper.[49] Even before the end of *Roe,* most US states had parental involvement laws affecting minors' abortion access, the effects of which were compounded when a young person was incarcerated and might have little to no (or deeply constrained) contact with their family. Now that many states have banned abortion, youth and adults incarcerated in those states are unable to travel to receive care.[50] They will be forced simply to continue the pregnancy to term in a place with inadequate prenatal care and poor nutrition and may have to give birth while shackled to a hospital bed—only to be denied the opportunity to parent by having the newborn immediately removed from their care.[51]

Much like their adult counterparts, young parents face myriad barriers to parenting during incarceration and after release. They are under hypersurveillance from the carceral functions of the child welfare system and the threat of permanently losing parental rights through the Adoption and Safe Families Act (which requires most states to automatically file a petition to terminate parental rights once a child has been in foster care for fifteen of the most recent twenty-two months). Their age and presumed inability to parent deeply intensifies this surveillance. Carceral institutions are also sites of gendered sexual violence. Sexual abuse committed by adult staff against incarcerated youth is widespread in juvenile facilities across the United States.[52] Although the Prison Rape Elimination Act (PREA) mandates data collection and strategies to curb sexual abuse in jails and prisons, correctional officers report viewing it as a burden on their work, and incarcerated people report that the policy is not taken seriously.[53] In an especially egregious 2019 case in Texas, a corrections officer was charged with having sex with an incarcerated girl who reportedly became pregnant following the abuse.[54]

REPRODUCTIVE INJUSTICE AND THE CHILD "WELFARE" SYSTEM

In 2021, Child Protective Services (CPS) in Manatee, Florida, took custody of the one-year-old son of former American Idol

YOUTH ACTIVIST SPOTLIGHT: ALYSSA (CHICAGO)

As a young person just getting started in activism, Alyssa believed they had to work separately on gender justice, racial justice, and all the other issues they cared about. Learning about reproductive justice brought all of it together for her as a Black queer person who has accessed abortion. Alyssa's work spans a variety of RJ issues, including emergency contraception access, sexual violence prevention and restorative justice, self-managed abortion training, and abortion storytelling. At the core of this work is a reproductive justice vision of "a world without prisons, without DCFS [Department of Children and Family Services], a world without ICE [Immigration and Customs Enforcement], and a world without borders in general." In this world, "all the criminalized people would be free and there would be access to free abortions and doulas."

Alyssa (now twenty-four) notes that parents and other adults often think they automatically have autonomy over young people's bodies when it comes to sexual and reproductive health care. "It's not talked about in the reproductive justice community," she observes, but youth in foster care, youth in detention facilities, and migrant youth are criminalized in their attempts to access abortion services. In their work with the Chicago Transformative Doula Network, Alyssa supports incarcerated people in accessing abortion care. This work includes tasks that people are unable to do from inside jails and prisons, such as researching appointments online or arranging transportation. "It's really just so many barriers to access care as well as currently being in a cage while you are pregnant and don't want to be," they explain. In Alyssa's view, abortion doulas are crucial to bridging the gaps in accessing care created by the prison industrial complex.

Like many young organizers, Alyssa has experienced tensions with and pushback from adults who don't share their vision of liberation, or who think young people are just apolitical. While working with other Black and brown students to implement a restorative justice response to sexual violence on her college campus, Alyssa experienced resistance from administrators who viewed the criminal legal system as the most appropriate response to survivor justice. "Students already have trauma from policing in their neighborhoods, . . . so we wanted to support survivors outside the carceral route." Alyssa also recalls a Twitter thread that demonstrates the tensions between youth organizers and their older counterparts. "This white feminist had tweeted something like, 'Oh, youth these days don't think reproductive rights are an important issue.' It was like, really? And then all the youth organizers on Twitter were like, 'Okay, most abortion funds are run by millennials.' It's stuff like that where we have these lived experiences and we should be able to take up the space no matter how old we are."

finalist Syesha Mercado, a Black woman. She had taken her son to the hospital to be treated for dehydration while she was transitioning him from breast milk to a solid food diet. While there, her son was assessed by a white doctor with a reputation for being quick to conclude that a child's health issue was the result of abuse. As Mercado later wrote in a GoFundMe campaign to raise money for her legal fees, "[My son was] forcefully and legally kidnapped from us by CPS, who claim we refused a B12 shot that was a matter of life and death, which is an absolute lie. We never refused a B12 shot, and at no point was he on the verge of death."[55] Later that year Mercado gave birth to her daughter while still fighting for custody of her son. In August police stopped Mercado's vehicle and conducted a surprise welfare check and took custody of her infant because she had failed to notify authorities that she had had another baby while being investigated for child abuse. While broadcasting the encounter on Instagram Live, she pleaded with the police not to take her infant. After allowing her to express some breastmilk for her daughter, the police took the baby away.[56]

Mercado's story is far from unique. Sociologist and legal scholar Dorothy Roberts has exposed the US child welfare system as a system of racialized reproductive coercion that monitors, regulates, and disrupts marginalized families—Black women's families in particular. What she calls the *family policing system* uses humiliating investigations, forced child removal, and impossible reunification plans to punish Black mothers, then blames them for their own structural dispossession. In this view, it's bad mothering that leads to Black mothers' overrepresentation in the child welfare system—not poverty and racism. "Stereotypes of maternal irresponsibility created and enforced by the child welfare system's disproportionate supervision of black children," Roberts explains, "help to sustain mass incarceration, and stereotypes of black female criminality help to sustain foster care."[57] The surveillance and punishment of the family policing system penalizes the most marginalized families while blaming them for a lack of dignified, living-wage employment opportunities, safe and affordable housing, access to addiction services, reliable public transit, and quality schools.[58] The family policing system, like the prison system, mutually reinforces private remedies for structural inequality and the punitive regulation of multiply marginalized communities. In the neoliberal age of eviscerated public resources such as housing, health care, and childcare assistance makes "excessive policing by foster care and prison seem necessary to protect children and the public from harm."[59]

In reality, this policing actively harms young people and their families. As in prisons, Black and Indigenous people in the United States are overrepresented in the family policing system. Whereas before the civil rights movement child welfare services essentially ignored Black children, by 2000 Black children made up the largest group of children in foster care. Today, over half of Black children in the United States will experience a child welfare investigation by their eighteenth birthday— double the rate for white children.[60] The cumulative risk that Black and Indigenous children face of being separated from their families and placed in foster care before they turn eighteen is also about double that for white children.[61] It takes a greater risk of child maltreatment for a white child to be placed in foster care than for a Black child.[62] Law enforcement personnel report rates of child maltreatment in Black and Indigenous families that are 66 percent and 38 percent higher, respectively, than the rate in white families. Black and Indigenous parents are not more likely than white parents to harm their children; rather, white supremacy and settler colonialism contribute to their overrepresentation in the family policing system. Black and Indigenous parents are also more likely than white parents to have their parental rights permanently terminated, a devastating outcome sometimes referred to as the "civil death penalty."[63] Statistics such as these illustrate how the policies and practices of child welfare agencies function much like the historical capture and enslavement of Black children and the removal of Indigenous children to boarding schools.

Poverty is also a main driver of family investigation and child removal. In 2019, 75 percent of confirmed child maltreatment cases in the United States involved neglect (not physical or sexual abuse), which, as defined by state statutes, is nearly synonymous with the conditions of racialized poverty.[64] Counties with more families living below the federal poverty line have a higher rate of child maltreatment investigations, while counties with higher family incomes have lower rates. Families describe being reported, investigated, and having children removed for incidents that would likely not be considered neglect in middle-class or wealthy families, such as running out of diapers or children injuring themselves while playing. Similarly, caseworkers and judges view parents experiencing drug and alcohol struggles as neglectful parents, regardless of whether their drug use affects their ability to parent and regardless of whether they are actively seeking or receiving treatment.[65] Because families who have limited economic resources or who use substances are more likely to rely on social services, they also have greater exposure to people who are mandated reporters and thus to more opportunities for their efforts to navigate poverty and addiction to be interpreted as neglect.[66]

We must think about the family policing system much as we do the school-to-prison nexus: as part of the carceral system that denies young people reproductive self-determination and bodily autonomy. Like the carceral system more generally, the family policing system polices and harms adults and youth, in both similar and distinct ways. Research shows that investigation, child removal, and life in the foster care system have detrimental effects on young people. The impact of family separation includes trauma, other mental health issues, homelessness, and school noncompletion.[67] Ironically, these experiences often circulate marginalized young people into other carceral systems that perpetuate additional reproductive injustices.

Paradoxically, the bureaucratic foster care system fails to provide adequate reproductive health services to the same young people it subjects to hypersurveillance of their sexual behavior and contraceptive decisions. Rates of unintended pregnancy and STIs are higher among youth in the foster care system than among youth in the general population—a result of the compounded effects of poverty, instability, and noncontinuity of health care.[68] Complex administrative rules govern the process through which youth in foster care access *any* kind of health care and are especially constraining when it comes to abortion access. Depending on the laws of the state in which they reside and the interpretation and discretion of the foster care agency (at a time when more such agencies are privatized and run by religious organizations that oppose abortion), youth face multiple barriers to obtaining an abortion. The parent(s) from whom the youth has been removed may be unavailable to provide consent in states with parental involvement laws. Foster parents may seek to block the young person's abortion by using the bureaucracy of the foster care system or the threat of a new placement or group home. Even when all parties support the minor's abortion, the diffusion of authority among legal parents, foster parents, and state agencies creates confusion and delays in obtaining consent.[69] In the post-*Roe* landscape where many people are financially and logistically burdened by the need to travel out of state for an abortion, foster care youth often face insurmountable barriers to abortion care.

These barriers to contraception and abortion contribute to higher rates of pregnant and parenting youth in the foster care system than outside it. Young women in foster care are more than twice as likely as their peers not in foster care to become pregnant as a minor.[70] Young women ages twenty to twenty-four who have aged out of the foster care system—a vulnerable time in which young adults are haphazardly transitioned into living independently—are also about twice as likely as their non–foster care peers to experience a pregnancy. Pregnant and parenting youth are often more difficult to place in foster homes, and those who become pregnant while in placement may experience greater instability depending on the foster parents' ability or willingness to care for their distinct needs. Young parents in the foster care system may have substantial needs for parenting support that the system is ill-equipped to provide. Pregnant and parenting youth in the foster care system are also at increased risk of having their child removed from their care because of enhanced state scrutiny and elevated contact with social service systems.

The heightened surveillance that young parents may face from their parents, caseworkers, teachers, or health care providers places them at greater risk of involvement with the family policing system. Pregnant and parenting youth may already be part of the system through their own foster placements, and are therefore more likely to be reported for child abuse and neglect than older parents (regardless of the veracity of those reports). As chapter 3 discusses, society is already predisposed to think of young people as always already neglectful parents solely by virtue of their age. Like parents of any age experiencing poverty, domestic violence, substance use, housing instability, or limited employment opportunities, family-policing systems punish young mothers for the structural conditions that make it difficult or impossible to raise children in healthy and sustainable communities. Young parents must navigate a complex bureaucracy that even many case workers agree is set up to fail them. For example, in an ethnography of a supervised independent living program for youth mothers who were involved with the child welfare or juvenile legal systems, anthropologist Lauren Silver shows how residents managed an impossible set of rules and regulations. At the same time that they were expected to engage in job training or employment, they had no access to quality affordable childcare and risked child removal if they left their children unsupervised.[71] My experiences as a young parent and my research with pregnant and parenting youth also demonstrate that the family policing system is a constant source of anxiety for young parents. As young parents, we knew that regardless of how well we took care of our children, the threat of getting entangled in the system's tentacles always loomed over our heads. Whether it was a pediatrician who thinks your baby has diaper rash because you never change him or a nosy neighbor who doesn't think you should have a social life, the relentless surveillance is exhausting.

YOUTH ORGANIZING AT THE INTERSECTION OF REPRODUCTIVE JUSTICE AND ABOLITION FEMINISM

A common critique of abolitionist politics is that abolition of the carceral state is impractical or impossible, or that abolitionists focus more on what they want to dismantle than on what they want to build. Angela Y. Davis, Gina Dent, Erica R. Meiners, and Beth E. Ritchie argue that this is hardly the case, as "abolition has always been as much about the work that focuses on building and experimenting as it has on what must be dismantled."[72]

ORGANIZATION SPOTLIGHT: RISE (NEW YORK CITY)

Rise was founded in 2005 for and by parents impacted by the family policing system. Like system-impacted parents across the United States, these families are disproportionately Black and/or navigating issues such as poverty, housing insecurity, domestic violence, and substance use. Rise envisions communities that are free from family policing and separation and a society that cultivates new ways of preventing and addressing harm. Its members' work stems from a radical commitment to ensuring that *all* families have what they need to live beyond survival and truly thrive. Rise organizes not only to abolish the family policing system but also to build a world where communities have the resources, support, and skills to raise families with dignity and support.

This transformative justice approach isn't focused just on dismantling the Administration for Children's Services, New York City's child welfare department; it also supports parents in family court, creates space for affected parents to tell their stories, and helps families get their health, housing, and childcare needs met without the surveillance of the system. Programs at Rise center families most impacted by the family policing system, including those who have experienced child welfare investigations, child removal, court-ordered supervision, and parental termination of rights. For instance, their peer supporter training helps to reduce system contact by building peer-to-peer care networks that connect parents under stress to trusted resources. Rise also provides parent organizing and leadership training to support system-involved parents in the movement to abolish family policing.

Rise engages young parents who've experienced the family policing system both as children and as parents. Since 2012, their writing workshop project "My Story, My Life" has trained young parents to speak about their experiences and become advocates for change. Two issues of Rise's magazine written by system-involved parents have focused on young parents who've experienced the family policing system from both ends. In addition to these workshops, Rise has conducted "Know Your Rights" workshops for young parents who grew up in foster care to prevent their own children from being unnecessarily removed from their homes.

For more on Rise, see its website, https://www.risemagazine.org/.

Celebrated abolitionist organizer and educator Mariame Kaba made this clear in a widely circulated *New York Times* op-ed published amid the nationwide uprisings following the police murder of George Floyd in June 2020. Titled, "Yes, We Mean Literally Abolish the Police," Kaba countered arguments that abolitionists merely want to abolish the police and call it a day. "We are not abandoning our communities to violence," she wrote; "we don't want to just close police departments." Instead, "we want to make them obsolete . . . [by redirecting] the billions that now go to police departments toward providing healthcare, housing, education, and good jobs."[73]

People who want to abolish prisons and policing acknowledge that those institutions and practices, along with the family policing system and school-to-prison nexus, aren't "broken" or "not working"; rather, they are working exactly as intended: they enforce white supremacy, anti-Blackness, heteronormativity, transphobia, ableism, and so on. Merely reforming these institutions by hiring more police officers of color or holding implicit-bias training sessions for child welfare caseworkers legitimizes and expands the carceral system instead of dismantling it.[74] As Dorothy Roberts puts it: "The only way to stop the destruction caused by family policing is to stop policing families."[75]

The following examples illustrate how youth and their adult co-conspirators bring the feminist abolitionist framework to bear on issues surrounding reproductive (in)justice and how they are building alternatives to the carceral state. No discussion of youth abolitionist organizing would be complete without naming the germinal work of Mariame Kaba's Project Nia, which Kaba founded in Chicago in 2009 with the goal of ending youth incarceration through transformative justice. As disability activist Mia Mingus explains, *transformative justice* is intimately connected to abolitionist politics. Transformative justice (TJ) "is a political framework and approach for responding to violence, harm, and abuse" without creating more violence.[76] Over the years, Project Nia has engaged in this work through a wide variety of projects and campaigns such as "Chicago Girl Talk," an outreach program supporting girls and young women in a juvenile detention center and "A World Without Prisons," an art exhibit bringing together the visions of incarcerated youth and people on the outside to imagine a world without prisons.

Supporting youth organizing and leadership has been key to Project Nia's work. Its Abolitionist Youth Organizing Institute (AYO-NYC!) was inaugurated in the summer of 2020 as a collaboration with EFA Project Space, a cross-disciplinary arts venue in New York City. Although originally intended to be a weeklong, in-person experience, the COVID-19 pandemic moved it to a remote format. As with the Trans Youth Justice Project described in chapter 4, the move to a remote platform enabled a larger and geographically broader group of young people to participate. AYO-NYC! raised nearly $100,000 to support the program, which hosted fifty virtual participants ages sixteen to twenty-four in July 2020. Youth participants received a $500 stipend. The objective of the institute is to support and nurture the next generation of abolitionist organizers in finding, defining, and sustaining their role within social justice movements. Institute sessions included "Mapping our Roles and Envisioning New Worlds," "Anti-oppression 101," "PIC Abolition and Queer + Trans Resistance to Policing," "Creative Resistance," and "Healing Justice," all of which were documented by Laura Chow Reeve of Radical Roadmaps. Using a graphic recording and illustration practice, Reeve creates accessible and visual political education tools that are used for both documentation and circulation. These maps, along with resources and content from the trainings, were made available for free online afterward (see https://padlet.com/ayonyc1). Following the institute, a small group of participants created a workbook, titled "Cosmic Possibilities: An Intergalactic Youth Guide to Abolition," that features content on engaging in care as an abolitionist practice, addressing harm, and undoing internalized carceral logic. The workbook is also available for free online (https://issuu.com/project-nia/docs/_2021__ayo-final-combined).

Advocates for Youth, the national youth sexual and reproductive health, rights, and justice organization (described in earlier chapters), also supports abolitionist youth organizing through leadership development. Its 2021 activist institute, "How to Get Police Out of Schools," was similar to AYO-NYC!'s training and outreach but drew explicit connections between divesting from police and investing in youth reproductive and sexual health, rights, and justice. The institute was open by application to youth ages fourteen to twenty-four; like AYO-NYC!'s program, it was hosted remotely and featured graphic recording from Radical Roadmaps. Videos of the institute are available on AFY's YouTube channel for all youth and their supporters to learn from. From the start, facilitators made explicit the connections between reproductive justice and getting police out of schools. Caro Hernandez of AFY's Young Womxn of Color Leadership Council explained:

> Not a single entity or person should ever have control over someone else's body and future, and for these basic reasons we think that reproductive health, rights, and justice are in direct alignment with the struggle for prison abolition. . . . When we are actively trying to work to dismantle these systems we are also actively working towards a more just and equitable world that creates safety, health, and autonomous futures for everyone . . . We need to try to create specific practices within ourselves, within our relationships, and our organizations to try to embody these values so that we can get to a future in which abolition is a reality—it's not just about abolishing physical buildings.[77]

Day 1 of the institute focused on political education about the problem of police in schools, day 2 focused on solutions for getting police out of schools, and day 3 featured Samantha Daley from Power U's campaign (described in chapter 2) discussing actions to get police out of schools. Daley broke down not only the campaign's specific organizing strategies but also the fundamentals of organizing more generally, such as defining the problem(s), facilitating a listening campaign, mobilizing stakeholders, making demands, and evaluating success. Modeling the abolitionist practice of both *dismantling* carceral practice and *building* the world we want to live in, Daley emphasized the campaign's actions, including paid trainings for teachers (who we know are deeply underpaid for their labor).

CONCLUSION

In February 2022, the New York Police Department posted a picture on its Twitter feed of items seized during a recent shoplifting operation in the Bronx. The photo showed officers proudly displaying the results of their "bust," only it wasn't the usual display of weapons or drugs. Instead, it was a large quantity of diapers, laundry products, and cold medicine. The tweet boasting that "the arrests made led to the closure of 23 warrants & the recovery of $1800 worth of merchandise" was quickly deleted after a decisive social media backlash. As one Twitter response put it: "When this is the photo the NYPD release about reclaimed stolen merchandise, you can't help but ask what kind of society we live in where police take back soap, infant diapers, OTC pain medication, and laundry detergent, and arrest and incarcerate the people who took them." Another tweet pointed out the hypocrisy that "if those parents didn't try to steal those diapers, soap, and medicine, you'd arrest them for child neglect." The user asked, "Are poor people just not allowed to have families and be happy?"[78]

I show this picture to my students when explaining the concept of criminalization. If a parent cannot afford diapers and steals them from a store, they are subject to arrest, fines, and possibly incarceration. It is not considered a crime that items like diapers are deemed "nonessential" and sold for a profit. Instead, the crime is to take them from the store when you can't afford them and know that your caseworker is going to check to see how many diapers you keep in the house on their next visit. Similarly, it is considered a crime when students repeatedly skip school, not when governments invest money in school police officers instead of teachers and counseling staff. The logic of the carceral state demands that individuals be held responsible for social inequality. From abortion bans to family policing, criminalization has long been a tactic of reproductive injustice. Like their adult counterparts, young people experience criminalization of their bodies, survival strategies, and identities—but with intensified surveillance, regulation, and punishment based on their structural position as youth. Analyzing youth criminalization through the reproductive justice framework enables us to see how policing and punishment are deeply entwined with the ability to create the families we want. Abolition feminism and transformative justice provide us with tools to imagine the world otherwise.

Epilogue

Let Them Lead the Way

A news story about a nearby grocery store caught my attention as I approached the completion of this book. Although the story was not explicitly about reproductive justice, it illustrates my analysis that all youth organizing is reproductive justice organizing. The grocery store is located in a predominately Latinx neighborhood and sits next to a large public housing complex. A group of youth organizers investigating the effects of inflation on low-income families discovered that this particular store—part of a large regional chain—charged as much as 18 percent more for the same products than it did at the chain's location in a neighboring, predominately white suburb where the median income is four times higher. As one of the youth explained, "Finding this out means that we've had our money stolen, that we've been ripped off."[1]

I was angered—though unsurprised—that the prices were inflated for the folks who were the most likely to face food insecurity and the least likely to be able to travel via the city's broken public transit system in search of better prices. I was also really impressed with these young people, who, once again, were doing the urgent work of pushing back against power. Then I did the thing you should never do when reading the news online: I read the comments. Perhaps I naively thought that some adult co-conspirators would share my anger, lack of surprise, and appreciation for the young people. News article comment sections are notorious for their racist, classist, sexist, and homophobic attacks, and this section was no exception. The mostly anonymous comments blamed the residents of the neighborhood for the inflated prices: if the Black and brown folks from the public housing complex would just stop being lazy and get a job and not steal from the store so much, then the company wouldn't have to raise its prices. Commenters who pointed out the obvious racism at play here were swiftly criticized as "woke liberals" and "reverse racists" who didn't understand how businesses operate.

The extent of the adultism in the comments on this story was especially hostile. With typical fervor, posters minimized the youth's work in every way possible: they were playing the victim, they didn't understand how basic economics work, their research methods were flawed, and so on. As one of the youth organizers told the reporter, "People think that just because we're young, we do not know what we're talking about." This is a classic example of how adultism is used to diminish youth resistance. In this view, youth cannot possibly know their own realities, and they certainly can't be trusted to make meaningful social change. Instead, adults see them as passive actors who must stay quiet and deal with the effects of adult-created inequalities—that is, if the adults are willing to acknowledge that the inequalities even exist. In this case, most commenters thought it was perfectly fine for the products to cost more at this location; after all, that's just how capitalism works.

I don't care at all whether the youth perfectly estimated the cost discrepancies. I'm interested in what their work illustrates about youth organizing and resistance. I imagine many of these young people grew up watching their female relatives struggle to make food budgets last until the next paycheck or the next month of food stamp benefits arrived. I imagine many of the youth had been dragged on an excruciatingly long bus ride by an adult trying to find deals elsewhere, because the kids were too young to be left home alone. Or perhaps the adults in their lives didn't feel their block was safe enough to leave their kids without supervision, or aging extended kin were not available because they needed care of their own. I also imagine that these young people watched as developers built luxury condos near the grocery store, driving up food prices and other basic costs of living like housing and health care while their schools got more police instead of more teachers. Multiply marginalized youth understand how interlocking systems of oppression structure the resources that contribute to bodily autonomy and self-determination. They know that access to affordable food for your family is reproductive justice.

APPENDIX

Supplementary Teaching Materials

These materials are aimed at educators in college and high school classes as well as staff in community and organizational settings. Individual readers may find them useful in deepening their learning, especially the recommendations for further reading. All discussion questions and activities assume you have read the corresponding chapter.

INTRODUCTION

Questions for Discussion and Reflection

1. Consider the author's provocation to analyze all youth organizing as reproductive justice organizing. How does this framing enable us to have a more expansive view of youth health, rights, and justice? What are some potential limitations of the approach?

2. Brainstorm a list of examples illustrating how the category of "youth" is socially constructed. Think about which social institutions (e.g., the family, schooling, media) contribute to these constructions and how.

3. The introduction quotes Audre Lorde as writing, "There is no such thing as a single-issue struggle because we do not live single-issue lives." Reflect on what this assertation means for

youth and social justice. For example, how do young people's intersecting identities affect how they view and experience the world? What interlocking systems of oppression structure their life chances, and how?

4. In this chapter the author reflects on how their social identities and experiences of both marginalization and privilege affect their research and writing. How do your intersecting identities affect your activism, career, or education?

Classroom Activity: Comparing Reproductive Health, Rights, and Justice

LEARNING OBJECTIVES

· Distinguish the central themes of the reproductive rights, reproductive health, and reproductive justice approaches.
· Describe the strategies that each approach uses to work toward reproductive freedom.
· Identify strengths and limitations in each approach.
· Apply the three approaches to examples from your own life or communities.

PROCEDURE (75 TO 90 MINUTES)

1. Preparation: Prior to the class session, participants should read the pivotal 2005 article by Asian Communities for Reproductive Justice (now called Forward Together), "A New Vision for Advancing Our Movement for Reproductive, Health, Rights, and Justice."

2. Interactive lecture and discussion: Clarify material from the article on the central themes of each approach. Reproductive health is a service delivery approach focused on addressing unmet reproductive health care needs. Reproductive rights is a legal and advocacy approach focused on maintaining the individual legal right to abortion, family planning, and so on. The reproductive justice approach is a vision, framework, and social movement with a goal of collective power.

	Reproductive Health	Reproductive Rights	Reproductive Justice
Level of analysis			
Central theme or tenet			
Analysis of the problem			
Strategies for advancing reproductive freedom			
Benefits and limitations			

3. Small group work: Using large sheets of paper or a digital spreadsheet prepared like the adjacent table, assign one approach each to small groups of three to five participants (for larger classes, more than one group will cover each approach). Instruct participants to brainstorm together and fill in the chart using examples from the reading, prior course materials, current events, and/or their own experiences. Have participants report back to the larger group.

Further Reading

Asian Communities for Reproductive Justice. 2005. "A New Vision for Advancing Our Movement for Reproductive Health, Reproductive Rights, and Reproductive Justice." Forward Together. https://forwardtogether.org/tools/a-new-vision/.
Although some of the language we use has shifted since this report was written, it is a go-to read for comparing and constrasting the differences between reproductive health, rights, and justice.

Cohen, Cathy J. 1997. "Punks, Bulldaggers, and Welfare Queens: The Radical Potential of Queer Politics?" *GLQ: A Journal of Lesbian and Gay Studies* 3 (4): 437–65.

This article marked a major turning point for queer studies and foreshadowed the body of work we now call *queer of color critique.*

Combahee River Collective. 2000. "The Combahee River Collective Statement." In *Home Girls: A Black Feminist Anthology,* edited by Barbara Smith, 264–74. New Brunswick, NJ: Rutgers University Press.
Originally published in 1977, this political manifesto is a key document in Black and women of color feminisms and remains as timely today as when it was first published.

Lorde, Audre. 1984. *Sister Outsider: Essays and Speeches.* Berkeley, CA: Crossing Press.
Another classic in Black and women of color feminisms, this collection of short speeches and essays had a profound effect on liberation movements and scholarship. Start with the essays "The Master's Tools Will Never Dismantle the Master's House," "Age, Race, Class, and Sex: Women Redefining Difference," and "Uses of the Erotic: The Erotic as Power."

Manalansan, Martin F. 2018. "Messing Up Sex: The Promises and Possibilities of Queer of Color Critique." *Sexualities* 21 (8): 1287–90.
If you're looking for a quick introduction to queer of color critique, this article is exactly what you need.

CHAPTER 1. ABORTION ACCESS
AND BEYOND
Questions for Discussion and Reflection

1. How have policies restricting minors' access to abortion incorporated dominant social and cultural ideas about youth, race, class, and gender?
2. As the research in this chapter explains, restricting minors' access to abortion does not do what proponents believe it does (i.e., strengthen families); instead, it worsens social and health

inequalities. Why do you think policies such as this persist even in the face of research that demonstrates their negative impact?

3. Consider the strategies that youth have employed to organize for abortion access, including college campus organizing, full-spectrum doula projects, mutual aid, and digital activism. What are some possibilities and limitations of each strategy?

Classroom Activity: Using Social Media to Organize for Abortion Access

LEARNING OBJECTIVES

· Identify the strengths and challenges of using social media as an organizing strategy.

· Describe how organizers have used memes and infographics as tools of resistance against abortion restrictions.

· Design a social media post that can be shared as a political education or mutual aid resource.

PROCEDURE (75 TO 90 MINUTES)

1. Preparation: Collect examples of active social media accounts that promote political education and mutual aid for abortion access. Some examples of accounts that were active at the time of this writing include @repromemes, @shoutyourabortion, and @plancpills.

2. Interactive lecture and discussion: Share examples from the social media accounts. Ask participants what they notice about the language, visuals, and content of the posts. Discuss what is useful and not so useful about each post.

3. Individual or small-group work: Ask participants, working alone or in small groups, to create a social media post of their own that is relevant to the local community or online communities they are part of. The post could share information, resources, or some combination of the two. It should be accessible and relevant to its

intended audience. Canva.com is a free-to-use web-based design program that is excellent for making social media posts. Encourage participants to use principals of universal design in their post (e.g., including alt-text descriptions).

4. Invite participants to share and discuss one another's posts, as in step 2.

Further Reading

Advocates for Youth. 2021. "Mutual Aid for Abortion Access." YouTube, February 4. https://www.youtube.com/watch?v=hYKJVNzKGKQ&t=216s.

Leaders from the Abortion Support Collective and the Womxn of Color Leadership Council discuss abortion mutual aid projects across the United States and argue that abortion legalization by itself is not access. 1 hour, 17 minutes in English with autogenerated captions.

Mahoney, Mary, and Lauren Mitchell. 2016. *The Doulas: Radical Care for Pregnant People.* New York: Feminist Press.

This book details the authors' experiences with creating an abortion doula project that later became a model full-spectrum doula project.

Spade, Dean. 2020. *Mutual Aid: Building Solidarity during This Crisis (and The Next).* London: Verso.

A short but comprehensive introduction to the history, philosophy, and practice of mutual aid that cautions against letting this radical practice be co-opted and watered down. Spanish translation available free online at https://www.deanspade.net/mutual-aid-building-solidarity-during-this-crisis-and-the-next/

Zoila Pérez, Miriam. 2012. *The Radical Doula Guide: A Political Primer for Full Spectrum Pregnancy and Childbirth Support.* N.p.: privately printed. https://radicaldoula.com/the-radical-doula-guide/.

Essential reading that details the radical politics of doula work and the potential of full-spectrum doula care.

CHAPTER 2. THE FIGHT FOR ACCURATE, AFFIRMING, AND LIBERATORY SEXUALITY EDUCATION

Questions for Discussion and Reflection

1. Many young people report learning about sex and sexuality from sources other than school. What formal and informal ways did you learn about sexuality growing up? What were some hidden or evaded lessons (see page 72)?

2. How has sexuality education been a response to real and imagined social problems throughout US history? How did this framing affect the objectives of sexuality education, how it was taught, and its content?

3. This chapter argues that school-based sexuality education serves to both reveal and reproduce social inequalities. Brainstorm a list of ways it does both of these. Use specific data and policies from your area(s) of expertise to illustrate.

4. Sexuality education has mostly focused on what it seeks to prevent, rather than on what it seeks to promote. What are some of the things that the activists and organizations described in the chapter want to promote? If you were designing a sexuality education program, what would you want to promote?

Classroom Activity (Can Be Adapted into a Written Assignment): Critiquing Youth Sexual Health Promotion

LEARNING OBJECTIVES

· Critique the form and content of sexual health promotion materials aimed at youth.
· Analyze sexual health promotion through an intersectional framework.
· Explain the difficulty of creating effective and inclusive health promotion material.

PROCEDURE (75 TO 90 MINUTES)

1. Preparation: Curate a selection of sexual health promotion materials aimed at young people (or ask participants to bring one to class). These materials can be found nearly anywhere, such as a health center or the side of a bus. Of course, you can also find numerous examples on the internet. Health promotion materials include things like brochures, zines, posters, websites, apps, and workshop curricula.

2. Discussion: Ask participants what they notice about the material. Questions might include:

Who is the target audience?

What is the objective or purpose?

What knowledge, attitudes, or behaviors does the material try to influence?

How does the material account for, or fail to account for, intersections of race, class, gender, sexuality, age, ability, and other differences?

What assumptions does the material make about youth and their bodies? Or about the category of youth more generally?

Do you think the material is effective? Why or why not? What would you change about it?

Further Reading

Barcelos, Chris. 2022. "The Politics of Race, Class, and Gender in Queer Safer Sex." In *Introducing the New Sexualities Studies,* 4th edition, edited by Nancy L. Fischer, Steven Seidman, Chet Meeks, and Laurel Westbrook, 721–29. New York: Routledge.
This accessible introduction to the intersectional politics of queer safer sex uses archival materials from the 1980s to the 2000s to show how safer-sex promotion is always connected to race, class, and gender.

Fields, Jessica, Jen Gilbert, and Michelle Miller. 2015. "Sexuality and Education: Toward the Promise of Ambiguity." In *Handbook of the*

Sociology of Sexualities, edited by John DeLamater and Rebecca F. Plante, 371–87. Cham, Switzerland: Springer.
A comprehensive and accessible, encyclopedic chapter that outlines research and debates in sexuality education.

García, Lorena. 2009. "'Now Why Do You Want to Know about That?' Heteronormativity, Sexism, and Racism in the Sexual (Mis) Education of Latina Youth." *Gender and Society* 23 (4): 520–41.
This frequently cited research article demonstrated how the racialization of young Latinas' sexuality contributes to health and social inequalities.

Guttmacher Institute. 2023. "Sex and HIV Education." September 1. https://www.guttmacher.org/state-policy/explore/sex-and-hiv-education.
An excellent resource in table format that tracks state policies on sex education and is updated regularly.

CHAPTER 3. DEPATHOLOGIZING TEEN PARENTING AND ABOLISHING TEEN PREGNANCY PREVENTION

Questions for Discussion and Reflection

1. Although teen pregnancy rates have been on the decline for decades, teen pregnancy is largely still considered a major social problem in the United States. Why do you think it is still seen as a problem? What are other social problems facing youth that this focus might distract from?

2. This chapter describes the #IntersectionalFail that occurred when trans activists called out a teen pregnancy prevention campaign for its transphobia but not its racism or adultism. What are some other intersectional fails you can think of? (Pro tip: intersectional fails happen on social media and in the news pretty much every day!)

3. Teen pregnancy is an issue that unites people across political divides: Democrats, Republicans, conservatives, and feminists alike have framed teen pregnancy as a serious social problem. What other issues can you think of that unite people across political divides? What can we learn by studying these issues?

4. What are some specific, concrete ways that you can push back against the pathologization of teen or youth childbearing? Similarly, what are specific, concrete steps you can take to support young pregnant and parenting youth in your community?

Classroom Activity: Critical Analysis of Media Portrayals of Teen and Young Moms

LEARNING OBJECTIVES

- Analyze the politics of race, class, gender, and sexuality in media about teen and youth moms.
- Identify how media portrayals can have real-world effects.
- Compare media *about* young parents with media *by* young parents.

PROCEDURE (75 TO 90 MINUTES, EXCLUDING THE FILM)

1. Preparation: First, choose a film or television show to watch together as a group or ask participants to watch beforehand. Letterboxd, for example, lists films in which teen or young pregnancy or parenting is a major part of the plot here: https:// letterboxd.com/mamadweezil/list/young-moms/. My personal favorite is *Quinceañera* (2006), which does an excellent job weaving together stories of youth pregnancy and queerness in a Latinx family while also critiquing gentrification and hegemonic whiteness. Most films about young parents do not depict this level of nuance. You can also screen episodes from the popular

MTV shows *16 and Pregnant* or *Teen Mom,* which scholars and
young moms have critiqued for their stigmatizing and unrealistic
portrayals. There is much scholarship on these shows, including
an edited volume of critical essays (see Guglielmo 2013; and
Greyson, Chabot, and Shoveller 2019).

2. Discussion

Invite general observations and reactions to the film or television
show.

What do you notice about how the film or show represents teen
or young parents?

Note such aspects as plot, character development, costuming,
casting, lighting, frame composition, motion.

What assumptions does it make about young parents' lives,
bodies, or relationships?

How does the film or show represent race and ethnicity,
gender, sexuality, and other social differences?

How does the film or show make you feel? What emotions come
up? How might it feel to view this film or show if you had
lived experience of being a young parent?

The effects of media on viewers are complex. How do you
imagine this film or show could impact social policy or
individual behavior? (Here is a place to review conflicting
research on *16 and Pregnant* or *Teen Mom.* See Greyson,
Chabot, and Shoveller 2019; and Kearney and Levine
2015.)

Contrast this film or show with media produced by young parents,
such as the #NoTeenShame campaign. What is similar and
different?

Further Reading

Cadena, Micaela, Raquel Z. Rivera, Tannia Esparza, and Denicia Cadena.
2016. *Dismantling Teen Pregnancy Prevention.* Albuquerque: Young Women
United.

This report from the organization now called Bold Futures is a must-read for understanding dismantling teen pregnancy prevention using a reproductive justice framework.

Geronimus, Arline T. 2003. "Damned If You Do: Culture, Identity, Privilege, and Teenage Childbearing in the United States." *Social Science and Medicine* 57 (5): 881–93.
This frequently cited article, written by an epidemidologist, was pivotal in calling attention to how commonly held assumptions about teen childbearing aren't support by robust research.

Pillow, Wanda. 2003. "'Bodies are Dangerous': Using Feminist Genealogy as Policy Studies Methodology." *Journal of Education Policy* 18(2): 145–159.
Another pivotal article in the critical approach to studying teen pregnancy, this article analyzes how educational policy discourses produce pregnant and parenting teen bodies as dangerous and abject.

Vinson, Jenna, and Clare Daniel. 2020. "'Power to Decide' Who Should Get Pregnant: A Feminist Rhetorical Analysis of Neoliberal Visions of Reproductive Justice." *Tense: A Journal of Rhetoric in Society* 8 (2).
An incisive critic of the National Campaign to Prevent Teen and Unplanned Pregnancy's rebrand as "Power to Decide."

CHAPTER 4. TRANSGENDER YOUTH, FAMILY MAKING, AND THE LIVABILITY OF TRANS LIVES

Questions for Discussion and Refection

1. Much of the opposition to transgender youth rights—and to sex education and access to abortion—frames its goal as "protecting children." Why is protecting children such a common policy strategy across the political spectrum? In what ways do these strategies ironically bring more harm to marginalized young people?

	State with a Ban	State without a Ban
Description of service and location		
How did you obtain the information? How difficult was it to find?		
Days/hours service is available		
Cost and which medical insurance accepted		
Transportation (is there parking, which bus lines go there, how often, etc.). How long would it take to get there from your current location?		
What kinds of barriers might prevent someone from accessing the service? For example, do you need a referral? Do you need pre-authorization from your health insurance company? Is there a waiting list? Do the providers speak languages other than English? Do providers employ people of color or trans-identified people?		
What community-based supports are available to assist trans youth and their families in navigating access to care?		

2. Reproductive justice and trans justice share similar theories of liberation, movement goals, and campaign issues. However, the two movements haven't always gotten along. Brainstorm a list of similarities and differences between reproductive justice and trans justice.

3. What could it look like to "protect trans kids" without falling into an adultist mindset that denies agency to trans youth? What are some specific, concrete steps you could take in your community to support trans youth?

*Classroom Activity: Accessing Gender-Affirming Health
Care for Trans Youth*

LEARNING OBJECTIVES

- Identify barriers faced by trans youth and their families when
  trying to access gender-affirming care.
- Explain the connection between barriers to gender-affirming
  care and interlocking systems of oppression.
- Identify strategies for building solidarity within a reproductive
  justice movement that includes trans youth.

PROCEDURE (75 TO 90 MINUTES)

1. Preparation: participants should have a general idea of what
   gender-affirming care for trans youth involves (reading the
   chapter is sufficient). Participants will need access to the internet.
2. Small-group activity: Separate participants into groups of three
   to four people. Explain that they will be researching access to
   trans youth gender-affirming care in states with and without a
   ban (for example, your state and a state with a ban). If you're in a
   state with a ban in place, the second location can be any US city
   of your choice (consider using a less restricted state). You can
   see an up-to-date map of bans here: https://www.lgbtmap.org
   /equality-maps/healthcare_youth_medical_care_bans.
3. Have participants, working in their groups, fill in the adjacent chart.
4. Ask groups to report back and reflect on the discussions they had
   in filling out the chart:

   What was it like doing this activity? What thoughts, feelings, or
      observations came up for you? What was (un)surprising?
   What barriers did you identify?
   How does the intersection of transphobia and adultism contrib-
      ute to these barriers? What about other systems of oppression?
   What are concrete, specific actions you could take to support
      trans youth in your community?

Further Reading

cárdenas, micha. 2016. "Pregnancy: Reproductive Futures in Trans of Color Feminism." *Transgender Studies Quarterly* 3 (1–2): 48–57.
This short essay includes poetry and analysis about the inclusion of trans women in reproductive justice by using the author's experience as a trans woman of color undergoing fertility preservation.

Seigel, Derek P. 2021. "Trans Moms Discuss Their Unique Parenting Challenges during the Pandemic—And What They Worry about When Things Go Back to 'Normal.'" *The Conversation*, March 20. https://theconversation.com/trans-moms-discuss-their-unique-parenting-challenges-during-the-pandemic-and-what-they-worry-about-when-things-go-back-to-normal-158857.
Using interview-based research with transgender mothers, this short, accessible article analyzes an infrequently studied reproductive justice topic.

Untorelli Press. 2013. "Street Transvestite Action Revolutionaires: Queer Antagonist Struggle." March 12. Archived at https://libcom.org/article/street-transvestite-action-revolutionaries-survival-revolt-and-queer-antagonist-struggle.
This electronic zine contains numerous speeches by Marsha P. Johnson and Sylvia Rivera that are hard to find elsewhere.

CHAPTER 5. CRIMINALIZED YOUTH AND ABOLITION FEMINISMS

Questions for Discussion and Reflection

1. The chapter defines criminalization as "the social and political processes through which individuals, groups of people, their bodies, or their behaviors become something to be managed through the tools of the carceral state: exclusion, punishment, and incarceration." What are some examples of criminalization you're familiar with that were not discussed in the chapter? How

do interlocking systems of oppression contribute to this
criminalization?

2. Using examples from the chapter (e.g., school policing, family
   policing), discuss how the prison industrial complex isn't a place
   but instead a set of relationships. It is helpful to draw these
   relationships out as a map with connecting lines to indicate
   connections and shared investments.

3. As the chapter explains, critics often argue that abolitionist
   politics are impractical or impossible. Critics also argue that
   abolitionist activists are focused too much on what they want to
   dismantle, and not enough on what they want to build.
   Brainstorm examples of what kinds of resources communities
   would need in order to make the carceral state obsolete.

Classroom Activity: Envisioning a World without Prisons and Policing

LEARNING OBJECTIVES

- Practice the abolitionist strategy of creating the world we want
  to live in.
- Apply the concept of transformative justice.
- Build hope for a better world.

PROCEDURE (75 TO 90 MINUTES)

1. Preparation: this vision board activity can be completed virtually
   using websites such as Kudoboard.com or Canva.com, which
   allow users to post images, videos, text, drawings, and so on.
   There are free versions with some limitations, as well as paid
   versions with additional features. Later, unless you delete it, the
   board will remain accessible to participants. You can also make a
   vision board the original way, with large sheets of paper and craft
   materials. Depending on the size of the group, you may wish to
   have more than one board.

2. Explain to participants that they are going to make a collaborative vision board about a world without prisons and policing. A vision board is a collage designed around a particular topic. For example, sometimes people make a vision board at the beginning of the year to manifest the changes in their life that they want to see in the new year. Give instructions relevant to the platform you are using. Encourage participants to get creative with images, drawings, and so forth. Encourage chatting while working on the board—it's collaborative! Remind participants that there are no right or wrong answers.

3. On the virtual board or on a sign in the room you're in, display the prompt: "Think about your vison of a world where prisons and policing are obsolete. Think about all forms of carcerality, from juvenile detention to migrant detention to the family policing system. What does the world look like? What does it feel like? Who is there? What resources do we have?"

4. After the vision board is complete, ask participants to take a moment to study it, and invite them to reflect on the process of completing the board and the steps we can take to make this world a reality.

Further Reading

Briggs, Laura. 2020. *Taking Children: A History of American Terror.* Oakland: University of California Press.
A decisive examination of how taking children away from their parents has long been part of the American experience, from chattel slavery to forced removal of migrant children along the Mexico-US border.

Davis, Angela Y., Gina Dent, Erica R. Meiners, and Beth E. Richie. 2022. *Abolition. Feminism. Now.* Chicago: Haymarket Books.
From leading scholar-activists on feminist abolition, this book is as generative for those new to abolition politics as it is for longtime activists.

Kaba, Mariame. 2021. *We Do This 'til We Free Us: Abolitionist Organizing and Transforming Justice.* Chicago: Haymarket Press.

This collection of essays, from one of the foremost abolitionst organizers, is required reading for anyone who wants to abolish the carceral state and build something new.

Roberts, Dorothy. 2022. *Torn Apart: How the Child Welfare System Destroys Black Families—And How Abolition Can Build a Safer World*. New York: Basic Books.

As detailed as it is heartbreaking, this book makes an impassioned call to action for distmantling the family policing system in the United States.

NOTES

INTRODUCTION

1. Freedom Inc. 2017.

2. See "Week of Action in Defense of Black Lives," M4BL, accessed June 9, 2024, https://m4bl.org/week-of-action/.

3. The term "accomplice" reframes the concept of "ally." An adult ally to youth takes on the role of an advocate or helper, generally on an individual level. Often, being an ally is an identity (a thing you are), rather than a process or action (a thing you do). In contrast, an adult accomplice to youth uses their privilege and power as an adult to work toward dismantling adultism and other systems of oppression. See Annalee Schafranek, "What's the Difference between an Ally and Accomplice?" YWCA Seattle, King, Snohomish, December 21, 2021, https://www.ywcaworks.org/blogs/ywca/tue-12212021-1103/whats-difference-between-ally-and-accomplice.

4. SisterSong: Women of Color Reproductive Justice Collective n.d.

5. See Tamar Sarai, "There's No Reproductive Justice without an End to Police Violence," *Prism*, May 21, 2021, https://prismreports .org/2021/05/21/ending-police-violence-is-integral-to-achieving-reproductive-justice/.

6. Briggs 2017, 4.

7. Gilliam 2020, 640.

8. See, for example, Earl, Maher, and Elliott 2017; Maher and Earl 2017; Taft 2011.

9. One exception is Patricia Zavella's 2020 book, *The Movement for Reproductive Justice: Empowering Women of Color through Social Activism*, which includes a chapter on youth mobilization. However, the chapter focuses specifically on youth empowerment through RJ organizations and only on the issues of sex education and abortion.

10. Author's calculations using ProQuest database.

11. See Ross and Solinger 2017, 63–66.

12. Luna 2020.

13. See SisterSong: Women of Color Reproductive Justice Collective n.d.

14. See Ross and Solinger 2017; Silliman et al. 2004; Luna 2020; Zavella 2020.

15. Asian Communities for Reproductive Justice 2005.

16. Luna 2020; Ross and Solinger 2017; Zavella 2020.

17. Luna 2020.

18. Glosser, Gardiner, and Fishman 2004. Depending on the state, people under the age of consent are allowed to consent to sexual activity if the age of the other person is within a certain number of years (e.g., in Alabama a person over 12 years old but under 16 can consent to having sex with someone no more than 2 years older than themselves). Scholars have pointed out that age of consent laws are disproportionately used to police and criminalize the sexuality of marginalized young people. See Sutherland 2002.

19. Walker-Harding et al. 2017.

20. Hardin et al. 2017.

21. See "YRBSS [Youth Risk Behavior Surveillance System] Overview," Centers for Disease Control: Adolescent and School Health, access June 9, 2023, https://www.cdc.gov/healthyyouth/data/yrbs/overview.htm.

22. Chavez-Garcia 2012.

23. Lesko 2012, 5.

24. Lesko 2012, 137.

25. Lira 2021.

26. Tuck and Yang 2014b, 17.

27. Tuck and Yang 2014a; Ginwright, Noguera, and Cammarota 2006.

28. DeJong and Love 2015, 536.

29. Gordon 2009, 9.

30. Gordon 2009, 8.

31. Barcelos 2022.

32. Fine 2014, 49.

33. Fine 2014, 47.

34. Ruglis 2011, 635.

35. Noguera 2014, 75.

36. Noguera and Cannella 2006, 334.

37. Tuck and Yang 2014b, 1.

38. Ginwright, Noguera, and Cammarota 2006.

39. Rodríquez 2017; Mananzala and Spade 2008.

40. Kwon 2013, 9.

41. Nair 2015.

42. Taft 2021, 194.

43. Taft 2021, 203.

44. Quoted in Western States Center 2011.

45. Luna 2020, 9.

46. cárdenas 2016.

47. Plaid and Macdonald-Dennis 2021.

48. Thompson 2002.

49. Lorde 1984, 112.

50. Lorde 1984, 138.

51. Combahee River Collective 2000.

52. Nash 2018.

53. Hong and Ferguson 2011, 2.

54. Manalansan 2018, 15.

55. C. Cohen 1997, 458.

56. Kafer 2013; Roberts and Jesudason 2013; Jarman 2015.

57. Kafer 2013.

58. Roberts and Jesudason 2013, 315.

59. URGE: Unite for Reproductive and Gender Equity 2020.

60. Moussawi and Vidal-Ortiz 2020, 14.

61. Advocates for Youth n.d.

CHAPTER 1. ABORTION ACCESS AND BEYOND

1. In 2020 the Massachusetts legislature overrode the governor's veto to enact a new law that removed the parental notification law for sixteen- and seventeen-year-olds.

2. Upadhyay et al. 2015.

3. Indeed, as I was finishing this book, RJ activists were awaiting the US Supreme Court's decisions in *FDA v. Alliance for Hippocratic Medicine* and *Idaho v. United States,* both of which could further restrict abortion access by limiting access to Mifepristone (one of the drugs used in a medical abortion) and restrict emergency abortion care, respectively. In both cases, the Court declined to hear oral arguments, on procedural grounds rather than on the merits of the cases; as a result, scholars and activists believe the fight to keep Mifepristone accessible is far from over.

4. Sins Invalid 2019, 59.

5. Silliman 2002, xi.

6. Brockell and Koh 2022; McClurg 2022.

7. Panich-Linsman and Kelly 2022.

8. Bellotti v. Baird, 443 U.S. 622 (1979).

9. Solinger 2005, 238.

10. Guttmacher Institute 2023a.

11. The "global gag rule" prohibits foreign nongovernmental organizations that receive financial assistance from the United States from counseling patients about abortion, even if the organization uses its own funding.

12. American Public Health Association 2011; American Medical Association n.d.; Braverman et al. 2017; American Academy of Pediatrics 2022.

13. American Academy of Pediatrics 2022, 2.

14. Boonstra 2014.

15. Epidemiological data use the word *women* to describe the people in the denominator of abortion and birth rates. At present it is not possible to know how many of these people are nonbinary people or transgender men.

16. Maddow-Zimet and Kost 2021.

17. Henshaw and Kost 1992; Ralph et al. 2014.

18. Hasselbacher et al. 2014.

19. Coleman-Minahan et al. 2019; Coleman-Minahan 2021.

20. Coleman-Minahan et al. 2019; Coleman-Minahan 2021.

21. Eskamani 2023.

22. Coleman-Minahan et al. 2021.

23. Begun et al. 2020; Murno et al. 2021; Ralph et al. 2021.

24. Dennis et al. 2009; Joyce, Kaestner, and Ward 2020; Naide 2020.

25. Ralph et al. 2021.

26. Engle and Freeman 2023.

27. Henshaw and Kost 1992; Ehrlich 2003a, 2003b; Janiak et al. 2019; White et al. 2022.

28. Janiak et al. 2019.

29. Duroseau et al. 2021

30. Kavanagh et al. 2012.

31. Begun et al. 2020.

32. Braverman et al. 2017; Ehrlich 2003a, 2003b.

33. Center for Information and Research on Civic Learning and Engagement 2022.

34. Ferguson 2018.

35. McMenamin 2024.

36. As in many RJ organizations, over the years, students and community members have questioned or criticized CLPP's commitment to racial justice and trans inclusion.

37. Poggi 1988.

38. Gupta 1994.

39. Belis 1994.

40. Lorde 1984, 119.

41. Gluckman and Trudeau 2002.

42. Crabtree 2002.

43. The word is also translated as "slave," and for this reason some people, especially those whose ancestors or whose clients' ancestors experienced enslavement, choose to use different terms for their work.

44. Kozhimannil et al. 2014.

45. Basile 2015.

46. Zoila Pérez 2012, 12.

47. Mahoney and Mitchell 2016, xx.

48. Zoila Pérez 2012, 5.

49. Mahoney and Mitchell 2016.

50. Spade 2020, 18.

51. Nelson 2011.

52. National Network of Abortion Funds n.d.

53. Apiary for Practical Support n.d.

54. Ely et al. 2018; Ely et al. 2017.

55. All quotes in this paragraph are from Advocates for Youth 2021b.

56. Advocates for Youth 2021b.

57. Advocates for Youth 2021b.

58. Bitman 2023; Li et al. 2018.

59. Nummi, Jennings, and Feagin 2019.

60. Tudoroiu 2014.

61. Holloway 2023.

62. Davis 2016.

63. Jenkins et al. 2016.

64. The use of the handkerchiefs is an homage to the Madres de Plaza de Mayo, who wore white headscarves as they protested the Argentine dictatorship's disappearance of their children in the late 1970s and early 1980s.

65. Anderson 2020; Chang, Mehta, and Kenin 2022; Harris 2021.

66. Salazar 2021.

67. Muliadi 2020.

68. Lewis 2023.

69. Sung 2020.

70. Although some people might view this tactic as problematic because it implicitly assumes that men with a small penis are less

desirable or masculine, I'd argue that these young people are playing into the men's belief in this assumption rather than asserting there is something wrong with different shapes and sizes of genitals.

71. Grose 2021.

72. Barcelos 2022.

73. Kaba 2021.

CHAPTER 2. THE FIGHT FOR ACCURATE, AFFIRMING, AND LIBERATORY SEXUALITY EDUCATION

1. Epstein 2022.

2. Forward Together 2012.

3. Epstein and Mamo 2017.

4. Fields, Gilbert, and Miller 2015, 271.

5. Gilbert 2010, 5.

6. García and Fields 2017; Fields 2008; Luker 2007; Lamb, Graling, and Lustig 2011; García 2009.

7. SIECUS: Sex Ed for Social Change 2021.

8. Moran 2002.

9. I first encountered this stigmatizing practice when I was a first-year PhD in public health and served as a teaching assistant for an undergraduate health course. Since then, countless students at every college or university where I've worked have shared their horror at having been forced to sit through the same.

10. Epstein 2022, 244.

11. Lord 2009.

12. Luker 2007, 60.

13. Patton 1996, 69.

14. Patton 1996.

15. Fields 2008.

16. For a review of this scholarship, see Fields, Gilbert, and Miller 2015.

17. Howell 2007. In the 2010s, proponents rebranded AOUM as "sexual risk avoidance programs." See Boyer 2018.

18. Santelli et al. 2006.

19. Barcelos 2020.

20. Future of Sex Education Initiative 2020.

21. O'Quinn and Fields 2020.

22. Centers for Disease Control and Prevention 2016.

23. Fields 2008.

24. Bustillos 2023.

25. Fields, Gilbert, and Miller 2015.

26. García 2009; Barcelos 2020.

27. Gill 2021, 3.

28. García 2009; Barcelos 2020.

29. Guttmacher Institute 2023b (data accurate as of December 2023); SIECUS: Sex Ed for Social Change 2022 (data accurate as of July 2022).

30. Nikkelen, van Oosten, and van den Borne 2020; Stevens 2017.

31. Power imbalances among youth may thwart these affinities. See Fields and Copp 2015.

32. Fowler, Schoen, and Morain 2021; Fowler et al. 2021; J. Johnston 2017; Stevens 2017; Yeo and Chu 2017.

33. Manduley et al. 2018; Gutiérrez 2011.

34. Craig et al. 2015; Manduley et al. 2018.

35. Lindberg and Kantor 2022.

36. Lindberg and Kantor 2022. The Healthy People objectives are simply to increase the percentage of adolescents who receive "formal instruction on delaying sex, birth control methods, HIV/AIDS prevention, and sexually transmitted diseases before they are 18 years old." See "Increase the Proportion of Adolescents Who Get Formal Sex Education before Age 18 Years—FP-08," Healthy People 2030, US Department of Health and Human Services, Office of Disease Prevention and Health Promotion, accessed June 20, 2024, https://health.gov/healthypeople/objectives-and-data/browse-objectives/family-planning/increase-proportion-adolescents-who-get-formal-sex-education-age-18-years-fp-08.

37. Lindberg and Kantor 2022.

38. Lindberg and Kantor 2022; Bradford et al. 2019; Gowen and Winges-Yanez 2014; Pampati et al. 2021; Roberts et al. 2020.

39. Kosciw et al. 2020.

40. Centers for Disease Control and Prevention 2013.

41. Howell, Pinckney, and White 2020.

42. Charlton et al. 2018; S.K. Goldberg, Reese, and Halpern 2016.

43. Arrington-Sanders et al. 2016; Pollitt and Mallory 2021.

44. Fields, Gilbert, and Miller 2015.

45. Goldfarb and Lieberman 2021.

46. Fields 2008.

47. Goldfarb and Lieberman 2021; Atkins and Bradford 2021; Santelli et al. 2006; Kirby, Laris, and Rolleri 2007.

48. Soyong Harley 2019.

49. Chicago Women's Health Center 2021, 202.

50. Chicago Women's Health Center 2021, 202.

51. URGE: Unite for Reproductive and Gender Equity 2021; Sex Education Collaborative 2022.

52. Chicago Women's Health Center 2021, 203.

53. Manalansan 2018, 1288.

54. Combahee River Collective 2000.

55. Chicago Women's Health Center 2021, 202.

56. Allen 2012; Lamb, Lustig, and Graling 2013.

57. Britzman 2012.

58. Lorde 1984, 54.

59. Cammarota and Fine 2010.

60. Krueger-Henney and Ruglis 2020.

61. Forward Together 2012.

62. Zavella 2020. As of August 2024 neither the House nor the Senate versions of this bill had made it out of committee.

63. California Department of Education 2022.

64. Oakland Unified School District n.d.

65. Advocates for Youth n.d., "Divesting from Police."

66. Kiema and Daley 2021.

67. See "About," Power U, accessed June 23, 2024, https://www.poweru.org/about/.

68. See Schools on Fire, accessed June 23, 2024, https://schoolsonfire.org/

69. Kiema and Daley 2021.

CHAPTER 3. DEPATHOLOGIZING TEEN
PREGNANCY AND ABOLISHING TEEN
PREGNANCY PREVENTION

1. Kingsbury 2008.

2. Benfer 2008.

3. Vinson 2018; Kaplan 1997.

4. Briggs 2017; Daniel 2017; J. Kim 2021.

5. Barcelos 2020; García 2009; Pillow 2004; Lubiano 1992; Tapia 2005.

6. Vinson and Daniel 2020.

7. Morse 2022.

8. Osterman et al. 2022.

9. Lincoln, Jaffe, and Ambrose 1976; Pillow 2004.

10. Pillow 2004.

11. Osterman et al. 2022.

12. Boonstra 2014.

13. Barcelos 2020.

14. Osterman et al. 2022.

15. Osterman et al. 2022.

16. Best 2007.

17. López 2014.

18. J. Kim 2021, 82.

19. Zane and Toppin 2022; Shaefer et al. 2019; Parolin 2019.

20. Santelli et al. 2017.

21. García 2009.

22. Guglielmo 2013.

23. Bonell 2004; Klein and Committee on Adolescence 2005; Penman-Aguilar et al. 2013; Rich-Edwards 2002; Sisson 2012.

24. Kirby 2001; Northridge and Coupey 2015; Parks and Peipert 2016.

25. D. Roberts 2016; Winters and McLaughlin 2020; Wu et al. 2019.

26. For a review of this research, see Geronimus 2003 and Sisson 2012.

27. Geronimus and Korenman 1992; Geronimus 1996, 2003.

28. Cadena et al. 2016, 7.

29. Hotz, McElroy, and Sanders 2005.

30. Wilson and Huntington 2006; Gubrium, Krause, and Jernigan 2014; Barcelos and Gubrium 2014; Luttrell 2014; Barcelos and Gubrium 2018b.

31. Barcelos and Gubrium 2018, 924.

32. Kwon 2013; Ray 2017.

33. Barcelos 2020, 58.

34. Fields, Gilbert, and Miller 2015.

35. Bernstein 2018, 65.

36. Bernstein 2018, 21.

37. Burns and Benz 2022.

38. Barcelos 2020, 70.

39. C. Cohen 1997, 458.

40. Lupton 2015.

41. Gunarata 2013.

42. Beauchamp 2013, 3.

43. Coren, Barlow, and Stewart-Brown 2003; Lupton 2015; Silver 2015.

44. Davis et al. 2022.

45. Cadena et al. 2016.

46. Crews n.d.

47. Piepmeier 2009.

48. The site stayed live until 2019, by which time a very different social world existed on the internet.

49. National Day to Empower Teen Parents 2003.

50. No Teen Shame n.d.

51. No Teen Shame n.d.

52. Zoila Pérez 2013.

53. Candie's Foundation 2015.

54. For a detailed discussion of #NoTeenShame's movement work, see Vinson 2018.

55. Jackson, Bailey, and Welles 2020, xxxviii.

56. Collins 2008.

57. Vinson 2018, 104.

58. Eisenstein 2019.

59. Vianna and Soyong Harley 2019.

60. Repro Jobs 2021.

61. O'Quinn and Fields 2020.

62. For a timeline of events, see "Trump's Teen Pregnancy Prevention Program Shift: A Timeline," SIECUS, 2019, https://siecus.org/resources/trump-shifts-teen-pregnancy-prevention-program/.

63. Weiss 2017.

64. Centers for Disease Control and Prevention 2021.

65. Vinson and Daniel 2020.

66. Paudel et al. 2022; Hamilton, Martin, and Osterman 2022.

CHAPTER 4. TRANSGENDER YOUTH, FAMILY MAKING, AND THE LIVABILITY OF TRANS LIVES

1. Movement Advancement Project 2024.

2. Mandler 2024.

3. Gluckman and Trudeau 2002, 7.

4. URGE: Unite for Reproductive and Gender Equity n.d.(b).

5. Yurcaba 2022.

6. Thomsen 2022.

7. cárdenas 2016.

8. Steinmetz 2014.

9. Guarino 2016; S. Goldberg 2017.

10. S. Goldberg 2017.

11. Guarino 2016.

12. Gill-Peterson 2018; Ellison et al. 2017; Lagos 2022.

13. Gossett, Stanley, and Burton 2017.

14. Gossett, Stanley, and Burton 2017.

15. Lovelock 2017; Glover 2016.

16. Gill-Peterson 2018, 2.

17. Hilliard 2022.

18. Movement Advancement Project 2021.

19. Kosciw et al. 2020.

20. Brown 2022.

21. Tannehill 2021.

22. Dugyala 2021.

23. Roberts 2014.

24. Thomas, Arkles, and Kant 2022, 18.

25. Thrasher 2022.

26. Collective Power for Reproductive Justice 2014.

27. Spade 2015; Westbrook 2020.

28. Turban and Ehrensaft 2018.

29. Turban and Ehrensaft 2018.

30. For youth, a diagnosis of gender dysphoria requires "persistent, insistent, and consistent" feelings that their gender does not match their sex assigned at birth. Scholars and activists have critiqued these criteria as a form of normalizing judgment to regulate trans youth. See Temple Newhook et al. 2018; and Pyne 2014.

31. Gridley et al. 2016.

32. Very occasionally a trans boy who did not take puberty blockers (or started late) may have a procedure to remove excess chest tissue before turning eighteen. Trans adults also experience a myriad of barriers in getting gender-affirming hormones and surgeries, with more adults desiring care than are able to access it. See James et al. 2016.

33. shuster 2021.

34. cárdenas 2016; Pfeffer et al. 2023.

35. Tishelman et al. 2019; Nahata et al. 2017; Chen et al. 2017.

36. Wierckx et al. 2012.

37. Reisner et al. 2015; Chodzen et al. 2019.

38. Johns et al. 2019.

39. Turban et al. 2020.

40. De Vries et al. 2014; Kuper et al. 2020.

41. shuster 2021.

42. Clark and Virani 2021.

43. Ikuta 2016; Vergani 2018.

44. Feinberg 2023.

45. The phrase is generally attributed to Micah Bazant and B Parker. See Katie Tandy, "Trans Day of Remembrance Is Resilience

Above All," *Medium*, November 20, 2015, https://medium.com/the-establishment/trans-day-of-remembrance-is-resilience-above-all-2e542fd6b147.

46. Snorton and Haritaworn 2013.

47. As Gill-Peterson (2018) points out, much of the research on Street Transvestite Action Revolutionaries (STAR) has focused on a handful of events—as I do here—likely because of limited archival resources.

48. For consistency I refer to Marsha and Sylvia under the "trans" umbrella, though the term was not in wide circulation at the time. Readers may notice that I refer to them by their first names, whereas this book refers to most people by their surnames. Marsha and Sylvia are historical figures widely referred to by their first names, and my use here is meant to signal that cultural familiarity.

49. Plaster 2023.

50. Ferguson 2018, 26.

51. Ferguson 2018, 23.

52. Untorelli Press 2013, 13.

53. Duberman 1994, 253.

54. Untorelli Press 2013, 13.

55. Nothing 2013.

56. Gill-Peterson 2018, 23

57. STAR [1970], Box 19, Street Transvestite Action Revolutionaries file, IGIC, Manuscripts and Archives, New York Public Library, cited in S. Cohen 2008.

58. SisterSong: Women of Color Reproductive Justice n.d.

59. Duberman 1994, 251.

60. Marvin 2019, 114.

61. Hillier et al. 2020, 385.

62. URGE: Unite for Reproductive and Gender Equity n.d.(a).

63. URGE: Unite for Reproductive and Gender Equity 2020, 8.

64. Barcelos et al. 2021.

65. See Trans Youth Justice Project, accessed July 4, 2024, https://transyouthjusticeproject.com/.

66. Thomas, Arkles, and Kant 2022, 3.

CHAPTER 5. CRIMINALIZED YOUTH
AND ABOLITION FEMINISMS

1. Brown-Long and Mauger 2019, 9.

2. Brown-Long and Mauger 2019; Sedlak and McPherson 2010.

3. Kaba and Schulte 2021.

4. Kaba and Schulte 2021.

5. Ritchie 2023.

6. Although some readers may be more familiar with the term *criminal justice system,* I use *criminal legal system* to refer to the system of policing, prosecution, courts, and corrections, as these systems do not deliver justice in the way critical scholars and activists see it.

7. Flavin 2010; Silliman et al. 2004; Charlton et al. 2018; D. Roberts 2002, 2016, 2022; Briggs 2020; Frunel and Lorr 2022.

8. Pregnancy Justice 2016.

9. Huss 2022.

10. Flavin and Paltrow 2010, 232.

11. Flavin and Paltrow 2010; Paltrow and Flavin 2013; Goodwin 2017.

12. Bridges 2020.

13. Paltrow and Flavin 2013; Briggs 2020; Goodwin 2017.

14. Critical Resistance n.d.

15. Davis et al. 2022, 2.

16. Stanley 2011, 11.

17. Ben-Moshe 2020.

18. Davis et al. 2022, 67.

19. Nocella, Parmar, and Stovall 2023.

20. Sojoyner 2016; Shange 2019; Quinn and Meiners 2009; Meiners 2016.

21. Meiners 2016, 9.

22. Annamma 2016; Dylan 2010; Vaught 2017; Goldman and Rodriguez 2022.

23. Stovall 2018, 57.

24. Annamma 2018.

25. Bradshaw et al. 2010; Skiba et al. 2002; Skiba et al. 2014; Wallace et al. 2008.

26. Annamma et al. 2019.

27. Snapp et al. 2015; Rosentel et al. 2021; Wozolek, Wootton, and Demlow 2017; Mountz 2020.

28. Snapp et al. 2015, 65.

29. Snapp et al. 2015, 66.

30. Robinson 2020.

31. Rosentel et al. 2021.

32. Pendharkar 2023.

33. Glickman 2016.

34. Morris 2016; Glickman 2016; National Women's Law Center 2018.

35. Painter et al. 2012.

36. Sosnaud 2019.

37. Sentencing Project 2024.

38. Nellis 2021.

39. Sawyer 2019.

40. Wang et al. 2022.

41. Sickmund et al. 2021.

42. Monazzam and Budd 2023.

43. Jones 2021.

44. Hunt and Moodie-Mills 2012.

45. Ben-Moshe 2013.

46. Mendel 2022.

47. Johnston et al. 2016.

48. Saar et al. 2015; Tolou-Shams et al. 2022.

49. Kasdan 2009.

50. Immediately following the *Dobbs* decision, President Joe Biden took steps to maintain abortion access for youth and adults in federal detention, including immigration detention, but as of this writing it is unclear how effective these protections will actually be.

51. Although the use of shackles during labor and delivery is banned in federal detention, these laws do not apply to state and local facilities, where the vast majority of people in the United States are incarcerated.

52. Mendel 2015, 2022.

53. Rudes et al. 2021; Lydon 2015.

54. Sandoval and Arango 2021.

55. Chuck 2021.

56. According to her GoFundMe page, as of October 2023, both of Mercado's children were back in her custody. See "Sing 2 the Children—Eye Am Nature Orphanage," accessed July 5, 2024, https://www.gofundme.com/f/bring-ra-home.

57. D. Roberts 2012, 1492.

58. D. Roberts 2022.

59. D. Roberts 2012, 1500.

60. Kim et al. 2017.

61. Minoff and Citrin 2022

62. D. Roberts 2012.

63. Brico 2020.

64. Naveed 2022.

65. Naveed 2022.

66. Cancian, Youn Yang, and Shook Slack 2010.

67. See D. Roberts 2002, 2022.

68. Ahrens et al. 2010

69. Aparicio et al. 2021; Wallis 2014.

70. Boonstra 2011.

71. Silver 2015.

72. Davis et al. 2022, 51.

73. Kaba 2021, 16.

74. Interrupting Criminalization, Project Nia, and Critical Resistance 2022.

75. Roberts 2022, 11.

76. Mingus 2019.

77. Advocates for Youth 2021a.

78. Flynn 2022.

EPILOGUE

1. Woodard 2023.

REFERENCES

Advocates for Youth. 2021a. "Day 1: The Problem with Police in Schools." YouTube, January 19. https://www.youtube.com/watch?v=VNEKSLB7A6k&list=PLIJ8QY62IB8RskH3wr6srEtji98XdWWYj&index=4.

Advocates for Youth. 2021b. "Mutual Aid for Abortion Access." YouTube, February 4. https://www.youtube.com/watch?v=hYKJVNzKGKQ&t=216s.

Advocates for Youth. 2023. "Abortion Out Loud." Accessed November 14. https://www.advocatesforyouth.org/abortion-out-loud/.

Advocates for Youth. n.d. "About Advocates for Youth." Accessed February 9, 2024. https://www.advocatesforyouth.org/about/.

Advocates for Youth. n.d. "Divesting from Police and Investing in Reproductive and Sexual Health, Rights, and Justice." Accessed June 20, 2024. https://www.advocatesforyouth.org/divesting-from-police-and-investing-in-reproductive-and-sexual-health-and-rights/.

Ahrens, Kym R., Laura P. Richardson, Mark E. Courtney, Carolyn McCarty, Jane Simoni, and Wayne Katon. 2010. "Laboratory-Diagnosed Sexually Transmitted Infections in Former Foster Youth Compared with Peers." *Pediatrics* 126 (1): e97–e103.

Allen, Louisa. 2012. "Pleasure's Perils? Critically Reflecting on Pleasure's Inclusion in Sexuality Education." *Sexualities* 15 (3–4): 455–71.

American Academy of Pediatrics, Committee on Adolescence. 2022. "The Adolescent's Right to Confidential Care When Considering Abortion." *Pediatrics* 150 (3): 1–9.

American Civil Liberties Union. 2021. "Special Report: Chase Strangio on the Legislative Assault on Trans Youth" (33:06). *At Liberty Podcast,* April 7. https://www.aclu.org/podcast/special-report-chase-strangio-legislative-assault-trans-youth-ep-149.

American Medical Association. n.d. "Opinion 2.2.3. Mandatory Parental Consent to Abortion." Accessed June 23, 2023. https://code-medical-ethics.ama-assn.org/ethics-opinions/mandatory-parental-consent-abortion.

American Public Health Association. 2011. "Ensuring Minors' Access to Confidential Abortion Services." APHA, November 1. https://www.apha.org/policies-and-advocacy/public-health-policy-statements/policy-database/2014/07/03/11/14/ensuring-minors-access-to-confidential-abortion-services.

Anderson, Cora Fernández. 2020. *Fighting for Abortion Rights in Latin America: Social Movements, State Allies, and Institutions.* New York: Routledge.

Annamma, Subini Ancy. 2016. "Disrupting the Carceral State through Education Journey Mapping." *International Journal of Qualitative Studies in Education* 29 (9): 1210–30.

Annamma, Subini Ancy. 2018. "Mapping Consequential Geographies in the Carceral State: Education Journey Mapping as a Qualitative Method with Girls of Color with Dis/abilities." *Qualitative Inquiry* 24 (1): 20–34.

Annamma, Subini Ancy, Yolanda Anyon, Nicole M. Joseph, Jordan Farrar, Eldridge Greer, Barbara Downing, and John Simmons. 2019. "Black Girls and School Discipline: The Complexities of Being Overrepresented and Understudied." *Urban Education* 54 (2): 211–42.

Aparicio, Elizabeth M., Olivia N. Kachingwe, John P. Salerno, Melanie Geddings-Hayes, and Bradley O. Boekeloo. 2021. "Addressing Sexual Health among Youth in Foster Care Group Homes: A Community-Engaged Grounded Theory Study." *Sexuality Research and Social Policy* 18 (4): 1136–47.

Apiary for Practical Support. n.d. "About." Accessed June 16, 2024. https://apiaryps.org/about-apiary.

Arrington-Sanders, Renata, Anthony Morgan, Jessica Oidtman, Ian Qian, David Celentano, and Chris Beyrer. 2016. "A Medical Care Missed Opportunity: Preexposure Prophylaxis and Young Black Men Who Have Sex with Men." *Journal of Adolescent Health* 59 (6): 725–28.

Asian Communities for Reproductive Justice. 2005. "A New Vision for Advancing Our Movement for Reproductive Health, Reproductive Rights, and Reproductive Justice." Forward Together. https://forwardtogether.org/tools/a-new-vision/.

Atkins, Danielle N., and W. David Bradford. 2021. "The Effect of State-Level Sex Education Policies on Youth Sexual Behaviors." *Archives of Sexual Behavior* 50 (6): 2321–33.

Barcelos, Chris A. 2020. *Distributing Condoms and Hope: The Racialized Politics of Youth Sexual Health.* Oakland: University of California Press.

Barcelos, Chris. 2022. "Saying 'Pregnant People' Is Even More Critical Post-'Roe.'" *Rewire News* (blog), July 27. https://rewirenewsgroup.com/2022/07/27/saying-pregnant-people-is-even-more-critical-post-roe/.

Barcelos, Chris A., and Aline C. Gubrium. 2014. "Reproducing Stories: Strategic Narratives of Teen Pregnancy and Motherhood." *Social Problems* 61 (3): 466–81.

Barcelos, Chris A., and Aline C. Gubrium. 2018. "Bodies That Tell: Embodying Teen Pregnancy through Digital Storytelling." *Signs: Journal of Women in Culture and Society* 43 (4): 905–27.

Barcelos, Chris, J. Nyla McNeil, Yanté Turner, and Edie Ma'iingan Redwine. 2021. "The Trans Youth Justice Project: A Political Education and Leadership Development Program." *Journal of LGBT Youth* 20 (2): 265–81.

Basile, Monica. 2015. "Reimagining the Birthing Body: Reproductive Justice and New Directions in Doula Care." In *Doulas and Intimate*

Labour: Boundaries, Bodies, and Birth, edited by Angela N. Castañeda and Julie Johnson Searcy. Toronto: Demeter Press.

Beauchamp, Toby. 2013. "Expectations: Trans Youth and Reproductive Politics in Public Space." *Media Fields Journal* 7: 1–9.

Begun, Stephanie, Katie Massey Combs, Kaitlin Schwan, Michaela Torrie, and Kimberly Bender. 2020. "'I Know They Would Kill Me': Abortion Attitudes and Experiences among Youth Experiencing Homelessness." *Youth and Society* 52 (8): 1457–78.

Belis, Noemi. 1994. "Speaking Out for Reproductive Freedom." *The Fight for Reproductive Freedom: A Newsletter for Student and Community Activists* 8 (3): 1–2.

Ben-Moshe, Liat. 2013. "Disabling Incarceration: Connecting Disability to Divergent Confinements in the USA." *Critical Sociology* 39 (3): 385–403.

Ben-Moshe, Liat. 2020. *Decarcerating Disability: Deinstitutionalization and Prison Abolition.* Minneapolis: University of Minnesota Press.

Benfer, Amy. 2008. "What's So Wrong with a Pregnancy Pact?" *Salon*, June 27. https://www.salon.com/2008/06/27/pregnancy_pact_2/.

Bernstein, Elizabeth. 2018. *Brokered Subjects: Sex, Trafficking, and the Politics of Freedom.* Chicago: University of Chicago Press.

Best, Joel. 2007. *Social Problems.* New York: W. W. Norton.

Bitman, Nomy. 2023. "'Which Part of My Group Do I Represent?': Disability Activism and Social Media Users with Concealable Communicative Disabilities." *Information, Communication, and Society* 26 (3): 619–36.

Bonell, Chris. 2004. "Why Is Teenage Pregnancy Conceptualized as a Social Problem? A Review of Quantitative Research from the USA and UK." *Culture, Health, and Sexuality* 6 (3): 255–72.

Boonstra, Heather. 2011. "Teen Pregnancy among Young Women in Foster Care: A Primer." *Guttmacher Policy Review* 14 (2): 8–19.

Boyer, Jesseca. 2018. "New Name, Same Harm: Rebranding of Federal Abstinence-Only Programs." *Guttmacher Policy Review* 21: 11–16.

Bradford, Nova J., James DeWitt, Jilyan Decker, Dianne R. Berg, Katherine G. Spencer, and Michael W. Ross. 2019. "Sex Education and Transgender Youth: 'Trust Means Material by and for Queer and Trans People.'" *Sex Education* 19 (1): 84–98.

Bradshaw, Catherine P., Mary M. Mitchell, Lindsey M. O'Brennan, and Philip J. Leaf. 2010. "Multilevel Exploration of Factors Contributing to the Overrepresentation of Black Students in Office Disciplinary Referrals." *Journal of Educational Psychology* 102 (2): 508.

Braverman, Paula K., William P. Adelman, Elizabeth M. Alderman, Cora C. Breuner, David A. Levine, Arik V. Marcell, and Rebecca O'Brien. 2017. "The Adolescent's Right to Confidential Care When Considering Abortion." *Pediatrics* 139 (2): 1–11.

Brico, Elizabeth. 2020. "'The Civil Death Penalty'—My Motherhood Is Legally Terminated." *Filter,* July 13.

Bridges, Khiara M. 2020. "Race, Pregnancy, and the Opioid Epidemic: White Privilege and the Criminalization of Opioid Use during Pregnancy." *Harvard Law Review* 133 (3): 770–851.

Briggs, Laura. 2017. *How All Politics Became Reproductive Politics: From Welfare Reform to Foreclosure to Trump.* Oakland: University of California Press.

Briggs, Laura. 2020. *Taking Children: A History of American Terror.* Oakland: University of California Press.

Britzman, Deborah P. 2012. "Queer Pedagogy and Its Strange Techniques." In *Sexualities in Education: A Reader,* edited by Erica Meiners and Therese Quinn, 292–308. New York: Peter Lang.

Brockell, Gillian, and Joyce Koh. 2022. "They Had Secret Abortions Pre-*Roe*; Now They Feel Compelled to Speak Out." *Washington Post,* November 1, 2022. https://www.washingtonpost.com/history/interactive/2022/secret-abortions-before-roe-wade/.

Brown, Sherronda J. 2022. "Gender Affirming Care Bans Are Cruel and Hypocritical Violations of Children's Autonomy." *Prism,* November 28. https://prismreports.org/2022/11/28/gender-affirming-care-intersex-trans-children/.

Brown-Long, Cyntoia, and Bethany Mauger. 2019. *Free Cyntoia: My Search for Redemption in the American Prison System.* New York: Atria Books.

Burns, Tara, and Allie Benz. 2022. "Four Years of FOSTA: The Survey." Call Off Your Old Tired Ethics Rhode Island. https://coyoteri.org/wp/wp-content/uploads/2022/09/FourYearsOfFosta.pdf.

Bustillos, Esteban. 2023. "A Worcester School Committee Candidate's Views on Sex Ed Have Rocked the Local Election." *GBH,* updated

August 9. https://www.wgbh.org/news/education-news/2021-10-29/a-worcester-school-committee-candidates-views-on-sex-ed-have-rocked-the-local-election.

Cadena, Micaela, Raquel Z. Rivera, Tannia Esparza, and Denicia Cadena. 2016. *Dismantling Teen Pregnancy Prevention.* Albuquerque: Young Women United.

California Department of Education. 2023. "Comprehensive Sexual Health and HIV/AIDS Instruction." Reviewed October 27. https://www.cde.ca.gov/ls/he/se/.

Cammarota, Julio, and Michelle Fine. 2010. "Youth Participatory Action Research: A Pedagogy for Transformational Resistance." In *Revolutionizing Education,* edited by Julio Cammarota and Michelle Fine, 9–20. New York: Routledge.

Cancian, Maria, Mi-Youn Yang, and Kristen Shook Slack. 2013. "The Effect of Additional Child Support Income on the Risk of Child Maltreatment." *Social Service Review* 87 (3): 417–37.

Candie's Foundation. 2015. "Mission." Accessed February 24, 2016. www.candiesfoundation.org/aboutUs_Mission.

cárdenas, micha. 2016. "Pregnancy: Reproductive Futures in Trans of Color Feminism." *Transgender Studies Quarterly* 3 (1–2): 48–57.

CIRCLE: Center for Information and Research on Civic Learning and Engagement. 2022. "Major National Issues like Abortion May Spur Youth Mobilization." Tufts University, Tisch College, June 28. https://circle.tufts.edu/latest-research/major-national-issues-abortion-may-spur-youth-mobilization.

Centers for Disease Control and Prevention. 2013. *Sexually Transmitted Disease Surveillance 2012.* Atlanta: US Department of Health and Human Services.

Centers for Disease Control and Prevention. 2016. "Results from the School Health Policies and Practices Study." https://www.cdc.gov/healthyyouth/data/shpps/index.htm.

Centers for Disease Control and Prevention, Division of Reproductive Health. 2021. "About Teen Pregnancy." Accessed February 23, 2023. https://www.cdc.gov/teenpregnancy/about/index.htm.

Chang, Alisa, Jonaki Mehta, and Justine Kenin. 2022. "What the U.S. Can Learn from Abortion Rights Wins in Latin America."

NPR, July 7. https://www.npr.org/2022/07/07/1110123695/abortion-roe-latin-america-green-wave.

Charlton, Brittany M., Andrea L. Roberts, Margaret Rosario, Sabra L. Katz-Wise, Jerel P. Calzo, Donna Spiegelman, and S. Bryn Austin. 2018. "Teen Pregnancy Risk Factors among Young Women of Diverse Sexual Orientations." *Pediatrics* 141 (4): e20172278.

Chavez-Garcia, Miroslava 2012. *States of Delinquency: Race and Science in the Making of California's Juvenile Justice System.* Oakland: University of California Press.

Chen, Diane, Lisa Simons, Emilie K. Johnson, Barbara A. Lockart, and Courtney Finlayson. 2017. "Fertility Preservation for Transgender Adolescents." *Journal of Adolescent Health* 61 (1): 120–23.

Chicago Women's Health Center. 2021. "10 Ways Sex Education Can and Should Be Abolitionist." In *Lessons in Liberation: An Abolitionist Toolkit for Educators,* edited by Education for Resistance Network and Critical Resistance Editorial Collective, 202–10. Chico, CA: AK Press.

Chodzen, Gia, Marco A. Hidalgo, Diane Chen, and Robert Garofalo. 2019. "Minority Stress Factors Associated with Depression and Anxiety among Transgender and Gender-Nonconforming Youth." *Journal of Adolescent Health* 64 (4): 467–71.

Chuck, Elizabeth. 2021. "Authorities Take Second Child from 'American Idol' Contestant, Prompting Outrage." *NBC News,* August 13. https://www.nbcnews.com/news/us-news/authorities-take-2nd-child-american-idol-contestant-prompting-outrage-n1276796.

Clark, Beth A., and Alice Virani. 2021. "'This Wasn't a Split-Second Decision': An Empirical Ethical Analysis of Transgender Youth Capacity, Rights, and Authority to Consent to Hormone Therapy." *Journal of Bioethical Inquiry* 18 (1): 151–64.

Cohen, Cathy J. 1997. "Punks, Bulldaggers, and Welfare Queens: The Radical Potential of Queer Politics?" *GLQ: A Journal of Lesbian and Gay Studies* 3 (4): 437–65.

Cohen, Stephan L. 2008. *The Gay Liberation Youth Movement in New York: "An Army of Lovers Cannot Fail."* New York: Routledge.

Coleman-Minahan, Kate. 2021. "Judicial Bypass Attorneys' Experiences with Abortion Stigma in Texas Courts." *Social Science and Medicine* 269, article 113508.

Coleman-Minahan, Kate, Amanda Jean Stevenson, Emily Obront, and Susan Hays. 2019. "Young Women's Experiences Obtaining Judicial Bypass for Abortion in Texas." *Journal of Adolescent Health* 64 (1): 20–25.

Collective Power for Reproductive Justice. 2014. "CLPP Conference 2014: Morgan Robyn Collado." YouTube, posted May 13. https://www.youtube.com/watch?v=66g_lR-I9AY.

Collins, Patricia Hill. 2008. *Black Feminist Thought: Knowledge, Consciousness, and the Politics of Empowerment*. New York: Routledge.

Combahee River Collective. 2000. "The Combahee River Collective Statement." In *Home Girls: A Black Feminist Anthology*, edited by Barbara Smith, 264–74. New Brunswick, NJ: Rutgers University Press.

Coren, Esther, Jane Barlow, and Sarah Stewart-Brown. 2003. "The Effectiveness of Individual and Group-Based Parenting Programmes in Improving Outcomes for Teenage Mothers and Their Children: A Systematic Review." *Journal of Adolescence* 26 (1): 79–103.

Crabtree, Sadie. 2002. "Finding Common Ground between Movements for Reproductive Freedom and Transgender/Transsexual Liberation." *The Fight for Reproductive Freedom: A Newsletter for Student and Community Activists* 16 (3): 9–11.

Craig, Shelley L., Lauren B. McInroy, Lance T. McCready, Dane Marco Di Cesare, and Lincoln D. Pettaway. 2015. "Connecting without Fear: Clinical Implications of the Consumption of Information and Communication Technologies by Sexual Minority Youth and Young Adults." *Clinical Social Work Journal* 43 (2): 159–68.

Crews, Allison. n.d. "Girlmom: We Are Young/Teen Moms and Pro-Choice." Pro Choice Education Project. Accessed October 31, 2023. https://www.protectchoice.org/article.php?id=127&printsafe=1.

Critical Resistance. n.d. "Political Education Overview." Accessed April 20, 2023. https://criticalresistance.org/popular-education-overview/.

Critical Resistance. n.d. "What Is the PIC? What Is Abolition?" Accessed April 20, 2023. https://criticalresistance.org/mission-vision/not-so-common-language/.

Ellis, Dale. 2023. "Federal Judge Strikes Down Arkansas' Gender-Affirming Health Care Ban as Unconstitutional." *Arkansas Demo-*

crat-Gazette (Little Rock), June 20. /news/2023/jun/20/judge-blocks-arkansas-ban-on-gender-affirming-care-for-transgender-minors/.

Daniel, Clare. 2017. *Mediating Morality: The Politics of Teen Pregnancy in the Post-welfare Era.* Amherst: University of Massachusetts Press.

Davis, Angela Y. 2016. *Freedom Is a Constant Struggle.* Chicago: Haymarket Books.

Davis, Angela Y., Gina Dent, Erica R. Meiners, and Beth E. Richie. 2022. *Abolition. Feminism. Now.* Chicago: Haymarket Books.

De Vries, Annelou L. C., Jenifer K. McGuire, Thomas D. Steensma, Eva C. F. Wagenaar, Theo A. H. Doreleijers, and Peggy T. Cohen-Kettenis. 2014. "Young Adult Psychological Outcome after Puberty Suppression and Gender Reassignment." *Pediatrics* 134 (4): 696–704.

DeJong, Keri, and Barbara J. Love. 2015. "Youth Oppression as a Technology of Colonialism: Conceptual Frameworks and Possibilities for Social Justice Education Praxis." *Equity and Excellence in Education* 48 (3): 489–508.

Dennis, Amanda, Stanley K. Henshaw, Theodore J. Joyce, Lawrence B. Finer, and Kelly Blanchard. 2009. *The Impact of Laws Requiring Parental Involvement for Abortion: A Literature Review.* Guttmacher Institute, March. https://www.guttmacher.org/report/impact-laws-requiring-parental-involvement-abortion-literature-review.

Duberman, Martin. 1994. *Stonewall.* New York: Plume.

Dugyala, Rishika. 2021. "Looking behind the Wave of Anti-trans Bills." *Politico,* July 16. https://www.politico.com/newsletters/the-recast/2021/07/16/imara-jones-anti-trans-bills-ideology-493614.

Duroseau, Nathalie, Miranda Loh, Leslie Sanders, and Martha Arden. 2021. "Options for Teens with No Options: A Self-Managed Second Trimester Abortion." *Journal of Pediatric and Adolescent Gynecology* 34 (2): 226–27.

Dylan, Rodríguez. 2010. "The Disorientation of the Teaching Act: Abolition as Pedagogical Position." *Radical Teacher* (88): 7–19.

Earl, Jennifer, Thomas V. Maher, and Thomas Elliott. 2017. "Youth, Activism, and Social Movements." *Sociology Compass* 11 (4): e12465.

Ehrlich, J. Shoshanna. 2003a. "Choosing Abortion: Teens Who Make the Decision without Parental Involvement." *Gender Issues* 21 (2): 3–39.

Ehrlich, J. Shoshanna. 2003b. "Grounded in the Reality of their Lives: Listening to Teens Who Make the Abortion Decision without Involving Their Parents." *Berkeley Women's Law Journal* 18: 61–180.

Eisenstein, Zach. 2019. "Introducing Sex Ed for All Month!" SIECUS: Sex Ed for All. https://siecus.org/siecus-observes-first-ever-sexed-for-all-month/.

Ellison, Treva, Kai M. Green, Matt Richardson, and C. Riley Snorton. 2017. "We Got Issues: Toward a Black Trans*/Studies." *TSQ: Transgender Studies Quarterly* 4 (2): 162–69.

Ely, Gretchen E., Travis Hales, D. Lynn Jackson, Eugene Maguin, and Greer Hamilton. 2017. "The Undue Burden of Paying for Abortion: An Exploration of Abortion Fund Cases." *Social Work in Health Care* 56 (2): 99–114.

Ely, Gretchen E., Travis W. Hales, D. Lynn Jackson, Jenni Kotting, and Kafuli Agbemenu. 2018. "Access to Choice: Examining Differences between Adolescent and Adult Abortion Fund Service Recipients." *Health and Social Care in the Community* 26 (5): 695–704.

Engle, Olivia, and Cordelia Freeman. 2023. "'All This Way, All This Money, for a Five-Minute Procedure': Barriers, Mobilities, and Representation on the US Abortion Road Trip." *Mobilities* 18, no. 2: 297–311.

Epstein, Steven. 2022. *The Quest for Sexual Health: How an Elusive Ideal Has Transformed Science, Politics, and Everyday Life*. Chicago: University of Chicago Press.

Epstein, Steven, and Laura Mamo. 2017. "The Proliferation of Sexual Health: Diverse Social Problems and the Legitimation of Sexuality." *Social Science and Medicine* 188: 176–90.

Eskamani, Anna. 2023. "Florida Judges Have the Power to Force Young People to Give Birth." *The Nation*, March 8, 2023.

Feinberg, Robbie. 2023. "Maine Expands Ability of Older Teens to Receive Gender-Affirming Care without Parents' Consent." WBUR, July 13. https://www.wbur.org/news/2023/07/13/teens-gender-affirming-care-parental-consent.

Ferguson, Roderick A. 2018. *One-Dimensional Queer*. New York: John Wiley & Sons.

Fields, Jessica. 2008. *Risky Lessons: Sex Education and Social Inequality.* New Brunswick, NJ: Rutgers University Press.

Fields, Jessica, and Martha Copp. 2015. "Striving for Empathy: Affinities, Alliances, and Peer Sexuality Educators." *Sex Education* 15 (2): 188–203.

Fields, Jessica, Jen Gilbert, and Michelle Miller. 2015. "Sexuality and Education: Toward the Promise of Ambiguity." In *Handbook of the Sociology of Sexualities*, edited by John DeLamater and Rebecca F. Plante, 371–87. Cham, Switzerland: Springer.

Fine, Michelle. 2014. "An Intimate Memoir of Resistance Theory." In *Youth Resistance Research and Theories of Change*, edited by Eve Tuck and K. Wayne Yang, 46–58. New York: Routledge.

Flavin, Jeanne. 2010. *Our Bodies, Our Crimes: The Policing of Women's Reproduction in America.* New York: New York University Press.

Flavin, Jeanne, and Lynn M. Paltrow. 2010. "Punishing Drug-Using Women: Defying Law, Medicine, and Common Sense." *Journal of Addictive Diseases* 29: 231–44.

Flynn, Shelia. 2022. "NYPD Blasted for Bragging Post about Arrests of People for Stealing Diapers and Medicine: 'This Is Not Public Safety.'" *The Independent.* https://www.independent.co.uk/news/world/americas/crime/nypd-twitter-seizure-diapers-medicine-b2017663.html.

Forward Together. 2012. *Let's Get It On: Oakland's Vision for Sex Ed.* Oakland, CA.

Fowler, Leah R., Lauren Schoen, and Stephanie R. Morain. 2021. "Let's Tok about Sex." *Journal of Adolescent Health* 69 (5): 687–88.

Fowler, Leah R., Lauren Schoen, Hadley Stevens Smith, and Stephanie R. Morain. 2021. "Sex Education on TikTok: A Content Analysis of Themes." *Health Promotion Practice* 23 (5): 739–42.

Franco, Mariel. 2012. *Supporting Latina/o Youth: Strengthening Latina/o Young Families and Communities; Justice for Young Families!* Issue Brief 1. Los Angeles: California Latinas for Reproductive Justice.

Freedom Inc. 2017. "About Freedom Inc.—Freedom, Inc." Accessed December 21. https://freedom-inc.org/index.php?page=about-us.

Frunel, L., and Sarah H. Lorr. 2022. "Lived Experience and Disability Justice in the Family Regulation System." *Columbia Journal of Race and Law* 12 (1): 477–95.

Future of Sex Education Initiative. 2020. "National Sex Education Standards: Core Content and Skills, K–12." 2nd edition. SIECUS. https://siecus.org/resources/national-sex-ed-standards-second-edition/.

García, Lorena. 2009. "'Now Why Do You Want to Know about That?' Heteronormativity, Sexism, and Racism in the Sexual (Mis) Education of Latina Youth." *Gender & Society* 23 (4): 520–41.

García, Lorena, and Jessica Fields. 2017. "Renewed Commitments in a Time of Vigilance: Sexuality Education in the USA." *Sex Education* 17 (4): 471–81.

Geronimus, Arline T. 1993. "Maternal Youth or Family Background? On the Health Disadvantages of Infants with Teenage Mothers." *American Journal of Epidemiology* 137 (2): 213–25.

Geronimus, Arline T. 1996. "What Teen Mothers Know." *Human Nature* 7 (4): 323–52.

Geronimus, Arline T. 2003. "Damned If You Do: Culture, Identity, Privilege, and Teenage Childbearing in the United States." *Social Science and Medicine* 57 (5): 881–93.

Geronimus, Arline T., and Sanders Korenman. 1992. "The Socioeconomic Consequences of Teen Childbearing Reconsidered." *Quarterly Journal of Economics* 107 (4): 1187–1214.

Gilbert, Jen. 2010. "Ambivalence Only? Sex Education in the Age of Abstinence." *Sex Education* 10 (3): 233–37.

Gill, Michael. 2021. *Already Doing It: Intellectual Disability and Sexual Agency*. Minneapolis: University of Minnesota Press.

Gilliam, Melissa. 2020. "Youth Reproductive Justice: Beyond Choice, toward Health Equity." *Health Education and Behavior* 47 (4): 640–41.

Gill-Peterson, Jules. 2018. *Histories of the Transgender Child*. Minneapolis: University of Minnesota Press.

Ginwright, Shawn, Pedro Noguera, and Julio Cammarota. 2006. *Beyond Resistance! Youth Activism and Community Change; New Democratic Possibilities for Practice and Policy for America's Youth*. New York: Routledge.

Glickman, Deanna J. 2016. "Fashioning Children: Gender Restrictive Dress Codes as an Entry Point for the Trans School to Prison Pipeline." *American University Journal of Gender, Social Policy, and the Law* 24 (2): 263–84.

Glosser, Asaph, Karen Gardiner, and Mike Fishman. 2004. "Statutory Rape: A Guide to State Laws and Reporting Requirements." Office of the Assistant Secretary for Planning and Evaluation, US Department of Health and Human Services, December 15. https://aspe.hhs.gov /reports/statutory-rape-guide-state-laws-reporting-requirements-1.

Glover, Julian Kevon. 2016. "Redefining Realness? On Janet Mock, Laverne Cox, TS Madison, and the Representation of Transgender Women of Color in Media." *Souls* 18 (2–4): 338–57.

Gluckman, Ryn, and Mina Trudeau. 2002. "Trans-itioning Feminism: The Politics of Transgender in the Reproductive Rights Movement." *Fight for Reproductive Freedom: A Newsletter for Student and Community Activists* 16 (3): 6–8.

Goldberg, Shoshana K., Bianka M Reese, and Carolyn T Halpern. 2016. "Teen Pregnancy among Sexual Minority Women: Results from the National Longitudinal Study of Adolescent to Adult Health." *Journal of Adolescent Health* 59 (4): 429–37.

Goldberg, Susan. 2017. "Why We Put a Transgender Girl on the Cover of *National Geographic.*" *National Geographic.* Accessed July 25, 2024. https://www.nationalgeographic.com/magazine/article/editors-note-gender.

Goldfarb, Eva S., and Lisa D. Lieberman. 2021. "Three Decades of Research: The Case for Comprehensive Sex Education." *Journal of Adolescent Health* 68 (1): 13–27.

Goldman, Margaret, and Nancy Rodriguez. 2022. "Juvenile Court in the School-Prison Nexus: Youth Punishment, Schooling, and Structures of Inequality." *Journal of Crime and Justice* 45 (3): 270–84.

Goodwin, Michele. 2017. "How the Criminalization of Pregnancy Robs Women of Reproductive Autonomy." *Hastings Center Report* 47 (S3): S19–S27.

Gordon, Hava R. 2009. *We Fight to Win: Inequality and the Politics of Youth Activism.* New Brunswick, NJ: Rutgers University Press.

Gossett, Reina, Eric A. Stanley, and Johanna Burton. 2017. "Known Unknowns: An Introduction to Trap Door." In *Trap Door: Trans Cultural Production and the Politics of Visibility,* edited by Reina Gossett,

Eric A. Stanley, and Johanna Burton, xv–xxvi. Cambridge, MA: MIT Press.

Gowen, L. Kris, and Nichole Winges-Yanez. 2014. "Lesbian, Gay, Bisexual, Transgender, Queer, and Questioning Youths' Perspectives of Inclusive School-Based Sexuality Education." *Journal of Sex Research* 51 (7): 788–800.

Greyson, Devon, Cathy Chabot, and Jean A. Shoveller. 2019. "Young Parents' Experiences and Perceptions of 'Teen Mom' Reality Shows." *Journal of Youth Studies* 22 (8): 1150–65.

Gridley, Samantha J., Julia M. Crouch, Yolanda Evans, Whitney Eng, Emily Antoon, Melissa Lyapustina, Allison Schimmel-Bristow, Jake Woodward, Kelly Dundon, and RaNette Schaff. 2016. "Youth and Caregiver Perspectives on Barriers to Gender-Affirming Health Care for Transgender Youth." *Journal of Adolescent Health* 59 (3): 254–61.

Grose, Jessica. 2021. "Abortion Rights Activists Are on TikTok." *New York Times*, updated September 3. https://www.nytimes.com/2020/12/10/style/abortion-rights-activists-tiktok.html.

Guarino, Ben. 2016. "Applause, Anger Greet Transgender Girl on January Cover of National Geographic." *Washington Post*, December 19. https://link.gale.com/apps/doc/A474426092/AONE?u=mlin_b_umass&sid=bookmark-AONE&xid=c7014b67.

Gubrium, Aline C., Elizabeth L. Krause, and Kasey Jernigan. 2014. "Strategic Authenticity and Voice: New Ways of Seeing and Being Seen as Young Mothers through Digital Storytelling." *Sexuality Research and Social Policy* 11: 337–47.

Guglielmo, Letizia. 2013. *MTV and Teen Pregnancy: Critical Essays on 16 and Pregnant and Teen Mom*. Lanham, MD: Rowman & Littlefield.

Gunaratna, Shanika. 2013. "Pregnant Boys? New Transit Ads Spark Dialogue." *WTTW News*, May 29. https://news.wttw.com/2013/05/29/pregnant-boys-new-transit-ads-spark-dialogue.

Gupta, Sarita. 1994. "Women of Color and Reproductive Rights." *The Fight for Reproductive Freedom: A Newsletter for Student and Community Activists* 9 (1): 1, 3, 6.

Guttmacher Institute. 2023a. "An Overview of Consent to Reproductive Health Services by Young People." Guttmacher, August 30.

https://www.guttmacher.org/state-policy/explore/overview-minors-consent-law.

Guttmacher Institute. 2023b. "Sex and HIV Education." Accessed December 22. https://www.guttmacher.org/state-policy/explore/sex-and-hiv-education.

Gutiérrez, Ramón A. 2011. "Afterword: Virtual Sex Ed." *Sexuality Research and Social Policy* 8 (1): 73–76.

Hamilton, Brady E., Joyce A. Martin, and Michelle J. K. Osterman. 2022. "Births: Preliminary Data for 2021." Hyattsville, MD: National Center for Health Statistics.

Hardin, Amy Peykoff, Jesse M. Hackell, Geoffrey R. Simon, Alexy Darlyn Arauz Boudreau, Cynthia N. Baker, Graham Arthur Barden, III, Kelley E. Meade, Scot Benton Moore, and Julia Richerson. 2017. "Age Limit of Pediatrics." *Pediatrics* 140 (3).

Harris, Rachel. 2021. "Green Scarves and Data Harvesting: How the Abortion Battle Has Gone Digital." *Harvard International Review* 42 (2): 29–33.

Hasselbacher Lee, A. Subini Deklevamma Anna, Sigrid Tristan, and Melissa Gilliam. 2014. "Factors Influencing Parental Involvement among Minors Seeking an Abortion: A Qualitative Study." *American Journal of Public Health* 104 (11): 2207–11.

Healthy and Free Tennessee. n.d. "Mission, Vision, and Values." Accessed November 10, 2023. https://www.healthyandfreetn.org/mission_vision_values.

Henshaw, Stanley K., and Kathryn Kost. 1992. "Parental Involvement in Minors' Abortion Decisions." *Family Planning Perspectives* 24 (5): 196–213.

Hilliard, David. 2022. "Protesters Target Children's Hospital as Hundreds Rally to Defend It." *Boston Globe*, September 18. https://www.bostonglobe.com/2022/09/18/metro/counterprotesters-gather-outside-childrens-hospital-anticipation-right-wing-demonstration/.

Hillier, Amy, Kel Kroehle, Hazel Edwards, and Giana Graves. 2020. "Risk, Resilience, Resistance, and Situated Agency of Trans High School Students." *Journal of LGBT Youth* 17 (4): 384–407.

Holloway, Kali. 2023. "Solidarity between BLM and Palestine Has Deep Roots." *The Nation,* October 30, 2023. https://www.thenation.com/article/society/black-lives-matter-israel-palestine/.

Hong, Grace Kyungwon, and Roderick A. Ferguson. 2011. "Introduction." *In Strange Affinities: The Gender and Sexual Politics of Comparative Racialization,* edited by Grace Kyungwon Hong and Roderick A. Ferguson, 1–22. Durham, NC: Duke University Press.

Hotz, V. Joseph, Susan Williams McElroy, and Seth G. Sanders. 2005. "Teenage Childbearing and Its Life Cycle Consequences: Exploiting a Natural Experiment." *Journal of Human Resources* 40 (3): 683–715.

Howell, Marcela. 2007. *The History of Federal Abstinence-Only Funding.* Washington, DC: Advocates for Youth.

Howell, Marcela, Jessica Pinckney, and Lexie White. 2020. *Black Youth Deserve Comprehensive Approaches to Sexual Health Education.* Washington, DC: In Our Own Voice: National Black Women's Reproductive Justice Agenda.

Hunt, Jerome, and Aisha C. Moodie-Mills. 2012. "The Unfair Criminalization of Gay and Transgender Youth." Center for American Progress (Washington, DC), June 29. https://www.americanprogress.org/article/the-unfair-criminalization-of-gay-and-transgender-youth/.

Huss, Laura. 2022. "Self-Managed Abortion Is Not Illegal in Most of the Country, but Criminalization Happens Anyway." If/When/How: Lawyering for Reproductive Justice, August 1. https://www.ifwhenhow.org/abortion-criminalization-new-research/.

Ikuta, Emily. 2016. "Overcoming the Parental Veto: How Transgender Adolescents Can Access Puberty-Suppressing Hormone Treatment in the Absence of Parental Consent under the Mature Minor Doctrine." *Southern California Interdisciplinary Law Journal* 25 (1): 179–228.

Interrupting Criminalization, Project Nia, and Critical Resistance. 2022. So Is This Actually an Abolitionist Proposal or Strategy? A Collection of Resources to Aid in Evaluation and Reflection. Interrupting Criminalization, June 30. https://criticalresistance.org/resources/actually-an-abolitionist-strategy-binder/.

Jackson, Sarah J., Moya Bailey, and Brooke Foucault Welles. 2020. *#HashtagActivism: Networks of Race and Gender Justice*. Cambridge, MA: MIT Press.

James, Sandy E., Jdoy L. Herman, Susan Rankin, Mara Keisling, Lisa Mottet, and Ma'ayan Anafi. 2016. *The Report of the 2015 U.S. Transgender Survey*. Washington, DC: National Center for Trans Equality.

Janiak, Elizabeth, Isabel R. Fulcher, Alischer A. Cottrill, Nicole Tantoco, Ashley H. Mason, Jennifer Fortin, Jamie Sabino, and Alisa B. Goldberg. 2019. "Massachusetts' Parental Consent Law and Procedural Timing among Adolescents Undergoing Abortion." *Obstetrics and Gynecology* 133 (5): 978–86.

Jarman, Michelle. 2015. "Relations of Abortion: Crip Approaches to Reproductive Justice." *Feminist Formations* 27 (1): 46–66.

Jenkins, Henry, Sangita Shresthova, Liana Gamber-Thompson, Neta Kligler-Vilenchik, and Arely Zimmerman. 2016. *By Any Media Necessary: The New Youth Activism*. New York: New York University Press.

Johns, Michelle M., Richard Lowry, Jack Andrzejewski, Lisa C. Barrios, Zewditu Demissie, Timothy McManus, Catherine N. Rasberry, Leah Robin, and J. Michael Underwood. 2019. "Transgender Identity and Experiences of Violence Victimization, Substance Use, Suicide Risk, and Sexual Risk Behaviors among High School Students—19 States and Large Urban School Districts, 2017." *Morbidity and Mortality Weekly Report* 68 (3): 67–71.

Johnston, Emily E., Bianca R. Argueza, Caroline Graham, Janine S. Bruce, Lisa J. Chamberlain, and Arash Anoshiravani. 2016. "In Their Own Voices: The Reproductive Health Care Experiences of Detained Adolescent Girls." *Women's Health Issues* 26 (1): 48–54.

Johnston, Jessica. 2017. "Subscribing to Sex Edutainment." *Television and New Media* 18 (1): 76–92.

Jones, Alexi. 2021. Visualizing the Unequal Treatment of LGBTQ People in the Criminal Justice System. Prison Policy Initiative (Northampton, MA), March 2. https://www.prisonpolicy.org/blog/2021/03/02/lgbtq/.

Joyce, Theodore J., Robert Kaestner, and Jason Ward. 2020. "The Impact of Parental Involvement Laws on the Abortion Rate of Minors." *Demography* 57 (1): 323–46.

Kaba, Mariame. 2021. *We Do This 'til We Free Us: Abolitionist Organizing and Transforming Justice.* Chicago: Haymarket Press

Kaba, Mariame, and Brit Schulte. 2021. "Not a Cardboard Cutout: Cyntoia Brown and the Framing of a Victim." In *We Do This 'Til We Free Us: Abolitionist Organizing and Transforming Justice,* edited by Mariame Kaba, 35–40. Chicago: Haymarket Books.

Kafer, Alison. 2013. *Feminist Queer Crip.* Bloomington: Indiana University Press.

Kaplan, Elaine Bell. 1997. *Not Our Kind of Girl: Unraveling the Myths of Black Teenage Motherhood.* Oakland: University of California Press.

Kasdan, Diana. 2009. "Abortion Access for Incarcerated Women: Are Correctional Health Practices in Conflict with Constitutional Standards?" *Perspectives on Sexual and Reproductive Health* 41 (1): 59–62.

Kavanagh, Erin K., Lee A. Hasselbacher, Brittany Betham, Sigrid Tristan, and Melissa L. Gilliam. 2012. "Abortion-Seeking Minors' Views on the Illinois Parental Notification Law: A Qualitative Study." *Perspectives on Sexual and Reproductive Health* 44 (3): 159–66.

Kearney, Melissa S., and Philip B. Levine. 2015. "Media Influences on Social Outcomes: The Impact of MTV's 16 and Pregnant on Teen Childbearing." *American Economic Review* 105 (12): 3597–632.

Kiema, Kinjo, and Samantha Daley. 2021. "Divesting from School Policing and Investing in Comprehensive Sex Education: A Campaign Toolkit for Activists." Advocates For Youth and Power U Center for Social Change. https://www.advocatesforyouth.org /resources/policy-advocacy/divest-from-police-and-invest-in-sex-ed-toolkit/.

Kim, Hyunil, Christopher Wildeman, Melissa Jonson-Reid, and Brett Drake. 2017. "Lifetime Prevalence of Investigating Child Maltreatment among US Children." *American Journal of Public Health* 107 (2): 274–80.

Kim, Jina B. 2021. "Cripping the Welfare Queen: The Radical Potential of Disability Politics." *Social Text* 39 (3 [148]): 79–101.

Kingsbury, Kathleen. 2008. "Pregnancy Boom at Gloucester High." *Time* Magazine, June 18.

Kirby, Douglas B. 2001. "Emerging Answers: Research Findings on Programs to Reduce Teen Pregnancy (Summary)." *American Journal of Health Education* 32 (6): 348–55.

Kirby, Douglas B., Ba A. Laris, and Lori A. Rolleri. 2007. "Sex and HIV Education Programs: Their Impact on Sexual Behaviors of Young People throughout the World." *Journal of Adolescent Health* 40 (3): 206–17.

Klein, Jonathan D., and Committee on Adolescence. 2005. "Adolescent Pregnancy: Current Trends and Issues." *Pediatrics* 116 (1): 281–86.

Kosciw, Joseph G., Caitlin M. Clark, Nhan L. Truong, and Adrian D. Zongrone. 2020. *The 2019 National School Climate Survey: The Experiences of Lesbian, Gay, Bisexual, Transgender, and Queer Youth in Our Nation's Schools.* New York: GLSEN. https://www.glsen.org/sites/default/files/2021-04/NSCS19-FullReport-032421-Web_0.pdf.

Kozhimannil, Katy B., Laura B. Attanasio, Judy Jou, Lauren K. Joarnt, Pamela J. Johnson, and Dwenda K. Gjerdingen. 2014. "Potential Benefits of Increased Access to Doula Support during Childbirth." *American Journal of Managed Care* 20 (8): e340.

Krueger-Henney, Patricia, and Jessica Ruglis. 2020. "PAR Is a Way of Life: Participatory Action Research as Core Re-training for Fugitive Research Praxis." *Educational Philosophy and Theory* 52 (9): 961–72.

Kuper, Laura E., Sunita Stewart, Stephanie Preston, May Lau, and Ximena Lopez. 2020. "Body Dissatisfaction and Mental Health Outcomes of Youth on Gender-Affirming Hormone Therapy." *Pediatrics* 145 (4): e20193006.

Kwon, Soo Ah. 2013. *Uncivil Youth: Race, Activism, and Affirmative Governmentality.* Durham, NC: Duke University Press.

Lagos, Danya. 2022. "Has There Been a Transgender Tipping Point? Gender Identification Differences in U.S. Cohorts Born between 1935 and 2001." *American Journal of Sociology* 128 (1): 94–143.

Lamb, Sharon, Kara Lustig, and Kelly Graling. 2013. "The Use and Misuse of Pleasure in Sex Education Curricula." *Sex Education* 13 (3): 305–18.

Lamb, Sharon, Kelly Graling, and Kara Lustig. 2011. "Stereotypes in Four Current AOUM Sexuality Education Curricula: Good Girls, Good Boys, and the New Gender Equality." *American Journal of Sexuality Education* 6 (4): 360–80.

Lesko, Nancy. 2012. *Act Your Age! A Cultural Construction of Adolescence*. 2nd edition. New York: Routledge.

Lewis, Rachel Charlene. 2023. "On TikTok, Teens Teach Us to Mock Pro-lifers." *Bitch Media*. Accessed February 3, 2023. https://www.bitchmedia.org/article/very-online/teens-on-tiktok-change-abortion-culture.

Li, Hanlin, Disha Bora, Sagar Salvi, and Erin Brady. 2018. "Slacktivists or Activists? Identity Work in the Virtual Disability March." *Proceedings of the 2018 CHI Conference on Human Factors in Computing Systems*. New York: Association for Computing Machinery.

Lincoln, Richard, Frederick S. Jaffe, and Linda Ambrose. 1976. *11 Million Teenagers: What Can Be Done about the Epidemic of Adolescent Pregnancies in the United States*. New York: Guttmacher Institute.

Lindberg, Laura D., and Leslie M. Kantor. 2022. "Adolescents' Receipt of Sex Education in a Nationally Representative Sample, 2011–2019." *Journal of Adolescent Health* 70 (2): 290–97.

Lira, Natalie. 2021. *Laboratory of Deficiency: Sterilization and Confinement in California, 1900–1950s*. Oakland: University of California Press.

López, Ian Haney. 2014. *Dog Whistle Politics: How Coded Racial Appeals Have Reinvented Racism and Wrecked the Middle Class*. New York: Oxford University Press.

Lord, Alexandra M. 2009. *Condom Nation: The U.S. Government's Sex Education Campaign from World War I to the Internet*. Baltimore: Johns Hopkins University Press.

Lorde, Audre. 1984. *Sister Outsider: Essays and Speeches*. Berkeley, CA: Crossing Press.

Lovelock, Michael. 2017. "'I Am …': Caitlyn Jenner, Jazz Jennings, and the Cultural Politics of Transgender Celebrity." *Feminist Media Studies* 17 (5): 737–54.

Lubiano, Wahneema. 1992. "Black Ladies, Welfare Queens, and State Minstrels: Ideological War by Narrative Means." In *Race-ing Justice,*

En-gendering Power: Essays on Anita Hill, Clarence Thomas, and the Construction of Social Reality, edited by Toni Morrison, 323–63. New York: Pantheon.

Luker, Kristin. 2007. *When Sex Goes to School: Warring Views on Sex—and Sex Education—since the Sixties.* New York: W. W. Norton.

Luna, Zakiya. 2020. *Reproductive Rights as Human Rights: Women of Color and the Fight for Reproductive Justice.* New York: New York University Press.

Lupton, Deborah. 2015. "The Pedagogy of Disgust: The Ethical, Moral, and Political Implications of Using Disgust in Public Health Campaigns." *Critical Public Health* 25 (1): 4–14.

Luttrell, Wendy. 2014. *Pregnant Bodies, Fertile Minds: Gender, Race, and the Schooling of Pregnant Teens.* New York: Routledge.

Lydon, Jason. 2015. *Coming Out of Concrete Closets: A Report on Black and Pink's National LGBTQ Prisoner Survey.* Black & Pink, October. https://www.blackandpink.org.

Maddow-Zimet, and Kathryn Kost. 2021. "Pregnancies, Births, and Abortions in the United States, 1973–2017: National and State Trends by Age." Guttmacher Institute. https://www.guttmacher.org/report /pregnancies-births-abortions-in-united-states-1973-2017.

Mandler, C. 2024. "What Happened to Nex Benedict?" NPR, updated March 22. https://www.npr.org/2024/03/15/1238780699/nex-benedict-nonbinary-oklahoma-death-bullying.

Maher, Thomas V., and Jennifer Earl. 2017. "Pathways to Contemporary Youth Protest: The Continuing Relevance of Family, Friends, and School for Youth Micromobilization." In *Social Movements and Media,* edited by Jennifer Earl and Deana A. Rohlinger, 55–87. Bingley, UK: Emerald.

Mahoney, Mary, and Lauren Mitchell. 2016. *The Doulas: Radical Care for Pregnant People.* New York: Feminist Press.

Manalansan, Martin F. 2018. "Messing Up Sex: The Promises and Possibilities of Queer of Color Critique." *Sexualities* 21 (8): 1287–90.

Mananzala, Rickke, and Dean Spade. 2008. "The Nonprofit Industrial Complex and Trans Resistance." *Sexuality Research and Social Policy* 5 (1): 53–71.

Manduley, Aida E., Andrea Mertens, Iradele Plante, and Anjum Sultana. 2018. "The Role of Social Media in Sex Education: Dispatches from Queer, Trans, and Racialized Communities." *Feminism and Psychology* 28 (1): 152–70.

Marvin, Amy. 2019. "Groundwork for Transfeminist Care Ethics: Sara Ruddick, Trans Children, and Solidarity in Dependency." *Hypatia* 34 (1): 101–20.

McClurg, Lesley. 2022. "Women Share Their Experience of Getting an Abortion before *Roe* Made It Legal." *Weekend Edition Sunday*, May 29, 2022. NPR. https://www.npr.org/2022/05/29/1101973218/women-share-their-experience-of-getting-an-abortion-before-roe-made-it-legal.

McMenamin, Lex. 2024. "From Mass Arrests to Human Barricades: What to Know about the Pro-Palestine Campus Encampments." *Teen Vogue*, April 24, 2024. https://www.teenvogue.com/story/palestine-encampments-protests-arrests-israel-divestment.

Meiners, Erica. 2016. *For the Children? Protecting Innocence in a Carceral State*. Minneapolis: University of Minnesota Press.

Mendel, Richard. 2015. *Maltreatment of Youth in US Juvenile Corrections Facilities*. Baltimore: Annie E. Casey Foundation.

Mendel, Richard. 2022. "Why Youth Incarceration Fails: An Updated Review of the Evidence." Sentencing Project, March 1. https://www.sentencingproject.org/reports/why-youth-incarceration-fails-an-updated-review-of-the-evidence/#executive-summary.

Mingus, Mia. 2019. "Transformative Justice: A Brief Description." transformharm.org. Accessed May 10, 2023. https://transformharm.org/tj_resource/transformative-justice-a-brief-description/.

Minoff, Elisa, and Alexandra Citrin. 2022. "Systemically Neglected: How Racism Structures Public Systems to Produce Child Neglect." Center for the Study of Social Policy (Washington, DC), March. https://cssp.org/resource/systemically-neglected/.

Monazzam, Niki, and Kristen M. Budd. 2023. "Incarcerated Women and Girls." Sentencing Project. https://www.sentencingproject.org/fact-sheet/incarcerated-women-and-girls/.

Moran, Jeffery. 2002. *Teaching Sex: The Shaping of Adolescence in the 20th Century*. Cambridge, MA: Harvard University Press

Morris, Monique. 2016. *Pushout: The Criminalization of Black Girls in Schools*. New York: The New Press.

Morse, Anne. 2022. "Stable Fertility Rates 1990–2019 Mask Distinct Variations by Age." United States Census Bureau, April. https://www.census.gov/library/stories/2022/04/fertility-rates-declined-for-younger-women-increased-for-older-women.html.

Mountz, Sarah. 2020. "Remapping Pipelines and Pathways: Listening to Queer and Transgender Youth of Color's Trajectories through Girls' Juvenile Justice Facilities." *Affilia* 35 (2): 177–99.

Moussawi, Ghassan, and Salvador Vidal-Ortiz. 2020. "A Queer Sociology: On Power, Race, and Decentering Whiteness." *Sociological Forum* 35 (4): 1272–89.

Movement Advancement Project. 2021. "LGBTQ Policy Spotlight: Efforts to Ban Health Care for Transgender Youth." April. www.lgbtmap.org/2021-spotlight-health-care-bans.

Movement Advancement Project. 2024. "Healthcare Laws and Policies: Bans on Best Practice Medical Care for Transgender Youth." July 19. https://www.lgbtmap.org/img/maps/citations-youth-medical-care-bans.pdf.

Muliadi, Bradian. 2020. "What the Rise of TikTok Says about Generation Z." *Forbes*, July 7. https://www.forbes.com/sites/forbestechcouncil/2020/07/07/what-the-rise-of-tiktok-says-about-generation-z/.

Murno, Sarah, Savvy Benipal, Aleyah Williams, Kate Wahl, Logan Trenaman, and Stephanie Begun. 2021. "Access Experiences and Attitudes toward Abortion among Youth Experiencing Homelessness in the United States: A Systematic Review." *PLoS ONE* 16 (7): 1–3.

Nahata, Leena, Amy C. Tishelman, Nicole M. Caltabellotta, and Gwendolyn P. Quinn. 2017. "Low Fertility Preservation Utilization among Transgender Youth." *Journal of Adolescent Health* 61 (1): 40–44.

Naide, Sophia. 2020. "'Parental Involvement' Mandates for Abortion Harm Young People, but Policymakers Can Fight Back." Guttmacher Institute, February. https://www.guttmacher.org/article/2020/02/parental-involvement-mandates-abortion-harm-young-people-policymakers-can-fight-back.

Nair, Yasmin. 2015. "Stop Fetishising Youth Organizers." *Yasmin Nair* (blog), September 3, 2015. https://yasminnair.com/stop-fetishising-youth-organisers/.

Nash, Jennifer C. 2018. *Black Feminism Reimagined: After Intersectionality.* Durham, NC: Duke University Press.

National Day to Empower Teen Parents. 2003. "National Day to Empower Teen Parents Mission Statement." Archived at Wayback Machine Internet Archive. Accessed October 31, 2022. https://web.archive.org/web/20031120032038/http://empowerteenparents.org/.

National Network of Abortion Funds. n.d. "Our Mission and Values." Accessed June 16, 2024. https://abortionfunds.org/our-mission-vision-and-values/.

National Women's Law Center. 2018. *Dress Coded: Black Girls, Bodies, and Bias in DC Schools.* Washington, DC.

Naveed, Hina. 2022. "'If I Wasn't Poor, I Wouldn't Be Unfit': The Family Separation Crisis in the US Child Welfare System." Human Rights Watch and the American Civil Liberties Union, November 17. https://www.hrw.org/report/2022/11/17/if-i-wasnt-poor-i-wouldnt-be-unfit/family-separation-crisis-us-child-welfare.

Nelson, Alondra. 2011. *Body and Soul: The Black Panther Party and the Fight against Medical Discrimination.* Minneapolis: University of Minnesota Press.

Nellis, Ashley. 2021. *The Color of Justice: Racial and Ethnic Disparity in State Prisons.* Sentencing Project, October 13. https://www.sentencingproject.org/reports/the-color-of-justice-racial-and-ethnic-disparity-in-state-prisons-the-sentencing-project/.

Nikkelen, Sanne W. C., Johanna M. F. van Oosten, and Marieke M. J. J. van den Borne. 2020. "Sexuality Education in the Digital Era: Intrinsic and Extrinsic Predictors of Online Sexual Information Seeking among Youth." *Journal of Sex Research* 57 (2): 189–99.

No Teen Shame. n.d. "About Us." Accessed October 31, 2022. http://www.noteenshame.com/about.

Nocella, Anthony J., II, Priya Parmar, and David Stovall. 2023. *From Education to Incarceration.* New York: Peter Lang.

Noguera, Pedro. 2014. "Organizing Resistance into Social Movements." In *Youth Resistance Research and Theories of Change*, edited by Eve Tuck and K. Wayne Wang, 71–81. New York: Routledge.

Noguera, Pedro, and Chiara M. Cannella. 2006. "Conclusion: Youth Agency, Resistance, and Civic Activism—The Public Commitment to Social Justice." *In Beyond Resistance! Youth Activism and Community Change*, edited by Shawn Ginwright, Pedro Noguera, and Julio Cammarota, 333–48. New York Routledge.

Northridge, Jennifer L., and Susan M. Coupey. 2015. "Realizing Reproductive Health Equity for Adolescents and Young Adults." *American Journal of Public Health* 105 (7): 1284.

Nothing, Ehn. 2013. "Queens Against Society." In *Street Transvestite Action Revolutionaries: Queer Antagonist Struggle*. [San Francisco:] Untorelli Press. Archived at Anarchist Library. Accessed July 4, 2024. https://theanarchistlibrary.org/library/ehn-nothing-untorelli-press-street-transvestite-action-revolutionaries.

Nummi, Jozie, Carly Jennings, and Joe Feagin. 2019. "#BlackLivesMatter: Innovative Black Resistance." *Sociological Forum* 34 (S1): 1042–64.

Oakland Unified School District. n.d. "Puberty and Sexual Health Education: FAQs about Our Curriculum." Accessed June 20, 2024. https://www.ousd.org/healthy-oakland-kids-and-teens/puberty-and-sexual-health-education/faqs-about-our-curriculum.

O'Quinn, Jamie, and Jessica Fields. 2020. "The Future of Evidence: Queerness in Progressive Visions of Sexuality Education." *Sexuality Research and Social Policy* 17: 175–87.

Osterman, Michelle J.K., Brady E. Hamilton, Joyce A. Martin, Anne K. Driscoll, and Claudia P. Valenzuela. 2022. "Births: Final Data for 2020." *National Vital Statistics Reports* 70 (17): 1–49.

Painter, Julia. E., Gina M. Wingood, Ralph J. DiClemente, Lara M. Depadilla, and Lashun Simpson-Robinson. 2012. "College Graduation Reduces Vulnerability to STIs/HIV among African-American Young Adult Women." *Women's Health Issues* 22 (3): e303–e310.

Paltrow, Lynn M., and Jeanne Flavin. 2013. "Arrests of and Forced Interventions on Pregnant Women in the United States, 1973–2005:

Implications for Women's Legal Status and Public Health." *Journal of Health Politics, Policy, and Law* 38 (2): 299–343.

Pampati, Sanjana, Michelle M. Johns, Leigh E. Szucs, Meg D. Bishop, Allen B. Mallory, Lisa C. Barrios, and Stephen T. Russell. 2021. "Sexual and Gender Minority Youth and Sexual Health Education: A Systematic Mapping Review of the Literature." *Journal of Adolescent Health* 68 (6): 1040–52.

Panich-Linsman, Ilana, and Lauren Kelly. 2022. "Opinion: The Women Who Had Abortions before *Roe v. Wade.*" *New York Times*, January 21, 2022. https://www.nytimes.com/interactive/2022/01/21 /opinion/roe-v-wade-abortion-history.html.

Parks, Caitlin, and Jeffrey F. Peipert. 2016. "Eliminating Health Disparities in Unintended Pregnancy with Long-Acting Reversible Contraception (LARC)." *American Journal of Obstetrics and Gynecology* 214 (6): 681–88.

Parolin, Zachary. 2019. "Temporary Assistance for Needy Families and the Black–White Child Poverty Gap in the United States." *Socio-economic Review* 19 (3): 1005–35.

Patton, Cindy. 1996. *Fatal Advice: How Safe Sex Education Went Wrong.* Durham, NC: Duke University Press.

Paudel, Alissa, Shannon M. Wentworth, Kimberly B. Fortner, Laurel Carbone, Cecil Nelson, Alicia Mastronardi, Nikki B. Zite, and Megan M. Lacy Young. 2022. "COVID-19 Pandemic and Adolescent Pregnancy: A Look at Urban vs Rural Appalachian Populations." *American Journal of Obstetrics and Gynecology* 226 (1): S370–S371.

Pendharkar, Eesha. 2023. "Nonbinary Child's Long Hair Results in Suspension; Dress Code Amended after Legal Battle." *Education Week*, updated March 31. https://www.edweek.org/leadership /nonbinary-childs-long-hair-results-in-suspension-dress-code- amended-after-legal-battle/2023/03.

Penman-Aguilar, Ana, Marion Carter, M. Christine Snead, and Athena P. Kourtis. 2013. "Socioeconomic Disadvantage as a Social Determinant of Teen Childbearing in the US." *Public Health Reports* 128 (2 suppl1): 5–22.

Pfeffer, Carla A., Sally Hines, Ruth Pearce, Damien W. Riggs, Elisabetta Ruspini, and Francis Ray White. 2023. "Medical Uncertainty and Reproduction of the 'Normal': Decision-Making around Testosterone Therapy in Transgender Pregnancy." *SSM—Qualitative Research in Health* 4.

Piepmeier, Alison. 2009. *Girl Zines: Making Media, Doing Feminism.* New York: New York University Press.

Pillow, Wanda S. 2004. *Unfit Subjects: Education Policy and the Teen Mother, 1972–2002.* New York: Routledge.

Plaid, Andrea, and Christopher Macdonald-Dennis. 2021. "'BIPOC' Isn't Doing What You Think It's Doing." *Newsweek,* April, 9.

Plaster, Joey. 2023. *Kids on the Street: Queer Kinship and Religion in San Francisco's Tenderloin.* Durham, NC: Duke University Press.

Poggi, Stephanie. 1988. "What's Choice Got to Do with It?" *The Fight for Reproductive Freedom: A Newsletter for Student and Community Activists* 2 (2).

Pollitt, A. M., and A. B. Mallory. 2021. "Mental and Sexual Health Disparities among Bisexual and Unsure Latino/a and Black Sexual Minority Youth." *LGBT Health* 8 (4): 254–62.

Pregnancy Justice. 2016. "Purvi Patel's Conviction for Feticide Overturned." Accessed May 9. https://www.pregnancyjusticeus.org/purvi-patels-conviction-for-feticide-overturned/.

Pyne, Jake. 2014. "The Governance of Gender Non-conforming Children: A Dangerous Enclosure." *Annual Review of Critical Psychology* 11: 79–96.

Quinn, Therese, and Erica Meiners, eds. 2009. *Flaunt It! Queers Organizing for Public Education and Justice.* New York: Peter Lang.

Ralph, Lauren J., Heather Gould, Anne Baker, and Diana Greene Foster. 2014. "The Role of Parents and Partners in Minors' Decisions to Have an Abortion and Anticipated Coping after Abortion." *Journal of Adolescent Health* 54 (4): 428–34.

Ralph, Lauren J., Lorie Chaiten, Emily Werth, Sara Daniel, Claire D. Brindis, and M. Antonia Biggs. 2021. "Reasons for and Logistical Burdens of Judicial Bypass for Abortion in Illinois." *Journal of Adolescent Health* 68 (1): 71–78.

Ray, Ranita. 2017. *The Making of a Teenage Service Class: Poverty and Mobility in an American City.* Oakland: University of California Press.

Reisner, Sari L., Ralph Vetters, M. Leclerc, Shayne Zaslow, Sarah Wolfrum, Daniel Shumer, and Matthew J. Mimiaga. 2015. "Mental Health of Transgender Youth in Care at an Adolescent Urban Community Health Center: A Matched Retrospective Cohort Study." *Journal of Adolescent Health* 56 (3): 274–79.

Repro Jobs. 2021. "Don't Be a Shitty Instagram Brand: An Interview with Activist Natasha Vianna." May 17. Accessed February 23, 2023. https://www.reprojobs.org/blog/good-instagram-brand-practices.

Rich-Edwards, Janet. 2002. "Teen Pregnancy Is Not a Public Health Crisis in the United States; It is Time We Made it One." *International Journal of Epidemiology* 31 (3): 555–56.

Ritchie, Andrea. 2023. Special Edition Newsletter: Connecting the Dots, May 10. Archived at https://mailchi.mp/interruptingcriminalization/connectingthedots.

Roberts, Calpurnyia, Lauren J. Shiman, Erin A. Dowling, L. Tantay, Jennifer Masdea, Jennifer Pierre, Deborah Lomax, and Jane Bedell. 2020. "LGBTQ+ Students of Colour and Their Experiences and Needs in Sexual Health Education: 'You Belong Here Just as Everybody Else.'" *Sex Education* 20 (3): 267–82.

Roberts, Dorothy E. 2002. *Shattered Bonds: The Color of Child Welfare.* New York: Civitas Books.

Roberts, Dorothy E. 2012. "Prison, Foster Care, and the Systemic Punishment of Black Mothers." *UCLA Law Review* 59: 1473–1500.

Roberts, Dorothy E. 2014. "Child Protection as Surveillance of African American Families." *Journal of Social Welfare and Family Law* 36 (4): 426–37.

Roberts, Dorothy E. 2016. *Killing the Black Body: Race, Reproduction, and the Meaning of Liberty* 20th Anniversary Edition. New York: Vintage Books.

Roberts, Dorothy E. 2022. *Torn Apart: How the Child Welfare System Destroys Black Families—And How Abolition Can Build a Safer World.* New York: Basic Books.

Roberts, Dorothy E., and Sujatha Jesudason. 2013. "Movement Intersectionality: The Case of Race, Gender, Disability, and Genetic Technologies." *Du Bois Review: Social Science Research on Race* 10 (2): 313–28.

Robinson, Brandon Andrew. 2020. "The Lavender Scare in Homonormative Times: Policing, Hyper-incarceration, and LGBTQ Youth Homelessness." *Gender & Society* 34 (2): 210–32.

Rodríquez, Dylan. 2017. "The Political Logic of the Non-profit Industrial Complex." In *The Revolution Will Not Be Funded: Beyond the Nonprofit Industrial Complex,* edited by INCITE! Women of Color Against Violence, 21–40. Durham, NC: Duke University Press.

Rosentel, Kris, Ileana López-Martínez, Richard A. Crosby, Laura F. Salazar, and Brandon J. Hill. 2021. "Black Transgender Women and the School-to-Prison Pipeline: Exploring the Relationship between Anti-trans Experiences in School and Adverse Criminal-Legal System Outcomes." *Sexuality Research and Social Policy* 18 (3): 481–94.

Ross, Loretta, and Rickie Solinger. 2017. *Reproductive Justice: An Introduction.* Oakland: University of California Press.

Rudes, Danielle S., Shannon Magnuson, Shannon Portillo, and Angela Hattery. 2021. "Sex Logics: Negotiating the Prison Rape Elimination Act (PREA) against Its Administrative, Safety, and Cultural Burdens." *Punishment and Society* 23 (2): 241–59.

Ruglis, Jessica. 2011. "Mapping the Biopolitics of School Dropout and Youth Resistance." *International Journal of Qualitative Studies in Education* 24 (5): 627–37.

Saar, Malika Saada, Rebecca Epstein, Lindsay Rosenthal, and Yasmin Vafa. 2015. *The Sexual Abuse to Prison Pipeline: The Girls' Story.* Washington, DC: Center for Poverty and Inequality, Georgetown University Law Center.

Salazar, Maria. 2021. "Texas Teen Uses TikTok to Sabotage Abortion Whistleblower Website." FOX26 Houston, September 8. https://www.fox26houston.com/news/texas-teen-uses-tiktok-to-sabotage-abortion-whistleblower-website.

Sandoval, Edgar, and Tim Arango. 2021. "In Texas' Juvenile Prisons, Allegations Paint Portrait of Violence and Sex Abuse." *New York Times,* October 16, A:20.

Santelli, John S., Leslie M. Kantor, Stephanie A. Grilo, Ilene S. Speizer, Laura D. Lindberg, Jennifer Heitel, Amy T. Schalet, Maureen E. Lyon, Amanda J. Mason-Jones, Terry McGovern, Craig J. Heck,

Jennifer Rogers, and Mary A. Ott. 2017. "Abstinence-Only-Until-Marriage: An Updated Review of U.S. Policies and Programs and Their Impact." *Journal of Adolescent Health* 61 (3): 273–80.

Santelli, John, Mary A. Ott, Maureen Lyon, Jennifer Rogers, Daniel Summers, and Rebecca Schleifer. 2006. "Abstinence and Abstinence-Only Education: A Review of US Policies and Programs." *Journal of Adolescent Health* 38 (1): 72–81.

Sawyer, Wendy. 2019. "Youth Confinement: The Whole Pie 2019." Prison Policy Initiative (Northampton, MA). https://www.prisonpolicy.org/reports/youth2019.html.

Sedlak, Andrea J., and Karla S. McPherson. 2010. *Youth's Needs and Services: Findings from the Survey of Youth in Residential Placement.* Washington, DC: US Department of Justice, Office of Juvenile and Delinquency Prevention.

Sentencing Project. 2024. "Growth in Mass Incarceration." Accessed April 1. https://www.sentencingproject.org/research/.

Sex Education Collaborative. 2022. "Comprehensive Means Intersectional: Moving Sex Education Forward." Posted to YouTube February 28. https://sexeducationcollaborative.org/comprehensive-means-intersectional.

Shaefer, H. Luke, Kathryn Edin, Vincent Fusaro, and Pinghui Wu. 2019. "The Decline of Cash Assistance and the Well-Being of Poor Households with Children." *Social Forces* 98 (3): 1000–1025.

Shange, Savannah. 2019. *Progressive Dystopia: Abolition, Antiblackness, and Schooling in San Francisco.* Durham: Duke University Press.

SIECUS: Sex Ed for Social Change. 2021. "History of Sex Ed: From Awkward and Exclusionary, to Affirmative and Empowering." Washington, DC. https://siecus.org/wp-content/uploads/2021/03/2021-SIECUS-History-of-Sex-Ed_Final.pdf.

SIECUS: Sex Ed for Social Change. 2022. Sex Ed State Law and Policy Chart SIECUS State Profiles: July 2022. Washington, DC. https://siecus.org/resource/2022-state-of-sex-education-legislative-look-ahead/.

SisterSong: Women of Color Reproductive Justice Collective. n.d. "What Is Reproductive Justice?" Accessed September 6, 2022. https://www.sistersong.net/reproductive-justice.

shuster, stef m. 2021. *Trans Medicine: The Emergence and Practice of Treating Gender.* New York: New York University Press.

Sickmund, Melissa, T.J. Sladky, Charles Puzzanchera, and W. Kang. 2021. *Easy Access to the Census of Juveniles in Residential Placement.* Pittsburgh: National Center for Juvenile Justice, Office of Juvenile Justice and Delinquency Prevention. https://www.ojjdp.gov/ojstatbb/ezacjrp/.

Silliman, Jael. 2002. "Introduction." In *Policing the National Body: Sex, Race, and Criminalization,* edited by Jael Silliman and Anannya Bhattacharjee. Boston: South End Press.

Silliman, Jael, Marlene Gerber Fried, Loretta Ross, and Elena R. Gutiérrez. 2004. *Undivided Rights: Women of Color Organize for Reproductive Justice.* Chicago: Haymarket Books.

Silver, Lauren J. 2015. *System Kids: Adolescent Mothers and the Politics of Regulation.* Chapel Hill: University of North Carolina Press.

Sins Invalid. 2019. *Skin, Tooth, and Bone: The Basis of Movement Is Our People—A Disability Justice Primer.* https://www.sinsinvalid.org/disability-justice-primer.

Sisson, Gretchen. 2012. "Finding a Way to Offer Something More: Reframing Teen Pregnancy Prevention." *Sexuality Research and Social Policy* 9: 57–69.

SisterSong: Women of Color Reproductive Justice Collective. n.d. "What Is Reproductive Justice?" Accessed September 6, 2022. https://www.sistersong.net/reproductive-justice.

Skiba, Russell J., Choong-Geun Chung, Megan Trachok, Timberly L. Baker, Adam Sheya, and Robin L. Hughes. 2014. "Parsing Disciplinary Disproportionality: Contributions of Infraction, Student, and School Characteristics to Out-of-School Suspension and Expulsion." *American Educational Research Journal* 51 (4): 640–70.

Skiba, Russell J., Robert S. Michael, Abra Carroll Nardo, and Reece L. Peterson. 2002. "The Color of Discipline: Sources of Racial and Gender Disproportionality in School Punishment." *Urban Review* 34: 317–42.

Snapp, Shannon D., Jennifer M. Hoenig, Amanda Fields, and Stephen T. Russell. 2015. "Messy, Butch, and Queer." *Journal of Adolescent Research* 30 (1): 57–82.

Snorton, C. Riley, and Jin Haritaworn. 2013. "Trans Necropolitics: A Transnational Reflection on Violence, Death, and the Trans of Color Afterlife." In *The Transgender Studies Reader Remix*, edited by Susan Stryker and Dylan McCarthy Blackston, 305–16. New York: Routledge.

Sojoyner, Damien M. 2016. *First Strike: Educational Enclosures in Black Los Angeles*. Minneapolis: University of Minnesota Press.

Solinger, Rickie. 2005. *Pregnancy and Power: A Short History of Reproductive Politics in America*. New York: New York University Press.

Sosnaud, Benjamin. 2019. "Inequality in Infant Mortality: Cross-State Variation and Medical System Institutions." *Social Problems* 66 (1): 108–27.

Soyong Harley, Christine. 2019. "Sex Ed Is a Vehicle for Social Change. Full Stop." SIECUS: Sex Ed for Social Change. https://siecus.org/sex-ed-is-a-vehicle-for-social-change/.

Spade, Dean. 2015. *Normal Life: Administrative Violence, Critical Trans Politics, and the Limits of Law*. Revised ed. Durham, NC: Duke University Press.

Spade, Dean. 2020. *Mutual Aid: Building Solidarity during This Crisis (and The Next)*. London: Verso.

Stanley, Eric A. 2011. "Introduction: Fugitive Flesh; Gender Self-Determination, Queer Abolition, and Trans Resistance." In *Captive Genders: Trans Embodiment and the Prison Industrial Complex*, edited by Eric A. Stanley and Nat Smith, 7–17. Oakland, CA: AK Press.

Steinmetz, Katy. 2014. "The Transgender Tipping Point." *Time*, May 29.

Stevens, Robin. 2017. "Social Media Use and Sexual Risk Reduction Behavior among Minority Youth Seeking Safe Sex Information." *Nursing Research* 66 (5): 368–77.

Stovall, David. 2018. "Are We Ready for 'School' Abolition? Thoughts and Practices of Radical Imaginary in Education." *Taboo* 17 (1): 51–61.

Sung, Morgan. 2020. "How a Group of Clinic Volunteers Use TikTok to Battle Anti-abortion Protesters." Mashable, September 11. https://mashable.com/article/tiktok-abortion-clinic-defenders-pro-choice.

Sutherland, Kate. 2002. "From Jailbird to Jailbait: Age of Consent Laws and the Construction of Teenage Sexualities." *William and Mary Journal of Women and the Law* 9: 313–49.

Taft, Jessica K. 2021. "Is It Okay to Critique Youth Activists? Notes on the Power and Danger of Complexity." In *Children and Youth as Subjects, Objects, Agents: Innovative Approaches to Research across Space and Time,* edited by Deborah Levison, Mary Jo Maynes, and Frances Vavrus, 193–207. London: Palgrave.

Tannehill, Brynn. 2021. "The Far Right and Anti-trans Movements' Unholy Alliance." *Dame,* June 24. https://www.damemagazine.com/2021/06/24/the-far-right-and-anti-trans-movements-unholy-alliance/.

Tapia, Ruby C. 2005. "Impregnating Images: Visions of Race, Sex, and Citizenship in California's Teen Pregnancy Prevention Campaigns." *Feminist Media Studies* 5 (1): 7–22.

Temple Newhook, Julia, Jake Pyne, Kelley Winters, Stephen Feder, Cindy Holmes, Jemma Tosh, Mari-Lynne Sinnott, Ally Jamieson, and Sarah Pickett. 2018. "A Critical Commentary on Follow-Up Studies and 'Desistance' Theories about Transgender and Gender-Nonconforming Children." *International Journal of Transgenderism* 19 (2): 212–24.

Thomas, Maria, Gabriel Arkles, and Jessica Kant. 2022. "We Must Fight in Solidarity with Trans Youth: Drawing the Connections between Our Movements." Interrupting Criminalization, June. https://www.interruptingcriminalization.com/solidarity-with-trans-youth.

Thompson, Becky. 2002. "Multiracial Feminism: Recasting the Chronology of Second Wave Feminism." *Feminist Studies* 28 (2): 337–60.

Thomsen, Carly. 2022. "The Spectre of the Pregnant Person." Paper presented at American Studies Association Annual Meeting, New Orleans, November 5.

Thrasher, Steven (@thrasherxy). 2022. "A defense of the criminalization of trans parents needs to draw on the criminalization of trans sex workers, poor Black queer ppl & HIV criminalization."

Twitter, March 2. https://twitter.com/thrasherxy/status /1499035427600228353

Tishelman, Amy C., Megan E. Sutter, Diane Chen, Amani Sampson, Leena Nahata, Victoria D. Kolbuck, and Gwendolyn P. Quinn. 2019. "Health Care Provider Perceptions of Fertility Preservation Barriers and Challenges with Transgender Patients and Families: Qualitative Responses to an International Survey." *Journal of Assisted Reproduction and Genetics* 36 (3): 579–88.

Tolou-Shams, Marina, Emily F. Dauria, Rochelle K. Rosen, Melissa A. Clark, Joanne Spetz, Andrew Levine, Brandon D.L. Marshall, Johanna B. Folk, Lakshmi Gopalakrishnan, and Amy Nunn. 2022. "Bringing Juvenile Justice and Public Health Systems Together to Meet the Sexual and Reproductive Health Needs of Justice-Involved Youth." *American Journal of Orthopsychiatry* 92: 224–35.

Tuck, Eve, and K. Wayne Yang, eds. 2014a. *Youth Resistance Research and Theories of Change.* New York: Routledge.

Tuck, Eve, and K. Wayne Yang. 2014b. "Introduction to Youth Resistance Research and Theories of Change." In *Youth Resistance Research and Theories of Change,* edited by Eve Tuck and K. Wayne Yange, 1–24. New York: Routledge.

Tudoroiu, Theodor. 2014. "Social Media and Revolutionary Waves: The Case of the Arab Spring." *New Political Science* 36 (3): 346–65.

Turban, Jack L., and Diane Ehrensaft. 2018. "Research Review: Gender Identity in Youth: Treatment Paradigms and Controversies." *Journal of Child Psychology and Psychiatry* 59 (12): 1228–43.

Turban, Jack L., Dana King, Jeremi M. Carswell, and Alex S. Keuroghlian. 2020. "Pubertal Suppression for Transgender Youth and Risk of Suicidal Ideation." *Pediatrics* 145 (2): e20191725.

Turley, Ruth N. López. 2003. "Are Children of Young Mothers Disadvantaged Because of Their Mother's Age or Family Background?" *Child Development* 74 (2): 465–74.

Untorelli Press. 2013. "Street Transvestite Action Revolutionaries: Queer Antagonist Struggle." March 12. Archived at https://libcom .org/article/street-transvestite-action-revolutionaries-survival-revolt-and-queer-antagonist-struggle.

Upadhyay, Ushma D., Sheila Desai, Vera Zlidar, Tracy A. Weitz, Daniel Grossman, Patricia Anderson, and Diana Taylor. 2015. "Incidence of Emergency Department Visits and Complications after Abortion." *Obstetrics and Gynecology* 125 (1): 175–83.

URGE: Unite for Reproductive and Gender Equity. 2020. *A Youth People's Reproductive Justice Policy Agenda.* Washington, DC.

URGE: Unite for Reproductive and Gender Equity. 2021. "Sex Education Is a Reproductive Justice Issue." June 8. https://urge.org/resource/sex-education-is-a-reproductive-justice-issue/.

URGE: Unite for Reproductive and Gender Equity. n.d.(a). "Mission and Values." Accessed December 20, 2023. https://urge.org/about/mission-and-values/.

URGE: Unite for Reproductive and Gender Equity. n.d.(b). "Our Folks: Voices of LGBTQ+ Youth of Color." Accessed January 3, 2023. https://urge.org/our-folks/.

Vásquez, Tina. 2021. "Meet the 21-year-old Helping to Fund Abortions in Texas." *Prism*, March 25. http://prismreports.org/2021/03/25/meet-the-21-year-old-helping-to-fund-abortions-in-texas/.

Vaught, Sabina A. 2017. *Compulsory: Education and the Dispossession of Youth in a Prison School.* Minneapolis: University of Minnesota Press.

Vergani, Federica. 2018. "Why Transgender Children Should Have the Right to Block Their Own Puberty with Court Authorization." *Florida International University Law Review* 13: 903–28.

Vianna, Natasha, and Christine Soyong Harley. 2019. "Long Overdue: A Call to Action for Shame-Free Sex Education." SIECUS: Sex Ed for All. https://siecus.org/long-overdue-a-call-to-action-for-shame-free-sex-education/.

Vinson, Jenna. 2018. *Embodying the Problem: The Persuasive Power of the Teen Mother.* New Brunswick, NJ: Rutgers University Press.

Vinson, Jenna, and Clare Daniel. 2020. "'Power to Decide' Who Should Get Pregnant: A Feminist Rhetorical Analysis of Neoliberal Visions of Reproductive Justice." *Tense: A Journal of Rhetoric in Society* 8 (2).

Walker-Harding, Leslie R., Deborah Christie, Alain Joffe, Josephine S. Lau, and Larry Neinstein. 2017. "Young Adult Health and Well-

Being: A Position Statement of the Society for Adolescent Health and Medicine." *Journal of Adolescent Health* 60 (6): 758–59.

Wallace, John M, Jr., Sara Goodkind, Cynthia M. Wallace, and Jerald G. Bachman. 2008. "Racial, Ethnic, and Gender Differences in School Discipline among US High School Students, 1991–2005." *Negro Educational Review* 59 (1–2): 47–62.

Wallis, Kara Sheli. 2014. "No Access, No Choice: Foster Care Youth, Abortion, and State Removal of Children." *CUNY Law Review* 18: 119–52.

Wang, Leah, Wendy Sawyer, Tiana Herring, and Emily Widra. 2022. "Beyond the Count: A Deep Dive into State Prison Populations." Prison Policy Initiative (Northampton, MA). https://www.prisonpolicy.org/reports/beyondthecount.html.

Weiss, Suzannah. 2017. "Trump Cuts over $200 Million from Teen Pregnancy Prevention Programs." *Teen Vogue*, July 16. https://www.teenvogue.com/story/teen-pregnancy-prevention-funding-trump-cuts.

Westbrook, Laurel. 2020. *Unlivable Lives: Violence and Identity in Transgender Activism*. Oakland: University of California Press.

Western States Center. 2011. "The Origin of the Phrase Women of Color." YouTube, February 15. https://www.youtube.com/watch?v=82vl34mi4Iw.

White, Kari, Subasri Narasimhan, Sophie A. Hartwig, Erin Carroll, Alexandra McBrayer, Samantha Hubbard, Rachel Rebouché, Melissa Kottke, and Kelli Stidham Hall. 2022. "Parental Involvement Policies for Minors Seeking Abortion in the Southeast and Quality of Care." *Sexuality Research and Social Policy* 19: 264–72.

Wierckx, Katrien, Eva Van Caenegem, Guido Pennings, Els Elaut, David Dedecker, Fleur Van de Peer, Steven Weyers, Petra De Sutter, and Guy T'Sjoen. 2012. "Reproductive Wish in Transsexual Men." *Human Reproduction* 27 (2): 483–87.

Wilson, Helen, and Annette Huntington. 2006. "Deviant (M)others: The Construction of Teenage Motherhood in Contemporary Discourse." *Journal of Social Policy* 35 (1): 59–76.

Winters, Della J., and Adria Ryan McLaughlin. 2020. "Soft Sterilization: Long-Acting Reversible Contraceptives in the Carceral State." *Affilia* 35 (2): 218–30.

Woodard, Tiana. 2023. "Teens Investigating Equity Find Stop & Shop Charges More in Jackson Square than at a More Affluent Suburb." *Boston Globe*, June 5. https://www.bostonglobe.com/2023/06/05/metro /were-being-ripped-off-teens-investigating-equity-find-stop-shop-charges-more-jackson-square-than-more-affluent-suburb/?event= event12.

Wozolek, Boni, Lindsey Wootton, and Aaron Demlow. 2017. "The School-to-Coffin Pipeline: Queer Youth, Suicide, and Living the In-Between." *Cultural Studies / Critical Methodologies* 17 (5): 392–98.

Wu, Justine, Yael Braunschweig, Lisa H. Harris, Willi Horner-Johnson, Susan D. Ernst, and Bethany Stevens. 2019. "Looking Back While Moving Forward: A Justice-Based, Intersectional Approach to Research on Contraception and Disability." *Contraception* 99 (5): 267–71.

Yeo, Tien Ee Dominic, and Tsz Hang Chu. 2017. "Sharing 'Sex Secrets' on Facebook: A Content Analysis of Youth Peer Communication and Advice Exchange on Social Media about Sexual Health and Intimate Relations." *Journal of Health Communication* 22 (9): 753–62.

Yurcaba, Jo. 2022. "Law Professor Khiara Bridges Calls Sen. Josh Hawley's Questions about Pregnancy 'Transphobic.'" *NBC News*, July 13. https://www.nbcnews.com/nbc-out/out-politics-and-policy/law-professor-khiara-bridges-calls-sen-josh-hawleys-questions-pregnanc-rcna38015.

Zane, Ali, and Cristina Toppin. 2022. *Research Note: Study Shows Why TANF Is Not the Success That Some Claim*. Washington, DC: Center on Budget and Policy Priorities.

Zavella, Patricia. 2020. *The Movement for Reproductive Justice: Empowering Women of Color through Social Activism*. New York: New York University Press.

Zoila Pérez, Miriam. 2012. *The Radical Doula Guide: A Political Primer for Full Spectrum Pregnancy and Childbirth Support*. N.p.: privately printed.

Zoila Pérez, Miriam. 2013. "NYC Teen Pregnancy Campaign Brings Shaming to Bus Shelters and Cell Phones." Rewire News Group, March 5. https://rewirenewsgroup.com/2013/03/05/nyc-teen-pregnancy-campaign-brings-shaming-to-bus-shelters-and-cell-phones/.

INDEX

Founded in 1893,
UNIVERSITY OF CALIFORNIA PRESS
publishes bold, progressive books and journals
on topics in the arts, humanities, social sciences,
and natural sciences—with a focus on social
justice issues—that inspire thought and action
among readers worldwide.

The UC PRESS FOUNDATION
raises funds to uphold the press's vital role
as an independent, nonprofit publisher, and
receives philanthropic support from a wide
range of individuals and institutions—and from
committed readers like you. To learn more, visit
ucpress.edu/supportus.